# WordPress 3
# for Business Bloggers

Promote and grow your WordPress blog with advanced
marketing techniques, plugins, advertising, and SEO

**Paul Thewlis**

[PACKT] open source*
PUBLISHING   community experience distilled

BIRMINGHAM - MUMBAI

# WordPress 3 for Business Bloggers

First published: December 2011

Production Reference: 1021211

Published by Packt Publishing Ltd.
Livery Place
35 Livery Street
Birmingham B3 2PB, UK.

ISBN 978-1-84951-132-2

www.packtpub.com

Cover Image by Vinayak Chittar (vinayak.chittar@gmail.com)

# Credits

**Author**
Paul Thewlis

**Reviewers**
Srikanth AD
John Eckman
Lee Jordan

**Acquisition Editor**
Usha Iyer

**Development Editor**
Swapna Verlekar

**Technical Editor**
Arun Nadar

**Project Coordinator**
Leena Purkait

**Proofreaders**
Karen Estrada
Lydia May Morris

**Indexer**
Tejal Daruwale

**Graphics**
Manu Joseph
Conidon Miranda

**Production Coordinator**
Aparna Bhagat

**Cover Work**
Aparna Bhagat

# About the Author

**Paul Thewlis** has worked as a web marketing professional in the public and private sectors. He is currently Online Marketing Director for HeadRed (`http://headred.net`), a leading digital agency in the UK. He began his web career as a Technical Editor, working on web design books for a well-known publisher. He has extensive experience of many content management systems and blogging platforms. He is an expert in SEO, online marketing, and the use of social media within corporate communications. He blogs about those subjects, as well as WordPress and the web in general, at `http://blog.paulthewlis.com`. Paul lives in Birmingham, England, with his wife, Zöe.

I would like to thank Matt Mullenweg and the WordPress development team, as well as all the hard-working members of the wider WordPress community, who created the plugins featured in this book. I would also like to thank my parents, Jack and Margaret, for their unending support, and my wonderful wife, Zöe, for putting up with so many late nights and lonely weekends during the writing of this book.

# About the Reviewers

**Srikanth AD** is a web developer and SEO consultant. He is passionate about web development and optimizing websites for better search engine visibility and ranking.

His portfolio is available at http://www.srikanth.me.

**John Eckman** has more than a decade of experience designing and building web applications for organizations ranging from small non-profit organizations to Fortune 500 enterprises. Currently a Digital Strategist at ISITE Design, John works with clients to develop sustainable, strategic approaches to managing their presence on the web. Prior to ISITE Design, he was Director of Ecommerce Strategy at Optaros, leading the development of applications focused on the intersection of community, content, and commerce. Previously he was the director of development at PixelMEDIA and a principal consultant in software engineering with Molecular, Inc.

He received a Bachelor of Arts from Boston University, a Masters in Information Systems from Northeastern University, and a Ph.D. from the University of Washington, Seattle. John is an active contributor to a number of open source communities, a founding organizer of WordCamp Boston (2010 and 2011), and the lead developer of the WPBook plugin for WordPress. Online, he can be found at johneckman.com, blogging at www.openparenthesis.org, and tweeting as @jeckman.

He also served as a technical reviewer for *WordPress 3 Ultimate Security*.

---

I'd like to thank the broader WordPress community — users and developers — without whom none of this would be possible.

---

**Lee Jordan** is a designer and new media developer. She brings a strong design background and concern for the visual and emotional impact of media to web-based projects. Experienced in multiple CMS platforms including Expression Engine, Plone, WordPress, PostNuke, and Google's Blogger, she has maintained, explored, and used most of them on a day-to-day basis. She spends her spare time as the leader of a local scout troop, taking long hikes with her family in the beautiful North Georgia woods, trying to taste test every variety of chocolate that exists, and playing with code and pixels. Design topics or whatever she can think of at the time are posted on her blog at http://leejordan.net.

Lee has written and co-authored several previous books with Packt Publishing: *Project Management with dotProject*, *WordPress Themes 2.8*, *Blogger: Beyond the Basics*, and *HTML5 Rich Media Applications*.

Business blogging is simple to start but difficult to master. A big thanks to all the professional bloggers out there who let me learn by example.

# www.PacktPub.com

## Support files, eBooks, discount offers and more

You might want to visit www.PacktPub.com for support files and downloads related to your book.

Did you know that Packt offers eBook versions of every book published, with PDF and ePub files available? You can upgrade to the eBook version at www.PacktPub.com and as a print book customer, you are entitled to a discount on the eBook copy. Get in touch with us at service@packtpub.com for more details.

At www.PacktPub.com, you can also read a collection of free technical articles, sign up for a range of free newsletters and receive exclusive discounts and offers on Packt books and eBooks.

http://PacktLib.PacktPub.com

Do you need instant solutions to your IT questions? PacktLib is Packt's online digital book library. Here, you can access, read and search across Packt's entire library of books.

## Why Subscribe?

- Fully searchable across every book published by Packt
- Copy and paste, print and bookmark content
- On demand and accessible via web browser

## Free Access for Packt account holders

If you have an account with Packt at www.PacktPub.com, you can use this to access PacktLib today and view nine entirely free books. Simply use your login credentials for immediate access.

# Table of Contents

# Preface

*WordPress for Business Bloggers* provides advanced strategies and techniques which will help you to take your WordPress business blog from average to extraordinary. Regardless of whether you already have a blog, or are still in the planning stages, this book will show you how to use WordPress to create a highly successful blog for your business.

This is a practical, hands-on book based around a fictitious case study blog, which you will build using a development server on your own computer. The vast majority of tutorials and examples will be applied to the case study blog. The case study grows chapter-by-chapter, from the installation of your local development server, right up to the finished blog. You will be installing and configuring a selection of WordPress plugins to improve the functionality of the case study blog.

You are provided with clear instructions and detailed screenshots, so you can see exactly what to do at each step of the build. When you have completed the case study, you will have the knowledge and confidence to apply all the techniques you have learned to your own WordPress business blog.

The author assumes you have basic experience with WordPress, already know how to set up a self-hosted WordPress blog, and are familiar with the basics: creating posts and pages, configuring blog settings, and so on. By the time you have finished the book you will have moved forward from WordPress novice to an advanced user of the software in a business context.

## What this book covers

*Chapter 1, A Blog Less Ordinary – What Makes a Great Blog?*; will allow you to examine many different types of business blog. You will be shown a selection of great business blogs and see what you can learn from them.

*Chapter 2, Introducing our Case Study — WPBizGuru* introduces you to the case study blog, and takes you through the process of developing strategic goals and your blog plan. You will learn that the planning process is important, even if your blog is already up and running.

*Chapter 3, Designing your Blog* will teach you the basics of blog design. You will work through a brief introduction to HTML and CSS, and see how easy it is to create your own custom design using the Thematic theme framework.

*Chapter 4, Images and Videos* teaches you some advanced image and video handling techniques, including setting up an image gallery and using video from third-party sources, such as YouTube and Google Video.

*Chapter 5, Content is King* focuses on the different techniques and methods required for creating the best possible content for your business blog.

*Chapter 6, Search Engine Optimization* covers some of the most important SEO strategies and how to apply them, as well as how to submit your blog to the search engines.

*Chapter 7, Supercharged Promotion* will teach you some advanced blog promotion techniques, including: advanced RSS with FeedBurner; submission to blog search engines, such as Technorati; using social networks, such as Facebook and Twitter; and using social bookmarks, such as Digg and Delicious.

*Chapter 8, Connecting with the Blogosphere* talks about the importance of connecting with other bloggers and playing an active role in the blogosphere to promote your business blog.

*Chapter 9, Analyzing your Blog Stats* will teach you how to analyze your blog's performance using tools such as Google Analytics and WordPress.com Stats.

*Chapter 10, Monetizing your Blog* introduces you to a variety of strategies to help you generate revenue from your blog, like using advertising and affiliate programs.

*Chapter 11, Managing Growth* will show you how to manage the growth of your blog by optimizing it for high traffic, and introducing multiple authors by setting up a network using WordPress Multisite.

# What you need for this book

The main thing you need for this book is a self-hosted WordPress blog. We will be using some other open source software and a local development environment for WordPress. Full details of where to get this software and how to set it up will be covered in the relevant chapters. All the open source software used in the book is free to download and use.

# Who this book is for

This book is for anybody running or starting a business blog using WordPress, whether you plan to use your blog for PR and marketing, or want to profit directly from blogging.

The book mainly focuses on a self-hosted WordPress installation, but some of the advice could also be applied to blogs on `WordPress.com`.

# Conventions

In this book, you will find a number of styles of text that distinguish between different kinds of information. Here are some examples of these styles, and an explanation of their meaning.

Code words in text are shown as follows: "We can include other contexts through the use of the `include` directive."

A block of code is set as follows:

```
#footer {
  border-top:0px;
  margin-top:22px;
}
#siteinfo {
  color:#b7c4cf;
  font-size:11px;
  line-height:18px;
  padding:22px 0 44px 0;
}
```

When we wish to draw your attention to a particular part of a code block, the relevant lines or items are set in bold:

```
#primary {
  border:0px;
  padding:18px 0 0 0;
  margin-bottom:22px;
}
```

**New terms** and **important words** are shown in bold. Words that you see on the screen, in menus or dialog boxes for example, appear in the text like this: "Click **Save the Replace Posts** option and view your home page".

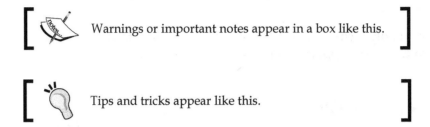

Warnings or important notes appear in a box like this.

Tips and tricks appear like this.

# Reader feedback

Feedback from our readers is always welcome. Let us know what you think about this book—what you liked or may have disliked. Reader feedback is important for us to develop titles that you really get the most out of.

To send us general feedback, simply send an e-mail to feedback@packtpub.com, and mention the book title via the subject of your message.

If there is a book that you need and would like to see us publish, please send us a note in the **SUGGEST A TITLE** form on www.packtpub.com or e-mail suggest@packtpub.com.

If there is a topic that you have expertise in and you are interested in either writing or contributing to a book, see our author guide on www.packtpub.com/authors.

# Customer support

Now that you are the proud owner of a Packt book, we have a number of things to help you to get the most from your purchase.

# Downloading the example code

You can download the example code files for all Packt books you have purchased from your account at http://www.PacktPub.com. If you purchased this book elsewhere, you can visit http://www.PacktPub.com/support and register to have the files e-mailed directly to you.

# Errata

Although we have taken every care to ensure the accuracy of our content, mistakes do happen. If you find a mistake in one of our books—maybe a mistake in the text or the code—we would be grateful if you would report this to us. By doing so, you can save other readers from frustration and help us improve subsequent versions of this book. If you find any errata, please report them by visiting http://www.packtpub.com/support, selecting your book, clicking on the **errata submission form** link, and entering the details of your errata. Once your errata are verified, your submission will be accepted and the errata will be uploaded on our website, or added to any list of existing errata, under the Errata section of that title. Any existing errata can be viewed by selecting your title from http://www.packtpub.com/support.

# Piracy

Piracy of copyright material on the Internet is an ongoing problem across all media. At Packt, we take the protection of our copyright and licenses very seriously. If you come across any illegal copies of our works, in any form, on the Internet, please provide us with the location address or website name immediately so that we can pursue a remedy.

Please contact us at copyright@packtpub.com with a link to the suspected pirated material.

We appreciate your help in protecting our authors, and our ability to bring you valuable content.

# Questions

You can contact us at questions@packtpub.com if you are having a problem with any aspect of the book, and we will do our best to address it.

# 1
# A Blog Less Ordinary—What Makes a Great Blog?

Blogging has been a part of the web landscape for over a decade now. From personal journals to big corporate marketing, the medium has matured to become a ubiquitous mode of live communication. The power of blogging has been recognized by the business community, and canny marketers view it as a powerful weapon in their digital arsenal.

If blogging is done well, it can bring myriad benefits to businesses of any size and if done badly, it can cause more harm than good. Central to the success of any business blogger is a thorough understanding of the technology he or she is using. This will give you a competitive advantage by being able to create a more engaging blog. You have wisely chosen WordPress as your blogging platform and this book will give you the in-depth knowledge of the software you need to take your blog from ordinary to exceptional.

This is not an introduction to WordPress; that is, we will not be covering the basics such as installation or how to post. Most readers will already have an established WordPress blog or will at least be in the advanced stages of planning one.

In this chapter, we will consider the essence of great blogs and the groundwork that is required to produce one. What separates the mediocre from the marvelous? What should you do to blast through the blogosphere and take your blog to the next level? We will look at some examples of the best blogs out there and see what we can learn from them. The principles outlined here are a jumping-off point for the techniques and methods that we will cover through the rest of the book. In this chapter, we cover:

- Where you fit into the business blogosphere
- How to identify your blog's strategic goals

- Some of the major categories of business blogs
- The tools and features in WordPress that help you to achieve your blog's goals

# You can stand out from the crowd

Let's begin with a quick pep talk.

Making a success of your blog can seem like an uphill struggle. It's easy to be disheartened in the early days because success rarely happens overnight. One of the first psychological stumbling blocks for many bloggers is the overwhelming size of the blogosphere. It's easy to feel like a small fish in a very big pond. However, that's not necessarily the case.

It's true; the blogosphere is a crowded place, with millions of blogs out there all clambering for attention.

At first this seems a little daunting. You may be wondering how you can stand out in such a crowded arena. With so much live information being constantly updated, is there room for any more? Does the world need another blog? Is the web-surfing public in danger of reaching blog-saturation or information-overload? I believe the answers to these questions are yes, yes, and no, respectively.

There are many out there, but *there are also a lot of web users hungry for information.*

As well as being big, the blogosphere is also diverse. There are millions of blogs, which cover an enormous spectrum of subjects and genres. However, the blogosphere can be almost endlessly segmented, which gives meaning to your activities as a business blogger. *You're not competing for audience share against the blogosphere as a whole.* Like most bloggers, you'll find your niche and realize success is within your grasp.

# Where do you fit in?

Blogging began very much as an exercise in personal publishing. It was an evolution of the personal home pages that have been with us since the early days of the Web. It's still true that the majority of blogs take the form of a personal journal, with no implicit business agenda. (However, many 'personal' bloggers have found ways to monetize their activity; there is now a growing breed of 'professional bloggers', who derive much, if not all of their income from blogging.)

It's widely believed that John Barger first used the term weblog in December 1997. Peter Merholz shortened it to blog in 1999, saying, "I've decided to pronounce the word 'Weblog' as 'wee-blog'. Or 'blog' for short."

It was politics and journalism that brought blogging into the mainstream, particularly in the wake of the 9/11 attacks of 2001. The 2004 US presidential elections marked a watershed as blogging became an increasingly normal part of the media landscape. Journalist, Andrew Sullivan, was a pioneer of the political blog, starting The Daily Dish in 2001. The following screenshot is of Andrew Sullivan's blog from September 30, 2001.

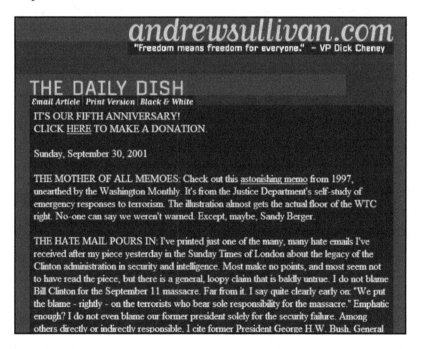

With politicians and influential journalists playing an active role in the blogosphere, it wasn't long until the business community recognized the potential benefits of blogging. Today, business blogging is commonplace with more and more web users expecting to see a 'Blog' link on company home pages.

In this very brief history of blogging we can already see three of the biggest blog genres: Personal Blogs, Political Blogs, and Business Blogs (there are, of course, many others). *Most readers of this book will fall into the 'Business' genre.*

# Not all business blogs are the same

So, you're a business blogger. However, that doesn't say very much about your specific goals and aspirations. All blogs are different. Their reasons for existence vary depending on what the publisher is trying to achieve. The key to the success of your blog is having a clear vision of what you want it to do for you. This is your **blogging strategy**. Once it's clear in your mind, you can start to set concrete **tactical** goals for your blog, which we'll cover in *Chapter 2, Introducing our Case Study — WPBizGuru*.

For now, consider the 'raison d'être' of your blog. Why are you putting your time, energy, and resources into it? What do you hope to achieve?

 One of the key drivers for many business bloggers is the fact that blogs can be a very inexpensive form of marketing — you can get a lot of value for a relatively small investment.

Obviously, not all business bloggers are trying to achieve the same things with their blogs, but here are a few of the more common strategic goals of business blogging:

- To increase sales
- To add value to your products and services
- To open a dialog with your customers
- To raise awareness of your company, products, and services
- To demonstrate your knowledge and expertise
- To provide customer service and support
- To improve public relations (for example, media relations, reputation management, crisis management, and so on)
- To drive traffic to your other website(s)
- To give some personality to your corporate image

You may well have several of these strategic goals in mind for your blog. There is no reason why your blog can't achieve a combination of these. Let's take a look at each of the goals in more detail with some examples of blogs that have them. (Not all of the example blogs here are created in WordPress; they're included as they are good illustrations of these strategic goals.)

# Increasing sales

A blog can be a great way of expanding and updating your online and offline sales literature. Posting about the benefits and features of your products or services can be a great way of converting leads into sales. This usually involves a simpler approach rather than a full-on hard sell. Your regular sales brochure, whether online or offline, will probably list your selling points with brief explanations, which for many customers, can seem rather over-hyped. A blog allows you to expand on your selling points and, in doing so, demonstrate that there is more to your products than just sales hype.

A great example of a 'sales' blog is that of GPS manufacturer, **Garmin** (`http://garmin.blogs.com`). Their blog not only gives background information about the products, it also shows innovative ways in which customers are using their GPS units, going beyond the scope of their regular sales literature. There are also plenty of customer testimonials and images of the products actually being used.

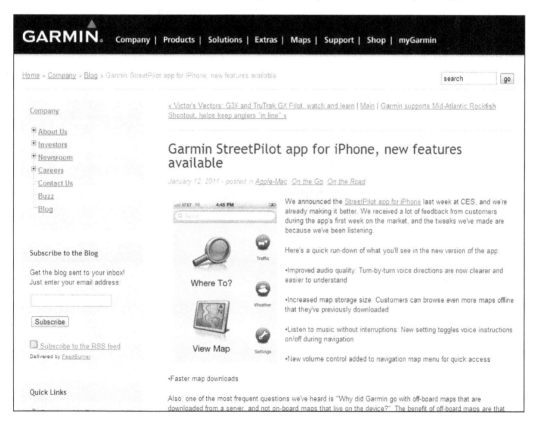

# Adding value

Your blog is a great place to tell customers about extra features and added benefits of your products and services. This is related to the idea of increasing sales, already mentioned, so your blog can probably kill two birds with one stone. Customers who use your products and services can learn ways of getting more out of them. For example, software developers might blog about hidden features that regular users might not otherwise know about.

A good example of this type of blog is the **37signals Product Blog** (`http://productblog.37signals.com/`). The company uses it to educate its customers about features in its range of online productivity software. The following screenshot illustrates this approach—who knew how to change time zones in Basecamp? As well as adding value for its existing customers, this kind of information is also sales material for prospective buyers.

# A dialog with your customers

Blogs provide the perfect environment for a genuine conversation with your customers. A key feature of any blog is the ability of readers to write comments about posts. Businesses can use this in-built technology to engage in a live conversation with their customers. It can be a great way of receiving feedback and testing opinions about new products and services, as well as finding out what your customers really want.

Obviously, opening up public communication channels with your customers can involve some risk—you may receive damaging comments. How to deal with negative feedback is a delicate issue that we'll look at in more detail in *Chapter 8, Connecting with the Blogosphere*. For this reason, many large businesses do not use comments on their blogs. A notable exception is Boeing, which does allow comments on its blog (`http://boeingblogs.com/randy/`).

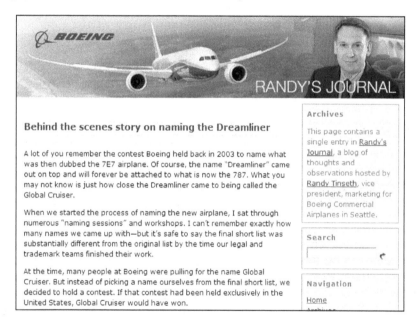

# Raising awareness

Blogs are a great way to raise awareness for your company and products. The nature of the blogosphere is that bloggers link to each other. This provides a great platform for spreading your message virally. Having your blog linked to and commented on by bloggers across the globe can spread the word quickly. It's a great form of **buzz marketing**, and many start-ups use a blog to create an air of anticipation about their forthcoming launch.

**Joost**, the web TV Company, used a blog in the lead-up to its launch, using the code name 'The Venice Project'. It helped to create a buzz and raised awareness for the company before it launched (http://joost.com/).

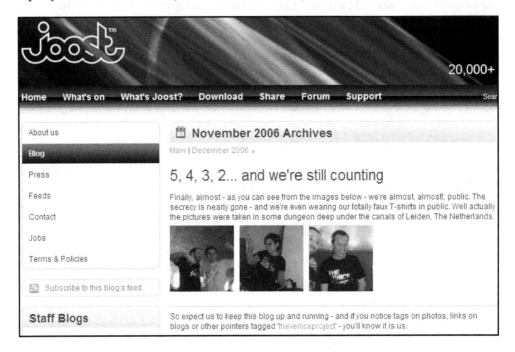

# Showing expertise

Demonstrating your professional knowledge and positioning yourself as an expert in your field is a great way of raising your business profile. This is particularly true for consultants and others who are hired because of their knowledge and experience. Web designers, academics, authors, life coaches, and software developers are just a few examples of the kinds of business people who may wish to demonstrate their expertise. Using a blog is a great way to achieve this because it provides a regularly updated outlet to showcase your professional activities and write about your achievements.

A great WordPress blog that demonstrates this is that of web designer, Jeffrey Zeldman (http://www.zeldman.com). He uses his blog to discuss issues in the web design arena and give his comment about what's happening in the industry.

# Providing customer service

Providing efficient customer service is the cornerstone of most successful businesses. Using a blog as part of your customer service provision can be a great help to both you and your customers. You can use your blog to provide answers to frequently asked customer service questions. Blogs are also great for quickly alerting your customers to product issues as they arise.

A great example of a customer services blog is Dell's **Direct2Dell** (`http://direct2dell.com/`).

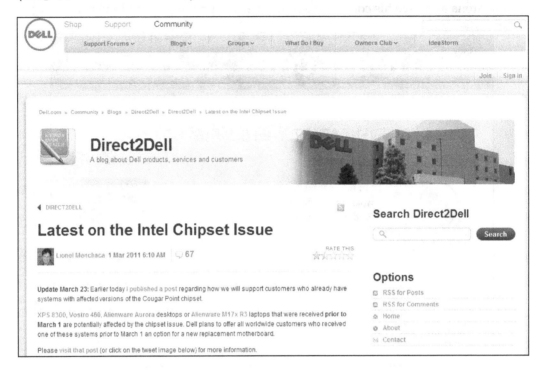

# Public relations

Your blog can provide a great window on your business. It can put a human face on the organization and provide a great way for both the public and media to get an understanding of what you're about. Blogs can also provide a means to transmit your company news, which can complement or maybe even replace the traditional press release. They also provide a forum to discuss and respond to any media coverage you receive, be it good or bad. A blog is also an invaluable tool for crisis management, as it enables you to provide instant updates about any negative situation you may find yourself in. Blogs allow you to control your corporate reputation.

Digg's blog has a strong public relations focus. It provides plenty of good-news stories, such as **awards** the company has picked up and enhancements to its service. It also uses it to respond quickly to any potentially damaging feedback it has received about its service. The blog also gives a good sense of the company's ethos and outlook, which is useful in managing its brand and reputation. All in all, the Digg blog is a great example of a WordPress blog with a PR-focus (`http://blog.digg.com/`):

# Driving traffic

Search engines love blogs. A continuous supply of frequently updated content is the key to improving search engine rankings. However, many company websites are updated infrequently, particularly if they are **brochure** style sites. A blog is a great way of bringing dynamic and fresh content into the mix. If you have a relatively lightweight company website that isn't updated too often, you'll find you get far better search engine success from a blog. It's basically down to the fact that search engines like fresh content to index.

This strategy would work particularly well if you keep your blog within your site's domain. So, rather than having www.mycompany.com and www.mycompanyblog.com as separate domains, consider placing your blog at http://blog.mycompany.com. This is becoming the standard approach for more and more company websites, who understand the importance of driving traffic from their blog to their main website (or vice versa—it works both ways).

An example of this approach is the blog set up by **Articulate**, an e-learning tools company (http://blog.articulate.com/). Not only are the blog pages within the main site's domain, they are also well integrated into the design and navigation of the main site. The blog and the main website have similar headers and menu bars.

# Add some personality

Blogging's evolution with its roots in personal journals means many blogs often take on a very conversational style. This lends itself very well to injecting a personal touch or a human face to corporate communications. Many companies use blogs to reveal some of the personalities behind the business. These days, many CEOs and senior executives blog on behalf of their companies. The topics discussed aren't necessarily related to company activities. These bloggers have the opportunity to write about their extra-curricular interests or anything else that takes their fancy.

This approach can be very useful in building a relationship with your customers. People are now far more used to informal communications with the organizations with which they do business. They like to get to know the people behind the corporate façade. Nevertheless, it's still important to gauge the tone correctly. If things get too informal or inappropriate content begins to creep in, you may end up upsetting or alienating some of your customers.

Bill Marriott, Chairman and CEO of Marriott International, maintains a blog at `http://www.blogs.marriott.com/`. The blog contains a mix of his personal musings as well as company news, and remains firmly under the Marriott brand. It's an excellent opportunity for a huge multi-national corporation to give a personal touch to its web communications.

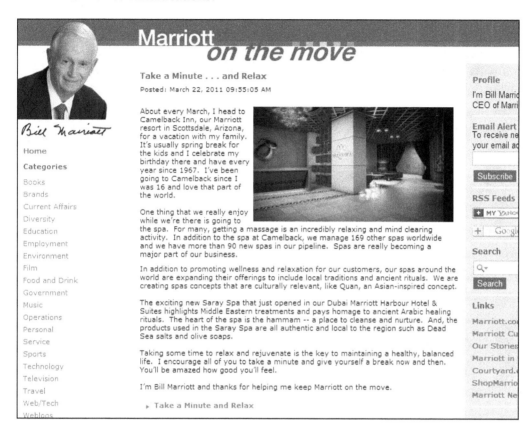

# Categorizing business blogs

So these are a few of the strategic goals that successful business blogs aspire to. They provide you with one method of analyzing your blog (and the blogs of others).

But we can also look at blogs in terms of their type. Looking around the blogosphere, we see many types or styles of blog. Each of these types of blog is likely to have its own set of strategic goals. By understanding what your strategic goals are, you can probably determine what type of blog you should have. We can measure the success of a blog by looking at its type and deciding whether it achieves the strategic goals for that particular blog type.

# Product blogs

These tend to simply focus on a company's product(s). They provide information on research and development, product features, user guides, where to buy, and anything else directly related to the product or service. They are usually regarded as a straightforward sales channel — their purpose is to close sales. The strategic goals that these blogs are trying to achieve are usually to increase sales and add value.

A great example of a product blog is the Amazon Web Services Blog, which the company uses to tell its customers about newly developed products and services (`http://aws.typepad.com/aws/`).

# Corporate or company blogs

This is probably the most diverse type of blog as it can fulfill many, if not all, of the strategic goals we highlighted previously. The corporate blog can take many forms and has many purposes.

These are at once the easiest kind of business blog to get started and the easiest to get wrong because remaining focused can be a challenge. They provide almost a completely blank canvas, so it's important to identify the strategic goals and stick to them.

General corporate blogs are probably the most common type of business blogs to be found on the web. They provide a great deal of flexibility and can cover a diverse range of subject matters.

If you have several strategic goals in mind for your blog, you will most likely end up with a general corporate blog. A great example of this type of blog, built using WordPress, is **Flickr** (`http://blog.flickr.com/en`).

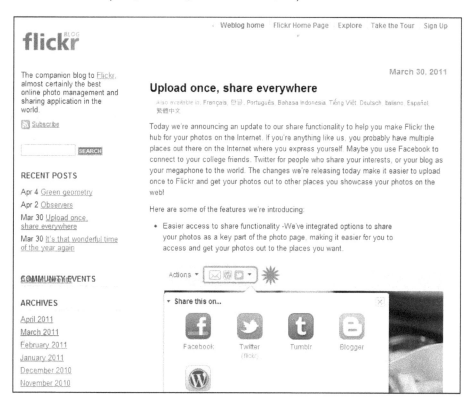

# News blogs

These are a slightly different type of blog as they can be a business in their own right.

They usually provide news coverage for a specific niche and may be run by an expert in that field or a team of experts. Many of the most popular blogs on the web take this form. A lot of these focus on internet and digital technologies. They are almost like online magazines or newspapers.

Because of the high traffic that these types of blogs can attract, many have become successful independent media businesses by raising revenue from advertising sales and corporate sponsorships.

In terms of the strategic goals behind this type of blog, it tends to show expertise and adding personality. However, as many of these are businesses in their own right, they also have the goal of increasing sales, that is, advertising sales.

Some notable blogs in this category are TechCrunch (`http://www.techcrunch.com/`), GigaOM (`http://gigaom.com/`), and Mashable (`http://mashable.com/`), all of which use WordPress.

# Expert blogs

These are written by pundits or experts in their field. They are usually aimed at promoting the business activity of the author. The experts behind these blogs may be freelance consultants, professional speakers, authors, or they may run their own companies.

Again, many of the most popular blogs on the web are of this type. Some expert bloggers derive a good income simply from running their blogs—they can monetize the high traffic they receive by selling advertising space.

The strategic goals behind these blogs are usually raising awareness of the expert's business activities, demonstrating knowledge and expertise, and driving traffic to the expert's other websites.

Expert blogs can also come under the auspices of large corporations who use the reputation of some of their senior employees to improve their company profile.

Some expert blogs have a long history coming directly from the tradition of the 'personal home page', which was instrumental in the development of blogging. Famous expert bloggers include Seth Godin (`http://sethgodin.typepad.com/`), Robert Scoble (`http://www.scobleizer.com/`), and Guy Kawasaki (`http://blog.guykawasaki.com/` — shown in the following screenshot).

These are just four, rather broad categories. It's easy to see that many blogs will fit into one or another of these types, but some blogs cross over and there are certainly other types of blogs that we haven't covered. The main point to understand is that having a clear idea of the type of blog you want to achieve, based on your strategic goals, is an important first step in making your blog a success.

# The WordPress arsenal

We've seen that successful blogs need clearly defined strategic goals and these goals will often determine the type of blog that will work best.

WordPress is one of the most powerful blogging platforms available, and it makes possible a number of techniques and methods that will help you put your strategic goals into practice. The tools, techniques, and methods you pull out of the WordPress arsenal will depend on your blog's strategic goals.

We'll be covering these techniques in detail throughout the rest of the book, but here are a few of them to give you a taste of what's to come.

# Good design

Whatever your strategic goals may be, design is going to be an important consideration—you must come up with a design that facilitates your strategic goals.

Luckily, WordPress gives you almost unlimited control over the look and feel of your blog. You may have already experimented with ready-made themes, of which there are thousands available from various sources. However, we'll be looking at how to modify WordPress themes so that you can develop a unique design that fits your purpose perfectly.

# Maximizing usability

This will be closely linked to the design of your blog. Ensuring that your blog is usable and accessible to everyone is a key to its success. Your readers must be able to navigate your blog and find the content easily.

WordPress has many built-in features that help to maximize usability. There are also several plugins that can be used to improve this. Throughout the book, we'll be looking at a selection of the best plugins, so that you can choose the ones you really need.

# Promoting your blog

Again, whichever strategic goals you are aiming for, a key factor to your blog's success will be getting it out to as big an audience as possible.

Promoting blogs is a wide-ranging skill that involves many techniques. For example, Search Engine Optimization (SEO) is central to any promotion strategy. There are many ways that you can use WordPress to improve the findability of your site and we will be covering these in detail.

WordPress also enables you to take advantage of social networking and social bookmarking. We will also be looking at syndication and submitting your blog to the various indices, such as **Technorati**. *Chapter 6, Search Engine Optimization* and *Chapter 7, Supercharged Promotion* will give you all the details on promoting your blog to the search engines and beyond.

# Analyzing the statistics

It is essential to monitor the progress of your blog, and WordPress offers many tools that enable you to do this. We will also look **Google Analytics**, a third-party statistics tool.

We will be looking at the various statistics that are available to you and examining how you can use the data to push your blog forward.

# Managing content

WordPress is a powerful content management system and we will be looking at the ways you can manage all types of content within your blog. Depending on your strategic goals, there may be many different types of content that you need to create. From static pages to image galleries and multimedia content, WordPress gives you the control you need.

We will also be developing the skills you need to create engaging and relevant content, including copywriting techniques, and how to manage categories.

# Monetizing your blog

WordPress provides you with a variety of options to develop revenue streams from your blog. There are several plugins and widgets that help you to do this.

In *Chapter 10, Monetizing your Blog*, we will be looking at creative methods of generating cash via your blog, which could go a long way towards covering its running costs or even develop into a significant revenue stream for your business.

# Measuring success

To ensure that your blog is a worthwhile use of your resources and is providing benefit to your business, you need to measure its success. It's also useful to be able to assess other blogs against yours, and against others within your market sector.

There are several tools that can be used to measure the success of blogs.

# Google PageRank

This is an algorithm that Google uses to rank web pages in its index. In very rough terms, the **PageRank** of a web page is assessed by the number of other pages that link to it. Google gives a numeric weighting from 0-10 for each web page on the Internet. The higher the PageRank, the higher up it appears in Google's search results. So, having a high PageRank helps you to achieve a better ranking in Google.

Taken on its own, *it is a matter of some debate how important PageRank actually is.* But as a general rule of thumb, PageRank is a good indicator of how well a page is doing. You can see the PageRank of any web page by installing the **Google Toolbar** (`http://toolbar.google.com/`).

# Alexa ranking

Alexa (`http://www.alexa.com/`) is a company that measures websites based on the traffic they receive. You can look up any website in Alexa to see how well it ranks. The higher up the list a website appears the more traffic it receives.

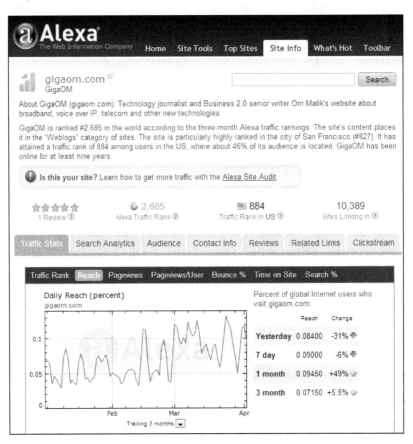

# Summary

In this chapter, we have considered what makes a great blog. We have looked at how the success of a blog depends on its strategic goals and how well it fulfils them. We outlined a number of strategic goals that are relevant to business blogs and saw examples of blogs that aspire to those goals.

We have also seen a number of blog types that are derived from the various strategic goals, and introduced some of the tools and features of WordPress that allow bloggers to realize them.

In the next chapter, you'll be introduced to the case study blog we'll be using throughout the book. You'll learn how to identify your own strategic goals and draw up your blog plan, by using the case study as an example.

# 2
# Introducing our Case Study—WPBizGuru

Throughout the book, we'll be using a case study based on a fictitious blog to demonstrate the concepts you'll be learning. It will be the basis for most of the tutorials in the rest of the book. In this chapter, we'll outline what we'll be doing to transform **WPBizGuru** from a mediocre blog into an all-singing, all-dancing traffic magnet.

As we discussed in *Chapter 1, A Blog Less Ordinary – What Makes a Great Blog?*, a successful business blog is achieved by identifying strategic goals and applying these to the type of blog you are publishing. We will work through this process for WPBizGuru to give us a detailed plan of how the blog should be developed. You will then be in a position to apply the planning process to your own blog and identify what needs to be done to improve it.

Even though you may already have a live blog, you should still work through the goal-setting process so that you have a clear road map of where your blog is going. This will be your **blog plan**. Think of it in the same way as you would treat your business plan. All businesses should regularly revisit and update their business plans. The same is true for blog plans. No matter how established your blog is, it needs a plan that is updated regularly and responds to your changing demands and business. In this chapter, we will cover:

- An introduction to our case study blog
- How to develop a detailed blog plan
- How to identify the specific goals that will enable us to achieve our blog plan
- An overview of how the case study blog will be implemented through the rest of the book

# WPBizGuru—the man behind the blog

Our (fictitious) eponymous hero is an expert in using WordPress to set up business blogs. Hence the name: 'WP' = WordPress, 'Biz' = Business, 'Guru' = Expert. So, **WP + Biz + Guru = WPBizGuru**.

He has spent several years applying his knowledge to help his clients use WordPress in their businesses. Now he is rebranding himself as the 'WPBizGuru'; the case study will follow him throughout the process of planning and building his new business blog.

If you want to find out a little more about him, take a look at the **About** page on the blog (`http://blog.wpbizguru.com`).

**Using a subdomain in your blog URL**

Many bloggers use a subdomain in the URL for their blog. This is particularly useful if you have a regular website running alongside your blog. You can have `www.yourdomain.com` pointing to your main home page and `http://blog.yourdomain.com` pointing to your blog.

If you set up a subdomain in your hosting control panel to point to your WordPress directory, remember that you also need to update **WordPress address (URL)** and **Blog address (URL)** on the **General Settings** page in your WordPress admin area:

| | |
|---|---|
| WordPress address (URL) | `http://blog.wpbizguru.com` |
| Site address (URL) | `http://blog.wpbizguru.com`  *Enter the address here if you want your site homepage to be different from the directory you installed WordPress.* |

# Before and after

If you take a look at the blog now (`http://blog.wpbizguru.com`), you'll see the finished version, which is the result of all the work we'll be doing in the chapters that follow.

But WPBizGuru didn't always look like this. Like most new WordPress blogs, WPBizGuru was using the default theme and had very few enhancements, such as plugins and widgets. What you now see came about by applying the methods and techniques you'll be learning through the rest of the book. The following screenshot shows the 'plain vanilla' version of WPBizGuru before it received its makeover:

# Goals and planning

Let's now look at WPBizGuru in more detail and see what business objectives he wants to achieve with his blog. We can apply a simple process here that should work with any business blog:

- Consider our business situation
- Decide on our strategic goals
- Come up with ideas based on those goals to give us a blog plan
- Decide how to implement the blog plan

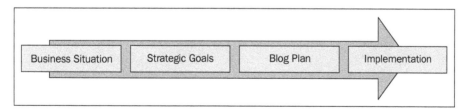

# Business situation

The first step is to stand back and analyze your business situation. WPBizGuru earns his living by setting up WordPress blogs for his clients, writing, speaking at events and shows, appearing on web TV, and selling a range of WordPress products. He is an expert in the WordPress community and has amassed a great deal of knowledge through his experience as a consultant, writer, and speaker.

Thinking back to the blog categories that we outlined in *Chapter 1, A Blog Less Ordinary – What Makes a Great Blog?*, it seems fairly obvious that WPBizGuru should be an 'Expert Blog'. He checks most of the boxes for that category (that is, demonstrating professional knowledge and positioning himself as an expert).

# Strategic goals

We can now think about the strategic goals that apply to this business situation. What does WPBizGuru want to achieve with his blog? This will probably begin with a brainstorming exercise. Make a list of all the strategic goals you can think of for your blog. For WPBizGuru, this will include the following:

- Finding new clients for his consultancy services
- Selling more books
- Announcing speaking events
- Getting more speaking engagements
- Selling WordPress products (for example, training videos, plugins, and themes)
- Building a brand
- Getting freelance writing work

And the list continues...

The following diagram is a 'Mind Map' showing all the strategic goals that WPBizGuru would like to achieve:

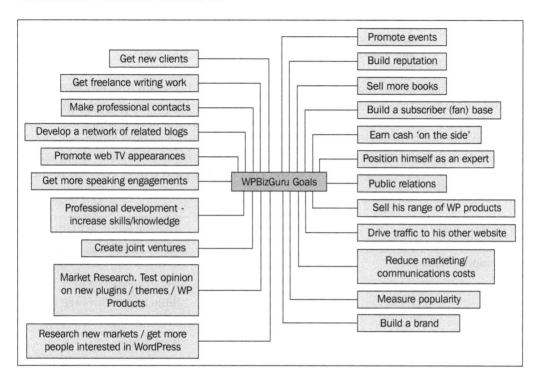

# The blog plan

Now that we have our strategic goals, it's time to think about how they can be realized. Some of these will be simpler than others. For example, for WPBizGuru to achieve his strategic goal of selling more books he may decide to simply set up a page on his blog that lists the books he has published. However, there may be better solutions that involve a bit more creative thinking. He may decide to add a 'book widget' in his blog sidebar. This will showcase his books right on the main blog page and link directly to Amazon.com.

At this point, it's worth formatting your blog plan into some kind of tabular structure. The blog plan for WPBizGuru is shown below. It has been broken down into three columns, showing each strategic goal, how these goals can be realized, and finally the specific implementation requirements.

Right now you may find it difficult to complete the third column for your own blog as your knowledge of WordPress may not be sufficient. However, as you work through the book and your WordPress skills improve, you will find solutions to your own implementation requirements and add them to your blog plan. Likewise, some of the details you see in the following WPBizGuru plan may not make a lot of sense right now. Don't worry—most items in the WPBizGuru plan will be covered in the rest of the book.

| Strategic goal | How to realize the goal | Specific implementation requirements |
| --- | --- | --- |
| **Get more clients** | Set up a 'Services' page | Create a static services page |
| | Make it easy to contact | Add a contact form |
| | Showcase previous work | Build a portfolio page |
| **Sell books** | Set up a 'Books' page | Create a static books page |
| | Amazon links in sidebar | Book widget |
| **Promote video appearances** | Have a 'video' category and announce upcoming appearances on the blog | Create a category called 'Video Appearances' |
| **Announce speaking events** | Integrate with some kind of calendar | Events calendar plugin |
| | Post announcements in the blog | |
| **Get more speaking engagements** | Make it easy to be contacted | Add a contact form |
| **Building buzz to draw in new traffic** | Get traffic from social news and bookmarking sites | **AddThis** plugin |
| **Build a subscriber base** | Encourage readers to subscribe with their e-mail address | 'Subscribe to comments' plugin |
| | | Set up FeedBurner e-mail subscriptions |
| **Sell WordPress products** | Make it easy for readers to buy WordPress products | WP e-Commerce plugin |

| Strategic goal | How to realize the goal | Specific implementation requirements |
| --- | --- | --- |
| **Build a brand** | Make an attractive design | Customize the theme with brand colors and images |
| | Use a logo / favicon | Install a favicon |
| | Use brand language | Apply a writing style guide |
| **Get freelance writing work** | Make it easy to contact | Add a contact form |
| | Have a portfolio of published work | Build a writing portfolio page |
| **Earn cash on the side** | Implement AdSense | AdSense manager plugin |
| | Sell banner ads | Implement a banner rotation script |
| | Affiliate marketing | Sign up with an affiliate network (for example, Amazon Associates) |
| **Public relations** | Integrate with offline and traditional PR methods | Create a 'Press' page or link to press page on his other website |
| **Build on reputation** | Build relationships with the movers and shakers in the WordPress community | Trackbacks to their blogs |
| | | Guest posts from other WP experts |
| **Market research (test opinion on WordPress products)** | Find out what readers think about new products | WP-Polls plugin |
| | | Ask for comments |
| **Position oneself as an expert** | Demonstrate good knowledge of WordPress | Maintain a short blogroll of other experts |
| | Provide original and top-quality content | Apply copywriting best practice and quality assurance |
| **Make professional contacts** | Build relationships with the movers and shakers in the WordPress community | Trackbacks to their blogs |
| | | Guest posts from other WP experts |
| **Measure popularity** | Find out visitor numbers | Implement Google Analytics or WordPress.com stats |

| Tactical goal | How to realize the goal | Specific implementation requirements |
| --- | --- | --- |
| Increase traffic | Use promotion techniques to drive traffic | Use RSS and FeedBurner |
| Maintain posting frequency | | Plan content ahead |
| | | Get into a routine of posting |
| Improve search engine rankings | | Use good permalinks |
| | | Employ SEO techniques |
| Maximize usability and accessibility | Maintain best practice in usability and accessibility | Use image alt tags properly |
| | | Have a good category list |
| | | Use tags correctly, (Configurable Tag Cloud widget) |
| | | Use an accessible color scheme |
| | | Don't break WP's valid code with poor quality plugins |

# Tactical goals

You will see a section headed **Tactical goals** at the bottom of the blog plan. These are generic goals that are not linked to any specific business goals. They are things that all blogs should be trying to do no matter what their strategic goals may be. For example, all blogs aim to increase traffic irrespective of what they may be trying to achieve from a business point of view. Even though they aren't specifically related to business objectives, these goals should feature in any good blog plan.

# Implementation

Once you have drawn up your blog plan, it's time to begin with the implementation. That's not to say you're done with the plan. You're likely to revisit it frequently as your blog takes shape, and make alterations and additions to it. The beauty of any kind of web publishing is that nothing is set in stone. If you find that some aspect of the original plan doesn't look right or doesn't work when you actually place it on your blog, you can always change your mind.

Implementation is the stage where we get our hands dirty and begin the real work of transforming your blog.

# An overview of the WPBizGuru makeover

Throughout the rest of the book, we will be seeing how the WPBizGuru blog plan is put into action. This will give you the practical skills you need to implement your own blog plan using WordPress.

# Design

The first stage of the makeover will be to implement an appropriate design. To achieve this, we will look at some of the principles of good design and how they should be applied to WPBizGuru. We will look at issues related to color schemes, layout, and typography. We will also be paying careful attention to usability and accessibility.

You will be introduced to advanced techniques for editing WordPress themes that will involve manipulating the source code. The following screenshot shows the finished design for WPBizGuru:

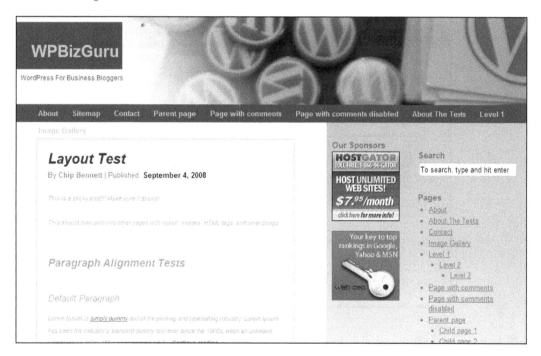

# Content

*Chapter 4*, *Images and Videos* and *Chapter 5*, *Content is King*, deal with all aspects of creating content and content management. Images and videos will be an important feature in the WPBizGuru blog and we will also be looking at a range of tools and techniques available in WordPress, which help us to manage this type of content.

We will learn how to present content, easily and efficiently, from a third-party website, such as YouTube. WPBizGuru will also feature a photo gallery, as you can see in the following screenshot. This will be achieved by the use of a powerful third-party plugin that makes managing an image gallery a breeze.

General content issues such as copywriting techniques and how to manage tags and categories will also be examined in detail. We will discuss the use of static pages within WordPress and the kinds of static content that might be required in the WPBizGuru blog. The importance of safeguarding content with appropriate back-up procedures will also be demonstrated.

# Promotion and analysis

A key element in the success of WPBizGuru, and indeed any blog, will be effective promotion. This subject will be looked at in detail in *Chapter 6, Search Engine Optimization* and *Chapter 7, Supercharged Promotion*. There is a wide range of techniques and tools to be employed to ensure WPBizGuru's promotional activity is as effective as possible.

We will examine the principles of effective SEO, including how to submit WPBizGuru to the search engines and directories. Understanding keywords and how they relate to SEO will be a fundamental lesson, as will the use of sitemaps and implementing a good permalink structure.

The importance of social networks and other social media will also be examined. We will see how the **AddThis** plugin can be used to promote the blog via social bookmaking sites.

One of the goals laid out in the blog plan is to effectively measure the popularity of WPBizGuru. We will be looking at the tools that enable us to achieve this, including a comparison between *WordPress.com* Stats and *Google Analytics*, in *Chapter 9, Analyzing your Blog Stats.*

# Generating revenue

Another goal in the WPBizGuru blog plan is to earn some revenue directly from the blog. We will be looking at some methods to achieve this. These include introducing a banner rotation system so that WPBizGuru can sell advertising and sponsorship banners directly. Revenue will also be generated by using advertising networks, such as **Google AdSense**.

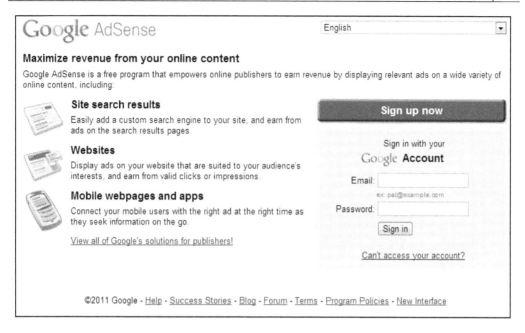

# Enabling growth

We will be looking at how to effectively manage the growth of the WPBizGuru blog. This includes practical considerations such as how to ensure smooth server operation when faced with high traffic. We will also examine options for expanding WPBizGuru's blogging activities. For example, we will see how the WordPress **Multisite** feature can be used as a tool for developing a network of linked blogs.

# Summary

In this chapter, we have introduced our case study blog—WPBizGuru. We have also seen how to develop a detailed **blog plan**. This began by analyzing our business situation and deciding what we want to achieve from our blog. We then identified the specific goals that will enable us to achieve this and how they might be realized by using WordPress. We also saw an overview of how the WPBizGuru blog will be implemented through the rest of the book.

Now is the time to sit down and work on your detailed blog plan before the practical work begins. In the next chapter, you will learn how to redesign the theme of a WordPress blog.

# 3
# Designing your Blog

In this chapter, we'll look at one of the most important aspects of your blog—design. We'll begin by considering some of the principles of good blog design. We'll then move on to apply some of those design principles to our WPBizGuru case study, based on the strategic goals we outlined in the previous chapters. Even if your blog is already up and running, this chapter will allow you to critically evaluate its design and replace your current theme with a custom-designed one. This chapter includes:

- The principles of blog design
- How to implement your blog design using CSS and HTML
- Setting up a local development environment
- Building a theme for our case study blog

## Blog design principles

Blogs tend to have a fairly simple, minimalist layout and design. This has always been one of their key characteristics. Blogs are all about frequently updated content, so the main purpose of their design is to present that content as efficiently and conveniently as possible. The vast majority of blogs present their most recent content on the page that visitors arrive at; hence, the front page contains the latest posts. There's no home page with a verbose welcome message and a long navigation menu to click through to the important stuff. The visitor gets straight into the meat of the blog. By default, this is the structure that WordPress provides. It is possible to set a static page as your blog's front page, but, in the vast majority of cases, I wouldn't recommend it.

So when considering the architecture of a blog, unlike other types of website, we don't have to worry too much about a complex navigation structure. There is a convention that we can follow. Yes, we may want to add some extra static pages, but probably only a few of these. What we are most concerned with in blog design is not a complicated navigation structure and how all the pages link together, but how the actual blog page should look and feel. This can be broken down into four key components, which we will examine, one by one:

- Layout
- Color
- Typography
- Usability and accessibility

# Layout

Good design is all about making something easy for people to use. Designers achieve this by employing standards and conventions. For example, cars have a standard design: four wheels, a chassis, a steering wheel, gas pedal, brake, gear shift, and so on. Car designers have stuck to this convention for many years. First, because it works well and second, because it enables us to drive any car we choose. When you sit down in any standard road car, you know how it works. You turn the key in the ignition, select a gear, hit the gas, and off you go. It's certainly not beyond the ken of car designers to come up with new ways for getting a car in motion (a joystick maybe, or a hand-operated brake) but this would make it more difficult for people to drive. Cars work reasonably safely and efficiently because we are all familiar with these conventions.

The layout of blog pages also tends to follow certain conventions. As with cars, this helps people to use blogs efficiently. They know how they work, because they're familiar with the conventions. Most blogs have a header and a footer with the main content arranged into columns. This columnar layout works very well for the type of chronological content presented in blogs.

Because of these conventions, the decisions about our blog layout are fairly simple. It's basically a case of deciding where we want to place all our page elements and content within this standard columnar layout. The set of page elements we have to choose from is also based on fairly well entrenched blogging conventions. The list of things we may want on our page includes:

- Header
- Posts
- Comments

- Static content (for example, the **About** page)
- Links to static pages (simple navigation)
- RSS feeds
- Search
- Categories
- Archives
- Blogroll
- Widgets and plugins
- Footer

There will be other elements to add to the page as we work through later chapters, but for now these should be enough for us to come up with a page layout. If we look at this list in more detail, we can see that these page elements can be grouped in a sensible way. For example:

- Group 1
    - Header
    - Links to static pages

- Group 2
    - Posts
    - Comments
    - Static content

- Group 3
    - RSS Feeds
    - Search
    - Categories

- Group 4
    - Archives
    - Blogroll
    - Widgets and plugins

- Group 5
    - Footer

This isn't the only possible grouping scheme we might come up with. For example, we may place the items in Groups 3 and 4 into a single larger group, or we may have widgets and plugins in a group on their own. From this grouping, we can see that the type of items in Group 2 are likely to be the main content on our page, with Groups 3 and 4 being placed in **sidebars**.

 Sidebars are areas on the page where we place ancillary content.

Having considered the elements we want on the page and how they might be grouped, we can think about possible layouts. Within the conventional columnar structure of blogs there are quite a few possible layout variations. We'll look at four of the most common. The first is a three-column layout.

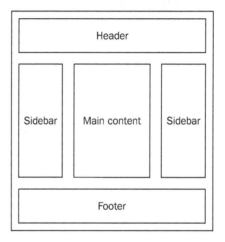

Here, we have two sidebars, one on either side of the main content. Using this type of layout, we would probably place the items in Groups 3 and 4 in the sidebars and Group 2 in the main content area.

A variation on the three-column layout is to have the two sidebars next to each other on one side of the page (usually the right), as shown in the following diagram. This is a popular layout for blogs, not just for aesthetics, but because the search engine spiders encounter the post column first as that content is at the top of the template. (You'll find out all about search engine spiders in *Chapter 6, Search Engine Optimization*, so if you don't know what they are right now, don't worry.)

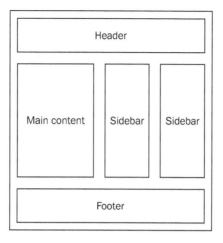

Using two sidebars is useful if you anticipate having a lot of ancillary content on your blog. The list of page elements given earlier is really the bare minimum you would want on your page. However, if you decide to use lots of widgets or have a long blogroll, it's a good idea to spread them across two sidebars (for more on blogrolls, see *Chapter 8, Connecting with the Blogosphere*). This means that more of your content can be placed *above the fold.*

The concept of *above the fold* in web design applies to content in a web page which is visible without having to scroll down, that is, the stuff in the top part of the page. It's a good idea to place the most important content above the fold so that readers can see it immediately. This is particularly true if you plan to monetize your blog by displaying adverts. Adverts that appear above the fold get the most exposure, and therefore, generate the most revenue (more on this in *Chapter 10, Monetizing your Blog*).

Another popular layout amongst bloggers has just two columns. In this layout, we would place the items in Groups 3 and 4 together in the one sidebar. It doesn't really matter which side of the page the sidebar is placed, but it seems more common to have it on the right. Studies have shown that a web user's eyes are most often focused on the top-left region of a web page, when they first open any page. So it makes sense to place your main content there, with your sidebar on the right.

Also, remember that the search engine spiders will find the leftmost content first. You want them to find your main content quickly, which is a good reason for placing your sidebar on the right, out of their way.

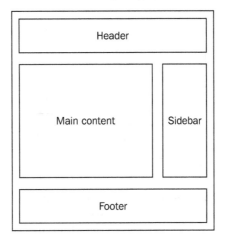

An important benefit of a two-column layout is that it allows more room for your main content area. This may be important, if you intend to use a lot of video or images within your blog posts. The extra room allows you to display this visual content bigger.

Many blogs place some of their ancillary content just above the footer, below the main content. This also has the advantage of leaving more space for the main content, as with the two-column layout. The following diagram shows this type of layout. Here, the content just above the footer isn't strictly speaking a sidebar, but I've labeled it this way because it's the terminology most often applied to this type of ancillary content.

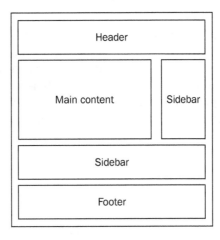

**Wireframing**

The layout diagrams we've just seen are referred to as wireframes by web designers. They give a simple overview of where the elements of a page should be placed. It would be a good idea for you to create your own wireframe for your blog design. This can be done using most graphic software packages or something like Microsoft Visio, or a simple pen and paper does the job equally well!

# Color

This is the next design principle we need to consider. It may be that you already have a corporate color scheme based on your company logo, stationery, or existing website. In this case, you'll probably want to continue that theme through your blog design. Even if you already have your corporate color scheme, this section may still be useful in case you decide to change your blog colors in the future.

The subject of color in design is a large one. Design students spend a great deal of time learning about the psychology and science of colors and techniques for achieving the best color schemes. Obviously, we don't have enough space to go into that kind of detail, but I will try to give you a few pointers.

The first thing to think about is the psychology of color, in particular, color associations. This is the idea that different colors evoke different feelings and emotions in the eye of the beholder. To a certain extent this can be rather subjective and it can also depend on cultural influences, but there are some generalities that can be applied. For example, red is often perceived as being exciting, passionate, or dramatic. Yellow is an active and highly visible color, which is why it is used in warning signs. It is also associated with energy and happiness. Blue is sometimes thought of as being *cold*. It can also be a calming color and may sometimes be seen as corporate or conservative. White, for many people, gives the idea of cleanliness, purity, and perfection. Black can be seen as strong, elegant, and chic. Obviously, these color associations can vary from person to person, so designers don't rely on them solely in their color decisions, but they are certainly worth bearing in mind.

There are more practical considerations regarding color that are probably more relevant than color psychology. For example, we all know that some color combinations don't work well together. There is a great deal of design theory aimed at devising good color combinations, but unless you're a professional designer, it's not really worth going into. Probably the best method for working out good color combinations is trial and error. If you're trying to figure out a background color and text color for your blog, simply test a few out. You could use a graphics package such as Photoshop or Microsoft Paint, or one of the many online color tools such as, `http://colorschemedesigner.com/` or Adobe's Kuler at `http://kuler.adobe.com`.

When choosing background and text colors you need to think about contrast. For example, yellow text on a white background can be very difficult to read. Some people also find light text on a black background a strain on their eyes.

It's also important not to use too many colors in your design. Try to limit your palette to a maximum of three or four. Sometimes you may only need two colors to make an attractive design.

One method for devising color combinations is to look for examples all around you, particularly in nature. Maybe look at a photograph of a landscape and pick out color combinations you like. Also consider the work of professional designers. Think about websites and blogs you like, and examine the color schemes they have used. You will also find good examples in offline design—pick up a book and see how colors have been used in the cover design.

 If you would like to base your blog's color scheme on your company logo, you could use lighter and darker versions of one color from the logo. Use the most vivid color in the logo for emphasis or headings.

## Web color theory

At this point, it's worth looking at the technical theory behind colors on the Web. Web browsers use the **Hexadecimal RGB** color system to render colors in web pages. This is because computer monitors use an RGB color model, which means every pixel is colored using a combination of red, green, and blue light (hence RGB). There are 256 different levels of red light, 256 different levels of green light, and 256 different levels of blue light. These can be combined to create 16,277,216 different colors, which are all available for your web browser.

The hexadecimal system gives us a way of counting from 0 to 255 using numbers and letters, which covers all 256 levels of RGB light. In the hexadecimal scale, 0 is 00 and 255 is FF. A six-character hexadecimal color code specifies the levels of red, green and blue, which form a particular color. For example, the color **white** combines red, green, and blue at their highest possible levels, that is 255. Remember that in hexadecimal 255 is FF, so the color code for white is **FFFFFF** (Red: FF, Green: FF, and Blue: FF). The color code for black is **000000** as the levels of red, green, and blue are set to their lowest, or 00 (in hexadecimal). The code for red is **FF0000**, blue is **0000FF**, and yellow is **FFFF00**, and so on.

*We can use six-character Hexadecimal RGB codes to define all of the 16,277,216 web colors.*

So how do we know the hexadecimal code for a particular color? Well, there are many tools available that define the Hexadecimal RGB codes for the colors you choose. Some are standalone applications for PC or Mac, and others are online. Take a look at www.colorpicker.com or do a quick search in Google on *color picker*. For more information on web colors, read the article at http://en.wikipedia.org/wiki/Web_colors.

# Typography

Another important consideration for your blog design is the fonts you use. Your choice of font will have a big impact on the readability of your blog. It's important to bear in mind that although there are literally thousands of fonts to choose from, only a small number of them are practical for web design. This is because a web browser can only display fonts that are already installed on the user's computer. If you choose an obscure font for your blog, the chances are that most users won't have it installed on their computer. If this is the case the web browser will automatically select a substitute font. This may be smaller or far less readable than the font you had in mind. It's always safest to stick to the fonts that are commonly used in web design, which are known as **web safe fonts**. These include the following:

- Arial
- Verdana
- Times New Roman
- Georgia

 There are two types of font, serif and sans-serif. Serif fonts have little flourishes at the end of the strokes whereas sans-serif fonts don't have this extra decoration. Arial and Verdana are sans-serif fonts, whereas Times New Roman and Georgia are serif fonts.

As you'll see later in the chapter, when we look at CSS, fonts are usually specified in groups or families. They are listed in the order of the designer's preference. For example, a designer may specify `font-family:"Georgia, Times New Roman, serif"`. This means when the browser renders the page it will first look for the Georgia font; if it isn't installed, it will look for the Times New Roman font and if that isn't installed, it will look for the computer's default serif font. This method gives the designer more control over the font choices the browser will make.

The size of your font is also an important factor. Generally speaking, the bigger it is, the easier it is to read. Computer displays are getting bigger and bigger but the default screen resolutions are tending to get smaller. In other words, the individual pixels on users' screens are getting smaller. This is a good reason for web designers to choose larger font sizes. This trend can be seen on many *Web 2.0* sites, which tend to use large and clear fonts as part of their design, for example `http://www.37signals.com`. But be careful not to go too big as this can make your design look messy and a little *childish*.

Remember that you're not limited to using just one font in your blog design. For example, you may decide to use a different font for your headings. This can be an effective design feature but don't go crazy by using too many fonts, as this will make your design look messy. Probably two, or at most three, fonts on a page are plenty.

# Font replacement

**Font replacement** refers to a relatively new group of technologies that are pushing the envelope of web typography. In theory, they allow designers to use any font in their web page designs. In practice, things are a little more complicated. Issues around browser compatibility and font licensing make font replacement technologies a bit of a minefield for anyone who is new to web design. It's true that, thanks to font replacement technologies, professional designers are no longer constrained by the notion of web safe fonts. But, if you are a web design novice, I recommend you stick to web safe fonts until your skills improve and you are ready to learn a whole new technology.

A full discussion on font replacement is way beyond the scope of this chapter; I mention it only to give you a better overview of the current state of web typography. But if you are interested in knowing more, three popular font replacement technologies are **Cufón** (`http://cufon.shoqolate.com`), **Font Squirrel** (`http://www.fontsquirrel.com`), and **Google Fonts API** (`http://code.google.com/apis/webfonts/`).

There is also something known as **@font-face**, which is part of CSS3, the latest specification of CSS. Again, it offers the tantalizing possibility of giving designers free rein in their choice of fonts. Sadly, @font-face is also hindered by browser compatibility and font licensing issues. The Font Squirrel technology, mentioned previously, resolves these issues to a certain extent, so this is something to be aware of as your web design skills develop. But for the time being, I recommend you concentrate on the basics of web typography and don't worry about @font-face until you feel ready.

# Usability and accessibility

This is another very important area to consider when designing your blog. Many people, who live with various disabilities, use a range of 'assistive' software to access the Web. For example, people with visual impairments use screen readers, which translate the text in a web browser into audible speech. There are also people who are unable to use a mouse, and instead rely on their keyboard to access web pages. It's the responsibility of web designers to ensure that their websites are accessible for these different methods of browsing. There's no sense in alienating this group of web surfers just because your blog is inaccessible to them.

There are also many other circumstances when your blog might be accessed by means other than a standard web browser, for example, via mobile phones, PDAs, or tablets. Again, a good designer will ensure that these modes of browsing are catered for. The web design industry has been well aware of these accessibility issues for many years and has come up with guidelines and technologies to help conscientious designers build websites that are **standards compliant**. These **web standards** help ensure best practice and maximize accessibility and usability.

Luckily, WordPress takes care of a lot of the accessibility issues simply by the way it's been developed and built. The code behind WordPress is valid XHTML and CSS, which means that it complies with web standards and is easily accessible. It's important, then, that you don't *break* the system by allowing bad practice to creep in.

Some of the things to bear in mind relate to a couple of design principles we've already discussed, for example, using a color scheme and font size that makes your text easy to read. Other issues include keeping the number of navigation links on your page to a minimum—a whole load of useless links can be annoying for people who have to *tab* through them to get to your main content.

You should also ensure that any third-party plugins you install are standards-compliant and don't throw up any accessibility problems. The same is true if you decide to use a ready-made theme for your blog design. Just make sure it's accessible and satisfies web standards. For more background reading on web standards, you could take a look at http://www.alistapart.com or the **World Wide Web Consortium (W3C)** website at http://www.w3.org.

# Implementing your blog design

We've now considered the principles involved in designing our blog. The next thing to decide is how we actually carry out the design work. There are three main options available, each of which involves varying degrees of work. However, they all require knowledge of the design principles we just covered.

The first approach is probably the easiest; it simply involves finding a readymade theme and installing it in WordPress. By working through the earlier design principles, you should have an idea of what you want your blog to look like and then you simply need to find a theme that matches your vision as closely as possible. A good place to start looking is the official WordPress **Free Themes Directory** at http://wordpress.org/extend/themes/. You'll also find many more theme resources by running a search through Google.

There are hundreds of very attractive WordPress themes available for free and many others which you can pay for. However, if you adopt this approach to your blog design, you won't have a unique or original blog. The chances are the theme you choose will also be seen on many other blogs.

At the other end of the scale, in terms of workload, is designing your own theme from scratch. This is a fairly complicated and technical process, and is well beyond the scope of this chapter. In fact, it's a subject that requires its own book. If you intend to build your own theme, I recommend *WordPress 2.8 Theme Design* by *Tessa Blakeley Silver* ISBN 978-1-849510-08-0 published by Packt Publishing.

The third approach is to modify a readymade theme. You could do this with any theme you choose, even the default *Twenty Ten* theme that ships with WordPress. However, if you edit a fully developed theme, you spend a lot of time unpicking someone else's design work and you may still be left with elements that are not completely your own. A better method is to start with a **theme framework**, which has been specially designed to be a *blank canvas* for your own design. This is the approach we'll use in the case study later in the chapter.

Over the last few years many WordPress theme frameworks have appeared, some free, some paid-for. Two of the most popular paid-for theme frameworks are **Thesis** (`http://diythemes.com/`) and **Genesis** (`http://www.studiopress.com/themes/genesis`), while popular free frameworks include **Hybrid** (`http://themehybrid.com/`), **Carrington** (`http://carringtontheme.com/`), and **Thematic** (see below).

In the case study later in this chapter, we will be using the **Thematic** theme framework built by Ian Stewart, who works for Automattic, the company that makes WordPress. The beauty of Thematic is that you can customize it just by modifying the CSS or stylesheets. You don't need to touch the other files that make up the theme, if you don't want to. However, you will need some understanding of CSS to achieve this, so before we begin with the case study, here's a crash course in CSS.

# A brief introduction to CSS

I would recommend anyone who is involved in web publishing, including all you business bloggers, to learn at least the basics of HTML and CSS. A full CSS tutorial is way beyond the scope of this chapter; in fact, there are many books that are exclusively devoted to the subject. However, I will attempt to give you a very rudimentary grounding in the principles of web design using HTML and CSS. For a more thorough tutorial, you can find many excellent online resources, such as `http://www.w3schools.com`.

# The early days of the web

The worldwide web was invented by academics in the early 1990's, who mainly used it to publish research papers via the Internet. Their layout requirements were fairly simple and early web pages usually contained nothing more than text arranged into headings and paragraphs.

 The technology that makes the Web work is **HyperText Markup Language (HTML)**, which tells web browsers, such as Internet Explorer and Mozilla Firefox, how to display content in a web page.

As the web grew in popularity, with more and more individuals and businesses using it to publish different types of content, web designers arrived on the scene and began to experiment with HTML to create more complex web pages. They wanted to create pages with images, lots of different colors, multiple columns, and more interesting layouts. It was possible to achieve this with HTML but it went way beyond what the language was originally intended for.

The main problem was that designers were forced to use the HTML `<table>` tag to create their complex page layouts. The `<table>` tag was only intended to present data in a tabular format. But by creating tables with hundreds of columns and rows, merging cells together, and nesting tables within tables, the designers could build the fancy-looking pages their clients demanded.

This was bad for a number of reasons. These huge complicated tables were slow to download. They were extremely difficult to maintain—making just one small change to a page could *break* the entire layout table. And, most importantly, they caused accessibility issues.

There was also a deeper *philosophical* dissatisfaction with using HTML for complicated web design—it simply isn't meant for it. HTML is the wrong tool for the job. The purpose of HTML is just to display content in a web browser, and not to format or style that content.

The W3C decided that something else was needed to handle the formatting and styling of web pages. So, in December 1996 it published the first specification for **Cascading Style Sheets (CSS)**.

# Content and style

The arrival of CSS meant that a web page's **content** could be separated from its **style**. HTML handles the content and CSS takes care of the style. The content of a web page includes things such as text, images, and links. The style of the page refers to things such as the colors, the typeface (font), the positioning, and the layout.

The following screenshot shows the content of a web page. No styling has been done—it just uses HTML to mark up the content into headings, links, and paragraphs.

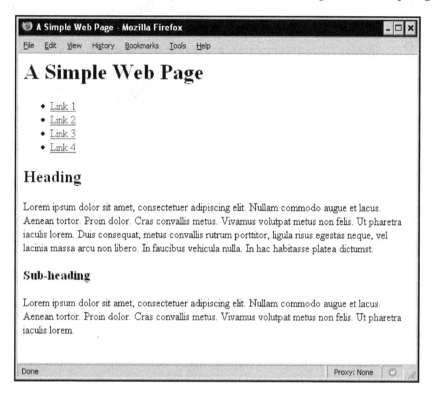

After making this simple page, we could add the following styling:

- Make the page heading white text on a dark gray background.
- Line up the links in a *navigation bar* under the header and make them bold.
- Give the body of the page a light gray background.
- Change the font to Arial.

In the bad old days, before CSS, all this styling would have been done by using HTML tags and tables. Nowadays, the correct way is to use CSS. The following screenshot shows the page after the CSS was added. *The changes you see have been achieved by just adding CSS to the web page – the HTML hasn't changed at all.*

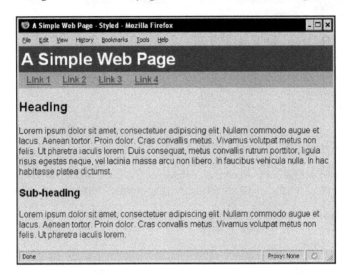

# Looking at the code

OK, let's look at the HTML and CSS used to make these simple web pages. You can download the example files from the Packt website: http://www.packtpub.com/ support?nid=8878/1322_Code.zip.

First, let's look at the HTML files. Once you've downloaded the code bundle, unzip it, and open the **CSS Example** folder. In it you will see three files: page.html, page_styled.html, and style.css:

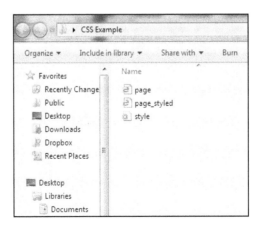

Double-click on page.html and it should open up in your default web browser. It looks like the first screenshot you saw below the *Content and style* section.

To view the HTML code that makes this page, go back to the **CSS Example** folder, right-click on page.html and select **Open With | Notepad**.

You will now see the following code in your Notepad window:

```html
<html>
<head>
<title>A Simple Web Page</title>
</head>

<body>
<h1>A Simple Web Page</h1>
<ul>
  <li><a href="http://www.packtpub.com">Link 1</a></li>
  <li><a href="http://www.packtpub.com">Link 2</a></li>
  <li><a href="http://www.packtpub.com">Link 3</a></li>
  <li><a href="http://www.packtpub.com">Link 4</a></li>
</ul>
<h2>Heading </h2>
<p>Lorem ipsum dolor sit amet, consectetuer adipiscing elit. Nullam
  commodo augue et lacus. Aenean tortor. Proin dolor. Cras convallis
  metus. Vivamus volutpat metus non felis. Ut pharetra iaculis lorem.
  Duis consequat, metus convallis rutrum porttitor, ligula risus
  egestas neque, vel lacinia massa arcu non libero. In faucibus
  vehicula nulla. In hac habitasse platea dictumst. </p>
<h3>Sub-heading</h3>
<p>Lorem ipsum dolor sit amet, consectetuer adipiscing elit. Nullam
  commodo augue et lacus. Aenean tortor. Proin dolor. Cras convallis
  metus. Vivamus volutpat metus non felis. Ut pharetra iaculis lorem.
</p>
</body>
</html>
```

**Downloading the example code**

You can download the example code files for all Packt books you have purchased from your account at http://www.PacktPub.com. If you purchased this book elsewhere, you can visit http://www.PacktPub.com/support and register to have the files e-mailed directly to you.

If you've never seen HTML before, this might look rather confusing. Don't worry, we'll go through it bit-by-bit.

The first thing you'll notice is lots of angle brackets: < >. These contain the HTML tags. Each HTML tag appears as a pair, with an opening tag < > and a closing tag </ >.

The very first tag you see is the `<html>` tag. This tag encloses the entire HTML document—you'll see the closing `</html>` tag is right at the bottom. The `<html></html>` tag simply tells the browser where the HTML document begins and ends.

All HTML documents are made up of two main parts, the **head** and the **body**. The head, also called the **header**, is contained in the `<head></head>` tag. The header gives information about the HTML document—this is known as **Metadata**. In our simple document the only information included in the header is the page title, which you can see in the `<title></title>` tag. The document title is shown in the title bar of your web browser as in the following screenshot:

Everything in the `<body></body>` tag is the main content of the page, which actually appears in the browser window. Our page begins with an `<h1></h1>` tag, which is a **level 1 heading**—it contains our main page heading. Next comes a `<ul></ul>` tag, which is an **unordered list** or bulleted list. Each item in the unordered list is placed in `<li></li>` tags. These are the four links at the top of the page.

Next you'll notice the `<a href></a>` tags. These are special tags for hyperlinks. Let's look at one of these in more detail:

```
<a href="http://www.packtpub.com">Link 1</a>
```

It begins with `<a href=`, which tells the browser that this is a hyperlink.

Next, between double quote marks we have the URL to which the link points `"http://www.packtpub.com"`. Then comes an angle bracket > which closes the first part of the tag. Now we have the link text that actually appears in the browser window. In this case, it is `Link 1`. And finally, there is the closing tag `</a>`, which tells the browser it's the end of the hyperlink.

We then have another heading tag, `<h2></h2>`—this time it's a **level 2 heading**, which appears in the browser slightly smaller than a level 1 heading. Next comes a `<p></p>` tag—these hold **paragraph** text. Then we see another heading, this time level 3 `<h3></h3>`, and then another paragraph.

Next, we have the closing body tag—`</body>`, as we have come to the end of our page's content. Finally, there's the closing `</html>` tag, as it's the end of the HTML document.

# The stylesheet

Now, let's look at the CSS, which gives the web page its style; that is the color and size of elements on the page and the layout, or placement of the elements on the page. In the **CSS Example** folder that you downloaded, right-click on the `style.css` file and select **Open With | Notepad**.

What you are now looking at is a **Cascading Style Sheet**. It actually comprises a number of **rules**, which tell web browsers how to display specific types of content structures. Our style sheet contains six **rules**.

Let's examine one of those rules in more detail:

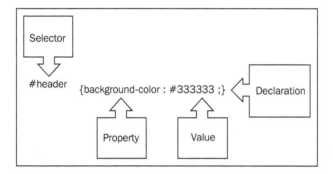

A CSS rule has **two parts**. The first part is the **selector**, which defines the HTML element to which the rule applies. There are various types of selectors, but we won't go into each type in detail as that would be the subject of a full CSS tutorial. Suffice to say that the selector in the preceding diagram is known as an **ID selector**—a # is used to identify this type of selector. I have defined this ID selector as `#header`; I could have chosen any ID which is appropriate and makes sense to me or anyone else who reads the stylesheet. Any word can be used to define an ID selector, there is no set vocabulary. `#goofy` or `#sandwich` would both work as ID selectors, but they may not make a lot of sense to someone else reading the stylesheet. Another common type of selector is called an **element selector**—these are based on standard HTML elements like `body`, `h1`, or `p`. In our stylesheet, the very first rule uses an element selector: `body`. All the other selectors here are ID selectors.

The second part of a CSS rule is known as the **declaration**, which is made up of a **property** and a **value**. The declaration describes the appearance of all the elements that match the selector.

There are hundreds of CSS properties available to web designers for use in their stylesheets. You can see a complete reference guide defining each and every available CSS property at: http://www.w3.org/TR/CSS2/propidx.html.

In this example, the **declaration** uses the background-color **property**, giving it a **value** of #333333. In CSS, the background-color property, fairly obviously, defines the background color of the selector. Colors can be defined using the RGB hexadecimal system. In this case, the hexadecimal value is #333333, which is a dark gray color.

So, in this example, the CSS rule states that *any HTML elements defined as #header will have a dark gray background*.

Let's examine another one of our CSS rules:

```
body {
    font-family: Arial, Helvetica, sans-serif;
    margin: 0;
    padding: 0;
    background-color: #CCCCCC;
    color: #000000;
}
```

This rule defines the body selector. As we've already seen, the HTML <body> element contains all the content for the web page. So, the styles defined here will apply to all the content in our HTML document. The first declaration in this rule refers to the font-family property, to which we have given the value, Arial, Helvetica, sans-serif. This means that all the text on our web page will appear in the **Arial** font.

The next two declarations deal with margin and padding. These affect the positioning of text (or other content) on the web page. Basically, by giving these two properties a 0 value, there is no space between the edge of the browser window and the content. Later on in this chapter, we'll adjust these values and see what happens.

 To fully understand about positioning in CSS, you need to know about something called the **CSS Box Model**. Again, it's beyond the scope of this chapter, but you can find excellent discussions on the CSS Box Model at http://www.brainjar.com/css/positioning/default.asp and http://www.w3schools.com/css/css_boxmodel.asp.

The next declaration uses the `background-color` property. We've seen this property before and here, it sets the background color for the whole page to light gray (#CCCCCC). The final declaration gives the `color` property a value of #000000. The `color` property applies to all the text on the page, making it black.

 As you become more experienced with CSS, you'll notice that different browsers display some CSS declarations in slightly different ways. This is why you should always test your web pages in as many different browsers as possible.

# Applying the stylesheet

So, we've seen the style sheet. Now you're probably wondering how these styles are applied to our HTML document, `page.html`.

There are three ways of adding CSS to an HTML document. The first is known as **Inline Declarations**. This method simply involves adding CSS styles throughout the HTML document as and when they are required. For example, each time we have an `<h2>` heading in our HTML document, we could add a CSS style direct to the `<h2>` tag, as follows:

```
<h2 style="color: #FF0000; font-size: 16px;">Level 2 Heading</h2>
```

This would give us a red heading with a size of 16 pixels. The problem with this method is that we would have to add the styling to each and every `<h2>` heading in our document. If we decided at a later date that we wanted our `<h2>` headings to be blue, we would have to go through the document and edit each and every `<h2>` style.

The next method of adding CSS to our HTML is known as **Embedded CSS**. This involves placing the CSS in the **header** of our HTML document, for example:

```
<html>
<head>
<title>A Simple Web Page</title>
<style type="text/css">
h2 {
  color: #FF0000;
  font-size: 16px;
}
</style>
</head>
```

This would also make all `<h2>` headings in our HTML document red with a size of 16 pixels. This is a slightly better approach because we only have to define our `<h2>` heading style once and it is automatically applied to every `<h2>` heading in the document. The downside with this approach is that the CSS has to be added to every page in our website — there might be dozens or hundreds of pages that need the CSS added to their headers. Once again, if we wanted to make our `<h2>` headings blue throughout the website, we would have to edit the **Embedded CSS** on every page.

The third approach is widely regarded as the best. It is called **External CSS**. This involves keeping your CSS in a completely separate file from your web page, for example, `style.css`. You then add a **link** to your CSS file in the header of each web page that requires those styles. The benefit here is that you just need to maintain one CSS file. If you want to change your `<h2>` headings to blue, you just make one change to the `style.css` file and the new style is automatically applied to every page in your website.

This is the approach we'll use in our simple web page example. So, let's work through the steps that will apply the stylesheet to our HTML document.

Go back to the `page.html` file and open it in Notepad. The first step is to link our style sheet to the HTML document. To do this, add the following line to the header just after the `<title>A Simple Web Page</title>` line:

```
<link rel="stylesheet" type="text/css" href="style.css" />
```

Your header should now look like this:

```
<html>
<head>
<title>A Simple Web Page - Styled</title>
<link rel="stylesheet" type="text/css" href="style.css" />
</head>
```

The link tag tells the browser that it needs to use an external stylesheet for this web page. The location of the stylesheet is specified by `href="style.css"`. In this case, `style.css` is in the same directory as our HTML document, so we just need the filename for the link to work. However, you can link to any `.css` file, which may be in another directory or on another web server. So, you could have a link like this: `href="http://www.anotherwebsite.com/style/style.css"`.

At this point let's take a look at the page. Save the file in Notepad, using **File | Save**. If you already have the page open in your browser, refresh or reload it. If it's not already open, go back to the `CSS Example` folder and double-click on `page.html`.

You'll see that the background color and font have already changed.

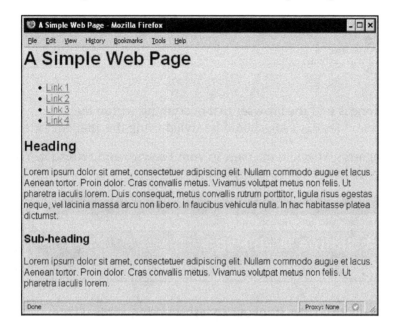

The web browser has already applied the first CSS rule in our stylesheet, because it's based on an **element selector**. Remember, these types of selectors apply to standard HTML elements and as we already have a `<body></body>` element in our document, the style for `body` has been applied.

The other rules in our stylesheet use **ID selectors**, so we need to tell the web browser which elements of our HTML we want these selectors to apply to. We do this by using **<div>** tags.

 `<div>` tags enable us to define **divisions** or regions of an HTML document.

Let's begin by defining the `#header` element and, in so doing, tell the browser where we want the `header` style to be applied.

Back in `page.html` in Notepad, add the following line immediately after the opening `<body>` tag:

```
<div id="header">
```

Now add a closing `</div>` tag after the `<h1>A Simple Web Page</h1>` heading. This section of code should now look like this:

```
<body>
<div id="header">
<h1>A Simple Web Page</h1>
</div>
```

What we've done is told the browser that everything within the `<div id="header"></div>` tag should be styled using the `#header` rule.

Save the file again, go back to the page in your browser and refresh it. You'll see that the `header` styles have now been applied:

There are actually two rules from our stylesheet being applied here:

```
#header {
    background-color: #333333;
}
```

and:

```
#header h1 {
    padding: 5px;
    margin: 0;
    color: #FFFFFF;
}
```

We have already looked at the first rule—it simply applies the dark gray background. The other rule uses a special kind of ID selector, known as a **descendent selector**. This **specifies** a rule for all `<h1>` elements that come within the `#header` ID. In this case, all `<h1>` elements within `#header` are white (#FFFFFF), with a `padding` of 5 pixels and a `margin` of 0.

Just to demonstrate that this only affects `<h1>` tags within `#header`, add this line immediately after the closing `</div>` tag:

```
<h1>Another H1 Heading</h1>
```

Now save `page.html` and refresh your browser. You will see another `<h1>` heading but it isn't styled the same as the heading in `#header`:

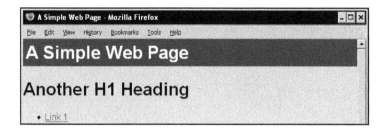

 You can delete the line we just added — it was only for demonstration.

Now we'll style the links to create the navigation bar. Once again, we need to create a `<div>` to tell the browser where to apply our `nav` styling. Add the following line just after the closing `</div>` tag for the `#header` element:

```
<div id="nav">
```

And then add a closing `</div>` tag straight after the closing `</ul>` tag. This section of code should now look like this:

```
<body>
<div id="header">
<h1>A Simple Web Page</h1>
</div>
<div id="nav">
<ul>
  <li><a href="http://www.packtpub.com">Link 1</a></li>
  <li><a href="http://www.packtpub.com">Link 2</a></li>
  <li><a href="http://www.packtpub.com">Link 3</a></li>
  <li><a href="http://www.packtpub.com">Link 4</a></li>
</ul>
</div>
```

Save `page.html` and refresh your browser. You should see the navigation bar just below the header. The browser has applied these three CSS rules to the `#nav` element:

```
#nav {
  font-weight: bold;
  background-color: #999999;
  padding: 5px;
```

```
    }
#nav ul{
    margin: 0;
    padding: 0;
    }
#nav li{
    display: inline;
    margin: 0;
    padding: 10;
    }
```

Hopefully, these CSS rules are starting to make a bit more sense now. You should be able to see what's going on in the first `#nav` rule. You may also have noticed that the other two contain more examples of **descendent selectors**. This time we're specifying styles that only apply to `<ul>` and `<li>` elements within `#nav`. If you added another unordered list (`<ul>`) elsewhere on the page, it would appear as a regular bulleted list.

In the `#nav li` rule, it's interesting to note the `display: inline;` declaration. This is what tells the browser to display the list items horizontally rather than in a vertical list.

That's our simple web page. I've included the finished HTML document (`page-styled.html`) in the CSS Example folder.

# Tweaking the styles

The last stage in this very brief introduction to CSS is to see what happens if we make some changes to the stylesheet. Go back to `style.css` in Notepad. First, let's see what happens if we change the values for `margin` and `padding` in the `body` rule. Change it to this:

```
body {
    font-family: Arial, Helvetica, sans-serif;
    margin: 10px;
    padding: 10px;
    background-color: #CCCCCC;
    color: #000000;
    }
```

Save `style.css` and refresh your browser. You should see some extra space around the edge of the browser window. This is the 10 pixels `margin` and `padding` we just added.

Now let's add a rule to change the styling of our `<h2>` heading. Add the following at the end of the stylesheet:

```
h2 {
    font-family: Courier New, Courier, mono;
    color: #0000FF;
}
```

After you've saved `style.css` and refreshed your browser, you'll see that our `<h2>` heading is now in **Courier** font and colored blue. This style will also apply to any other `<h2>` headings we add to the document.

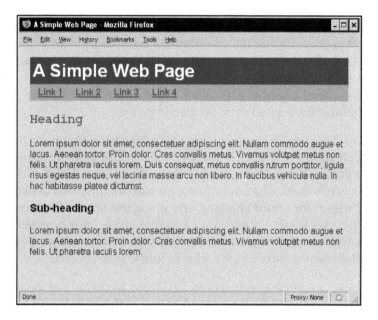

That was a very brief introduction to HTML and CSS and you'll probably want to supplement it with some further reading. It's a large subject and there is no way you could become an expert after such a short introduction. The aim of this brief tutorial was to teach you what HTML and CSS code looks like and how the two technologies work together to create web pages. Admittedly, much of the detail has been glossed over. However, this overview should enable you to follow the work we'll be doing in the case study as it involves editing the stylesheets for the Thematic theme framework (I will provide all the CSS; to see it working, you just need to paste it into the case study stylesheets). But before we move on to that, you may want to set up an environment on your own computer that allows you to run WordPress locally.

# Setting up a local development environment

If you are considering making big changes to your blog, particularly ones that require editing the WordPress source files, it's worth considering setting up a development environment on your local computer. This has a number of benefits. First, if you mess up and cause irreparable damage to the WordPress files, you haven't broken your live blog. Second, you don't have to take your blog offline while you're playing around *under the hood*. Third, you don't have to keep FTPing files to your remote server to view the changes.

Admittedly, most of the editing we'll be doing in the rest of this chapter could be done using the Theme Editor in the WordPress administration area. If you follow through the case study example at the end of this chapter, it will probably only take half an hour or so. However, if you do decide to design your own theme the chances are it could take several hours or even days. Much of the work will involve trial and error — saving your changes and then previewing them.

Since WordPress 2.6, tweaking a theme became a lot easier, thanks to the Theme Previewer, which allows you to view a theme as it would actually appear with your content, before you install it. However, using the WordPress Theme Editor to do a lot of editing work is not ideal. The editor is not as user-friendly as a desktop text editor (it's really only meant for minor changes) and using the Theme Previewer repeatedly during the design process is not as easy as just refreshing your browser window. This is why it's well worth using a local development environment. You may also find your development environment useful in future web projects.

To run WordPress you need a **web server**, **PHP**, and **MySQL**. For the web server I recommend **Apache** as it's widely regarded as one of the best. It's also open source (as are PHP and MySQL), so it's free to download and use. These are the components we will install to set up our development environment.

It is possible to download Apache, PHP, and MySQL as separate components and then install and configure them one by one. However, this can be quite a complicated process that requires a fair amount of technical knowledge. Luckily there are a number of open source Apache distributions that come bundled with PHP and MySQL pre-configured. They also include an installer, which makes setting up your server a breeze. One of the best is **XAMPP**, from Apache Friends, and it's the one we'll be using for our development environment. XAMPP is available for the most popular desktop operating systems including Windows, MAC OS X, Linux, and Solaris.

> XAMPP stands for: X (any of the four operating systems supported), A (Apache), M (MySQL), P (PHP), and P (Perl).

# Installing XAMPP

We will now run through the process of installing XAMPP on your computer.

1.  Go to `http://www.apachefriends.org/en/xampp.html` and click on the link for your operating system. We'll be working through the installation for Windows, but there are installation instructions for the other operating systems on the Apache Friends website.

2.  On the **XAMPP for Windows** page, choose to download the latest stable release of the **XAMPP Installer** and save it to your desktop. The file is about 66 MB, so this may take some time depending on the speed of your connection.

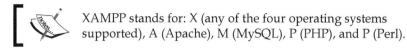

3.  Click on the XAMPP Installer icon on your desktop and, when prompted, choose your preferred language. The **XAMPP Setup Wizard** will now begin.

4.  Click **Next** and then choose the location for your XAMPP installation. I recommend using `C:\xampp`. Click **Next**.

5.  On the next screen, I recommend you stick with the defaults. Do not install the components as services. (If they are installed as services, they will start automatically every time you turn on your computer.) Click **Install** and wait for the various packages to be extracted and installed. If the Command Prompt window opens, don't touch it, just let it run.

6.  Click **Finish** and select **Yes** to start the **XAMPP Control Panel**.

7. Start the servers by clicking the **Start** buttons next to **Apache** and **MySQL** in the **Control Panel**. (If prompted by Windows Firewall, allow access to the Apache server.)

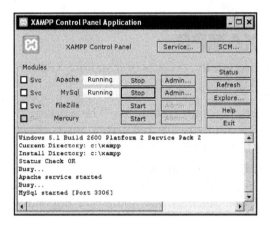

8. Open your web browser and enter the address `http://localhost/`. If your installation has worked properly, XAMPP should now be visible in your browser. If you can't see XAMPP, refer to the FAQs and help on the Apache Friends website.

Congratulations you now have an Apache / MySQL / PHP web server running on your computer!

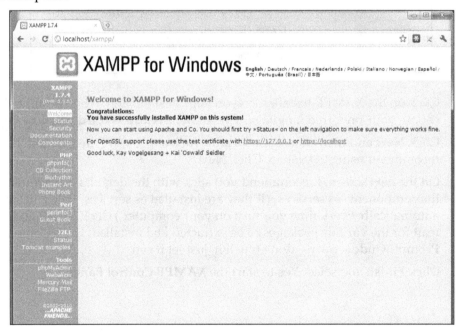

# Setting the 'root' password for MySQL

By default, when you install XAMPP there is no password set for the *root* MySQL user. This isn't a major security problem when you're only running a local server, but we'll fix it anyway.

1.  Open your web browser and go to `http://localhost/`. On the XAMPP welcome page, select **Security** under **Welcome** in the left-hand menu.

2.  You will see a table showing various security settings for XAMPP. Underneath the table, click on the link to fix security problems:

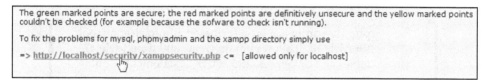

3.  Enter a password and click the **Password changing** button:

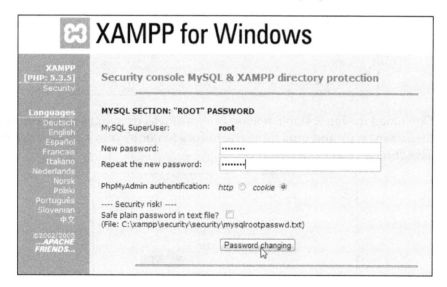

4.  You've now set a password for the **root** MySQL user.

We're now ready to install WordPress.

# Installing WordPress locally

You've probably installed WordPress at least once on a remote server and the principle is exactly the same for installing it on your local server.

1.  First, let's create a MySQL database for your WordPress installation. Open your web browser and go to `http://localhost/`. From the XAMPP welcome page, select **phpMyAdmin** under **Tools** in the left-hand menu. You'll now see the phpMyAdmin home page, where you will be prompted to login. Enter the username `root` and the password you chose for the root MySQL user (shown previously).

     phpMyAdmin is a browser-based administration tool for MySQL. It allows you to create and drop (delete) tables and databases, and run SQL statements right from your browser.

2.  Once you're logged in, locate **Create new database** and enter a name for your database in the input box. Click **Create**.

    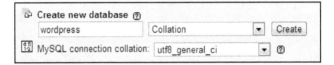

3.  Download the latest stable release of WordPress from `http://wordpress.org/download/` and unzip it to the **htdocs** folder in your **xampp** directory. This should be at `C:\xampp\htdocs`.

The htdocs folder in XAMPP is the same as the www, httpdocs, or htdocs directory on your remote web server. It's where you must place all the files you want to *publish* so that you can view them as web pages in your browser.

4. In the **wordpress** folder, open the wp-config-sample.php file using Windows Notepad or any other text editor. Edit the configuration details for the MySQL database we created earlier. These should be:

   ° DB_NAME = 'wordpress'

   ° DB_USER = 'root'

   ° DB_PASSWORD = 'yourpassword' (This is the MySQL password we set for the 'root' user earlier).

5. You can leave the other configuration settings as they are.

6. Save the file as wp-config.php. If you're using Notepad, in the **Save As** dialog box, remember to set **Save as type** to **All Files**.

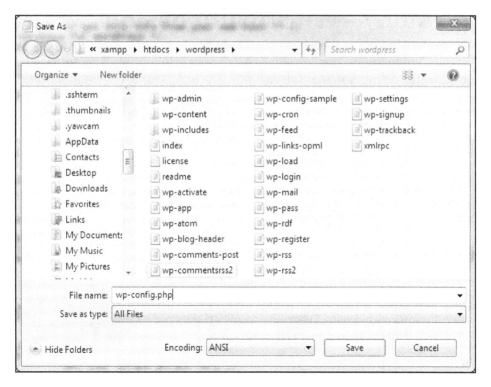

7.  Point your web browser to `http://localhost/wordpress/` and you will see the familiar WordPress installation screen. Enter your blog title (call it **WPBizGuru**), admin username, password, e-mail address, and click **Install WordPress**.

You now have a fully functional copy of WordPress on your own computer.

Note that the e-mail functions in WordPress won't work with your local server. This is because we haven't configured a mail server and we would need one for PHP to handle outgoing mail. Setting up an outgoing mail server is complicated and for many people it's impossible because their ISP won't allow them to run an SMTP server over their standard internet connection.

Not having the mail function in WordPress shouldn't be too much of a problem for the majority of things you're likely to be doing locally. *However, do ensure that you don't lose or forget your password as WordPress won't be able to email a reminder to you!*

# Case study—WPBizGuru design

As I mentioned earlier, we'll be using the Thematic theme framework to apply a custom design to the WPBizGuru blog. All the design work we'll be doing will only require changes to the stylesheets.

**Child themes**

In version 2.7, WordPress introduced the concept of **child themes**. This means you can create a new theme that uses an existing theme as its base, or **parent**. The beauty of this is that you don't have to edit the parent theme. All you need to do is create a new stylesheet (`style.css`) for your child theme, which will override the stylesheet of the parent. In effect, WordPress is using the templates and functionality from the parent theme and applying the styles from the child theme.

This means that if the developers of your parent theme make an update, you can just update the parent and the changes will be automatically applied to the child theme. We will be creating a child theme, with the Thematic framework as its parent. We will then edit the stylesheets of the child theme to create our new design (see the WordPress Codex for more on child themes: `http://codex.wordpress.org/Child_Themes`).

# Setting up a child theme

To begin, we'll install the Thematic theme framework in your local copy
of WordPress.

Log in to the dashboard of your local WordPress installation (`http://localhost/`
`wordpress/wp-admin/`). Select **Themes**, under **Appearance** in the left-hand menu,
and click the **Install Themes** tab. Enter **thematic** in the search box and click the
**Search** button (you must be connected to the internet for WordPress to search for
themes remotely). You should see the Thematic theme in the search results. Just
click **Install**, followed by **Install Now** in the pop-up window. The theme will be
downloaded and installed in your local copy of WordPress; click **Activate**. If you
view your blog, you'll see the Thematic theme in action.

## WPBizGuru

*Just another WordPress site*

Sample Page

## Hello world!

*By* ADMIN *| Published:* MAY 8, 2011 *| Edit*

Welcome to WordPress. This is your first post. Edit or delete it, then start
blogging!

Posted in *Uncategorized | 1 Comment | Edit*

If you wish, you can read some background information about the
Thematic theme at the official website (`http://themeshaper.`
`com/thematic/`) or by viewing the *ReadMe* file included with
the theme (`http://localhost/wordpress/wp-content/`
`themes/thematic/readme.html`).

# Dummy content

Your default installation of WordPress contains very little content; just a 'Hello
World!' post, a comment, and a short 'Sample Page'. When you're working on a
theme design, it's useful to have plenty of content to see how your stylesheet affects
the many different elements available in WordPress.

`WordPress.org` provides some test content for theme developers. This is how to install it:

1. Go to `http://codex.wordpress.org/Theme_Unit_Test`. Near the top of the page, locate the link to download the test data and save it to your desktop.

2. In your WordPress admin area, in the left-hand menu, select **Tools | Import**.

3. You will see a list of systems to import from. Click on **WordPress**.

4. A pop-up window will appear for you to install the WordPress Importer. Click **Install Now**.

5. When the plugin has downloaded, click **Activate Plugin & Run Importer**.

6. Choose the test data file you saved to your desktop and click **Upload file and import**.

7. On the next screen, under **Assign Authors**, leave the default settings. This will create new users for each of the authors in the test data. Under **Import Attachments**, select the **Download and import file attachments** checkbox. Click **Submit**.

8. It will take a few seconds for WordPress to install the test data.

9. Once the installation is complete, view your blog to see how the test data looks.

I have deleted the original *Sample Page,* so that the pages fit nicely on one line in the top menu:

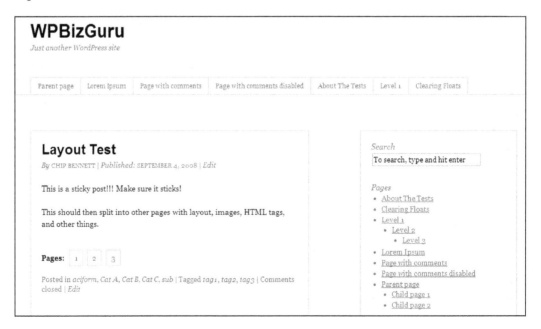

# Installing a new text editor

Now we'll download and install a decent text editor. A good text editor makes it far easier to work with code files such as `style.css`, which we'll be editing shortly. In our brief introduction to CSS we used Notepad to edit the CSS documents. That was fine with such small files, but now that we'll be working on more complex CSS, Notepad is not ideal. You may already have another text editor or a fully-blown HTML editor such as the Dreamweaver; if so, use that. Otherwise, for Windows, I recommend **Notepad++**, which is a good free option (`http://notepad-plus-plus.org/download/`). Once downloaded, install it on your PC. For Mac OS X or Linux, try Emacs (`http://www.gnu.org/software/emacs/`).

# Creating your child theme

Thematic provides us with a quick head start for creating a child theme. Take a look inside the Thematic theme folder (`C:\xampp\htdocs\wordpress\wp-content\themes\thematic`). Don't worry about all the theme files right now, just look for the folder called `thematicsamplechildtheme`. To set up our new child theme, copy `thematicsamplechildtheme` and paste it into the WordPress themes folder (`C:\xampp\htdocs\wordpress\wp-content\themes`). Rename it `wpbizguru`, which will be the name of our new child theme.

In WordPress themes, the stylesheet has a header, which gives WordPress some meta-information about the theme. This includes things like the theme's author, version number, and most importantly for child themes, the name of the theme template. This is the first part of the stylesheet we'll edit.

Fire up your new text editor (Notepad++) and open the `style.css` file in the `wpbizguru` child theme folder (`C:\xampp\htdocs\wordpress\wp-content\themes\wpbizguru`).

You'll notice that Notepad++ shows the line numbers down the left-hand margin of the text editor window, for easy reference. Editing is also made easier with Word Wrap switched on. This breaks long lines of code so you don't have to scroll horizontally to read them; select **View | Word Wrap**.

Lines 1-13 in `style.css` provide the meta-information for our new WPBizGuru theme. Each line is fairly self-explanatory. Edit the section similar to the following code (if you like, you can replace my name and website with your own):

```
/*
Theme Name: WPBizGuru
Theme URI: http://blog.wpbizguru.com
Description: A custom theme for the WpBizGuru blog.
```

```
Author: Paul Thewlis
Author URI: http://blog.paulthewlis.com
Template: thematic
Version: 1.0
Tags: Thematic, WPBizGuru,

.

WPBizGuru theme is © Paul Thewlis http://blog.paulthewlis.com/

.

*/
```

The information in this section of code appears next to each theme in the **Appearance | Themes** section of the WordPress dashboard, with the exception of two sections. The `Template:` line tells WordPress to use Thematic as the parent theme. The line with the copyright information is somewhere you can put comments or instructions—this area can contain any information you like. Save `style.css`.

We can now activate our new theme. Go to your admin area and select **Appearance | Themes** (if you were already in **Themes**, you'll need to refresh your browser). You should now see **WPBizGuru** listed under **Available Themes**:

Click the **Activate** link so we can start using our new theme.

 Now that we have the theme activated, we can view the progress of our design as we continue to work on the stylesheets.

# A closer look at style.css

At this point, it's worth having a look at the rest of the code in `style.css`:

```
/* Reset browser defaults */
@import url('../thematic/library/styles/reset.css');

/* Apply basic typography styles */
@import url('../thematic/library/styles/typography.css');

/* Apply a basic layout */
@import url('../thematic/library/layouts/2c-r-fixed.css');

/* Apply basic image styles */
@import url('../thematic/library/styles/images.css');

/* Apply default theme styles and colors */
/* It's better to actually copy over default.css into this file (or
link to a copy in your child theme) if you're going to do anything
outrageous */
@import url('../thematic/library/styles/default.css');

/* Prepare theme for plugins */
@import url('../thematic/library/styles/plugins.css');
```

What's going on here—where are all the CSS rules that give the theme its style? Well, instead of placing all the CSS rules in a single file, the Thematic developers have decided to split them up into a number of stylesheets. This prevents `style.css` from becoming a very long file. It also makes it easier to find the CSS rules you need. For example, the CSS rules that style images in the theme have been placed in a stylesheet called `images.css`. The images stylesheet is **imported** into `style.css`. That's what all the `@import` rules in `style.css` are for. You'll get a better idea of how this works as we start editing the individual stylesheets for the theme.

# The page layout

We're now getting into the meat of the CSS and the code will begin to get a little more complicated. Once again, a detailed explanation of the code would be in the realm of a more complete CSS tutorial, but I will give a summary explanation of the various sections of the stylesheets we are editing. As you edit the stylesheets, you should see how the chunks of code affect the design of the blog, even if you don't fully understand the intricacies of the CSS.

All the CSS selectors we'll be using are already coded into the template files for the Thematic theme—open up `index.php` in your text editor and you will see some of the elements that the selectors refer to.

The next stage is to give some structure to the blog page by designing the layout. Having considered WPBizGuru and its strategic goals, I think there may be quite a lot of content to go in the sidebar. This is largely because it's a case study blog and we'll be adding lots of functionality throughout the rest of the book. Because of the quantity of sidebar content, I think we need two sidebars and they should go on the right-hand side of the page, for the reasons we discussed earlier in the chapter (that is, it's best to have the main content on the left, because that's where people's eyes are likely to be drawn when they first open the page, and the search engine spiders will find it first). Out of the four wireframes we looked at earlier, the one that we'll apply to WPBizGuru is this:

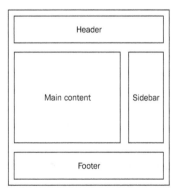

Thematic provides a number of readymade layouts. To apply the three-column layout we want for WPBizGuru, it's simply a matter of using one of the readymade Thematic layouts. Find this section of code on lines 21 and 22 of `style.css`:

```
/* Apply a basic layout */
@import url('../thematic/library/layouts/2c-r-fixed.css');
```

Then simply change the layout stylesheet to `3c-r-fixed.css`:

```
@import url('../thematic/library/layouts/3c-r-fixed.css');
```

Now if you view your blog, you will see the layout changes.

**Comments**

Line 21 is a comment. Comments are enclosed within an opening comment tag /* and a closing comment tag */. They are ignored by web browsers and can only be read by humans. They are most often used to notate CSS code so that other people reading it can follow the original author's thoughts. You can type anything you like within comment tags; it won't affect the way the web browser displays the CSS. In this case, the comment tells us that the proceeding line applies our layout.

# The default stylesheet

For the rest of the theme design, we will be editing the CSS rules contained in Thematic's `default.css` stylesheet. In `style.css` you can see that `default.css` is imported from the Thematic library—see lines 27-29 of `style.css`:

```
/* Apply default theme styles and colors */
/* It's better to actually copy over default.css into this file (or
link to a copy in your child theme) if you're going to do anything
outrageous */
@import url('../thematic/library/styles/default.css');
```

We'll follow the very sensible advice from the Thematic developers and, instead of editing `default.css` in the parent theme, we will copy the file over to our child theme. This means the original styles in the parent theme remain unchanged. So, copy `default.css` from `C:\xampp\htdocs\wordpress\wp-content\themes\thematic\library\styles` and paste it into our child theme folder at `C:\xampp\htdocs\wordpress\wp-content\themes\wpbizguru`. Then change the import URL on line 29 of `style.css` (in the WPBizGuru theme), so that our new `default.css` is imported:

```
/* Apply default theme styles and colors */
/* It's better to actually copy over default.css into this file (or
link to a copy in your child theme) if you're going to do anything
outrageous */
@import url('default.css');
```

Now open up your new `default.css` stylesheet in Notepad++ and we can begin editing it, safe in the knowledge that the parent theme styles will remain unchanged.

# The header

The next part of the theme design we'll work on is the header. We'll add a background image and apply some new styles to the blog title and blog description. The background image is included in the code file for this chapter—it's called wpbadges.jpg. Copy it into the wpbizguru theme folder (C:\xampp\htdocs\ wordpress\wp-content\themes\wpbizguru). In the default.css stylesheet for the WPBizGuru child theme, locate the section that begins /* =Header (it should be on or around line 56). You'll notice that the Thematic developers have used comments to divide default.css into logical sections, which makes it easier to find the CSS you're looking for. Now replace all the code in the header section with the following:

```css
#header {
    z-index:2;
    height: 200px;
    background: transparent url('wpbadges.jpg') center top no-repeat;
/* This image is derived from an image licensed under creative
    commons by Flickr user "whiteafrican" -
    http://www.flickr.com/photos/whiteafrican/2570514012/
    http://creativecommons.org/licenses/by/2.0/ */
    position: relative;
    width: 960px;
    margin: 0 auto;
}
#blog-title {
    font-family:Arial, Helvetica, sans-serif;
    position: absolute;
    top: 20px;
    left: 0px;
    width: 140px;
    text-align: right;
    font-size:30px;
    font-weight:bold;
    line-height: 35px;
    padding: 35px 30px 15px 30px;
    background: #3d4245;
}
#blog-title a {
    color:#b7c4cf;
    text-decoration:none;
}
#blog-title a:active,
#blog-title a:hover {
    color: #fff;
}
```

```
#blog-description {
  font-family:Arial, Helvetica, sans-serif;
  color:#3d4245;
  display: inline;
  position: absolute;
  top: 95px;
  left: 0px;
  width: 200px;
  text-align: left;
  font-size: 12px;
  padding: 15px 10px;
}
```

Save `default.css` and view the WPBizGuru blog in your browser (remember to refresh the page, if it's already open). You should be able to see the header's background image and the new styles for the blog title and blog description. Don't worry if the menu looks a bit weird, we'll fix that next.

# The menu

We'll add some background color and text color to the menu and make sure it's positioned correctly just below the header.

Locate the section of code for the menu styles—it begins at the `/* =Menu` comment. Replace this rule:

```
#access {
  border-bottom:1px solid #ccc;
  height:32px;
  font-size:13px;
  overflow:visible;
  z-index:100;
}
```

with the following:

```
#access {
  height:32px;
  font-size:13px;
  overflow:visible;
  z-index:100;
  position: absolute;
  bottom: 0px;
  left: 0px;
  right: 0px;
```

```
    padding-left: 30px;
    background: #3d4245;
}
```

Now skip down to the section of code that begins /*** THEMATIC SKIN ***/ and ends a couple of lines above /* =Content. Replace the whole section with the following:

```
/*** THEMATIC SKIN ***/
.sf-menu {
    float:left;
}
.sf-menu a {
  padding:9px 13px;
  text-decoration:none;
  color: #b7c4cf;
  font-weight: bold;
}
.sf-menu .current_page_item a,
.sf-menu .current_page_ancestor a,
.sf-menu .current_page_parent a {
  font-weight: bold;
}
.sf-menu a, .sf-menu a:visited  {
  color: #b7c4cf;
  border-bottom:none;
}
.sf-menu li:hover, .sf-menu li.sfHover,
.sf-menu a:focus, .sf-menu a:hover, .sf-menu a:active {
  background: #557792;
  color: #fff;
  outline: 0;
  text-decoration: underline;
}
.sf-menu li:hover ul,
.sf-menu li.sfHover ul {
  top:32px; /* overriding essential styles */
  background: #557792;
}
.sf-menu li li:hover a,
.sf-menu li li.sfHover a {
  background: #557792;
  color: #fff;
}
```

Once again, save `default.css` and view the blog in your browser, remembering to refresh if necessary. You should see the menu is now positioned below the header and its background colors have been applied.

# Colors and fonts

Based on the subject matter of WPBizGuru, I decided on a color scheme that uses gray and blue tones. This gives the blog a business-like feel, which makes sense considering it's aimed at a business audience. The blues and grays are also reminiscent of the WordPress corporate color scheme. I also decided to add a colored background to the blog, to make the main content area stand out. I chose a simple Arial font because it is readable and gives the design a clean, contemporary look.

We'll begin applying the fonts, colors, and background color by editing the global elements section right at the top of `default.css`. So, scroll back to the top of the stylesheet and locate the block of code that begins with `/* =Global Elements` and ends a couple of lines above `/* =Header`. Replace the whole section of code with the following:

```
/* =Global Elements
---------------------------------------------------------- */

#container {
  padding: 0;
}
body, input, textarea {
  font: 15px Arial, Helvetica, sans-serif;
  line-height:22px;
}
body {
  background: #555555;
  color: #020659;
}
p, ul, ol, dd, pre {
  margin-bottom:22px;
}
pre, code {
  font:14px Monaco, monospace;
  line-height:22px;
}
blockquote {
  color:#666;
  font-style:italic;
}
```

```
table {
  border:1px solid #ccc;
  border-width:1px 1px 0 1px;
  font-size:13px;
  line-height:18px;
  margin:0 0 22px 0;
  text-align:left;
}
caption {
  text-align:left;
}
tr {
  border-bottom:1px solid #ccc;
}
th, td {
  padding: .7em 1.25em;
}
hr {
  background-color:#ccc;
  border:0;
  color:#ccc;
  height:1px;
  margin-bottom:22px;
}
a:link {
  color:#004B91;
}
a:visited {
  color:#743399;
}
a:active,
a:hover {
  color: #b7c4cf;
}
```

Once again, save `default.css` and review the changes in your browser. You'll notice that the background color has been applied and the fonts have changed. Now we need to turn our attention to the main content area.

# The main content area

We're going to make the background color of the main content area white and add a background gradient behind the sidebars, to differentiate them from the rest of the content. We'll also apply a few styles to the text. First, you'll need to place the gradient image in the WPBizGuru theme folder. In the code download, locate gradient.png and paste a copy of it in C:\xampp\htdocs\wordpress\wp-content\themes\wpbizguru.

Now find the section of code that begins at the /* =Content comment and ends a couple of lines above /* =Attachments. As you can see, this is a pretty long section of code, so you might want to cut and paste it from the finished default.css file that's included with the code download for this chapter. You need to replace the whole section with the following:

```
/* =Content
-------------------------------------------------------------- */

#main {
  clear:both;
  padding:30px 0;
  background: #fff url('gradient.png') top right no-repeat;
  color: #222;
}
#content {
  padding: 0px 30px;
}
.attachment .page-title {
  font-style:italic;
}

.page-title a {
  color:#666;
  text-decoration:none;
}
.page-title a:active,
.page-title a:hover {
  color: #b7c4cf;
}
.page-title span {
  font-style:italic;
}
.page-title .meta-nav {
  font-style:normal;
}
```

```
.hentry {
  padding:0 0 22px 0;
}
.single .hentry {
  padding:0;
}
.home #content .sticky {
  border:1px solid #ccc;
  margin:0 0 66px 0;
  padding:22px 20px 0 20px;
}
.entry-title {
  font-family:Arial,sans-serif;
  font-size:26px;
  font-weight:bold;
  line-height:26px;
  padding:0 0 7px 0;
  color:#020659;
}
.entry-title a {
  color:#020659;
  text-decoration:none;
}
.entry-title a:active,
.entry-title a:hover {
  color: #b7c4cf;
}
.entry-meta {
  color:#666;
  font-size:13px;
  font-style:normal;
  line-height:18px;
}
.entry-meta .author {
}
.entry-meta .n {
  font-size:13px;
  font-style:normal;
  letter-spacing:0.05em;
  text-transform:none;
  font-weight:bold;
}
.entry-meta a {
  color:#bf5b04;
```

```
    text-decoration:none;
    font-weight:bold;
}
.entry-meta a:active,
.entry-meta a:hover {
  color: #b7c4cf;
  font-weight:bold;
}
.entry-meta abbr {
  border:none;
  cursor:text;
  font-size:13px;
  font-style:normal;
  font-weight:bold;
  letter-spacing:0.05em;
  text-transform:none;
  color:#000;
}
.entry-content {
  padding:22px 0 0 0;
}
.entry-content h1,
.entry-content h2 {
  font-family:Arial,sans-serif;
  font-size:19px;
  font-weight:bold;
  padding:28px 0 14px 0;
}
.entry-content h3 {
  font-size:17px;
  font-style:italic;
  padding:28px 0 14px 0;
}
.entry-content h4 {
  font-size:11px;
  font-family:Arial,sans-serif;
  font-weight:bold;
  text-transform:uppercase;
  letter-spacing:0.05em;
}
.entry-content table {
  margin-left:1px;
}
.entry-content embed {
```

```css
    margin:0 0 22px 0;
  }
.entry-utility {
  clear:both;
  color:#666;
  font-size:13px;
  line-height:18px;
  margin:0 0 44px 0;
}
.entry-utility a {
  color:#666;
  font-style:italic;
  text-decoration:none;
}
.entry-utility a:active,
.entry-utility a:hover {
  color: #b7c4cf;
}
.edit-link {
  clear:both;
  display:block;
}
.page-link {
  font-size:13px;
  font-weight:bold;
  line-height:18px;
  margin:0 0 22px 0;
  padding:22px 0 0 0;
  word-spacing:0.5em;
}
.page-link a {
  border:1px solid #ccc;
  color:#666;
  font-weight:normal;
  padding:0.5em 0.75em;
  text-decoration:none;
}
.page-link a:active,
.page-link a:hover {
  color: #b7c4cf;
}
ul#links-page,
ul#archives-page {
  list-style:none;
```

```
    margin-left:0;
    overflow:hidden;
}
li.content-column {
  float:left;
  margin-right:20px;
  width:45%;
}
.gallery {
  display: block;
  clear: both;
  overflow: hidden;
  margin: 0 auto;
  padding:0 0 22px 0;
    }
.gallery .gallery-row {
  display: block;
  clear: both;
  overflow: hidden;
  margin: 0;
    }
.gallery .gallery-item {
  overflow: hidden;
  float: left;
  margin: 0;
  text-align: center;
  list-style: none;
  padding: 0;
    }
.gallery .gallery-item img, .gallery .gallery-item img.thumbnail {
  max-width: 89%;
  height: auto;
  padding: 1%;
  margin: 0 auto;
  border: none !important;
    }
.gallery-caption {
  margin-left: 0;
    }
.wp-caption-text,
.gallery-caption {
  color:#666;
  font-size:13px;
  line-height:18px;
```

```
}
#author-info {
   margin:0 0 44px 0;
   overflow:hidden;
}
#author-info .avatar {
   float:left;
   margin:.3em 1em 0 0;
}
```

Phew! That was a lot of code. Save your work and check the results in your browser. You'll see that the main content area has been styled. Notice how the gradient image is being used as the background for the sidebars.

## The sidebars

We'll tidy up the sidebars by removing the border around the right-hand sidebar and applying some text styles. Locate the section of code that begins at the /* =Asides, Sidebars & Widget-Ready Areas (it should be on or around line 697). We're only making a couple of minor changes here, so I'll just run through the rules we need to change rather than giving the whole section of code.

First locate the following rules:

```
.aside .current_page_item a {
   color: #FF4B33;
}
.aside .current_page_item .page_item a {
   color:#666;
}
.aside .current_page_item .page_item a:hover,
.aside .current_page_item .page_item a:active {
   color: #FF4B33;
}
.aside {
   color:#666;
}
.aside a {
   color:#666;
}
.aside a:active,
.aside a:hover {
   color: #FF4B33;
}
```

```
.aside h3 {
  font-size:15px;
  font-style:italic;
  line-height:22px;
}
```

And replace with the following:

```
.aside .current_page_item a {
  color: #020659;
}
.aside .current_page_item .page_item a {
  color:#666;
}
.aside .current_page_item .page_item a:hover,
.aside .current_page_item .page_item a:active {
  color: #020659;
}
.aside {
  color:#666;
}
.aside a {
  color:#666;
}
.aside a:active,
.aside a:hover {
  color: #020659;
}
.aside h3 {
  font-size:15px;
  font-style:none;
  font-weight:bold;
  line-height:22px;
}
```

Now find the following rule, which should be on or around line 808:

```
#primary {
  border:1px solid #ccc;
  padding:18px 0 0 0;
  margin-bottom:22px;
}
```

And change it to the following:

```
#primary {
  border:0px;
  padding:18px 0 0 0;
  margin-bottom:22px;
}
```

Save your work and take a look at the changes in your browser.

You may notice that the search box is a bit too large for the sidebar. Unfortunately, this is something we can't change in the stylesheets. To fix this, use Notepad++ to open up `functions.php`, which you'll find in the `wpbizguru` theme folder. Scroll down to line 36, just before the closing PHP tag `?>`. Add a line break (by hitting **Enter** on your keyboard) and then insert the following code:

```
// change search input size
function child_search_widget($search_form) {
  $search_form = str_replace('size="32"', 'size="25"' ,
  $search_form);
  return $search_form;
}
add_filter('thematic_search_form', 'child_search_widget');
```

Save `functions.php` and take a look at the blog — the search box now fits the sidebar much better.

# The footer

OK, we're nearly finished. There are just a few styles to be applied to the footer. Locate the section of code that begins at the `/* =Footer` comment (which should be on or around line 843) and ends a couple of lines above `/* =PageNavi`. Replace the whole section with this:

```
#footer {
  border-top:0px;
  margin-top:22px;
}
#siteinfo {
  color:#b7c4cf;   font-size:11px;
  line-height:18px;
  padding:22px 0 44px 0;
}
#siteinfo a {
```

```
   color:#b7c4cf;
}
#siteinfo a:active,
#siteinfo a:hover {
   color: #fff;
}
```

Save your work and view the blog in your browser to see the new styling in the footer.

You can change the footer text by going to **Appearance | Thematic Options** in the WordPress Dashboard. I changed the footer text to this:

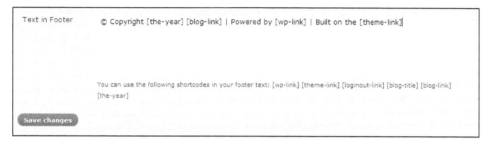

# The finished theme

You should now have something that resembles this:

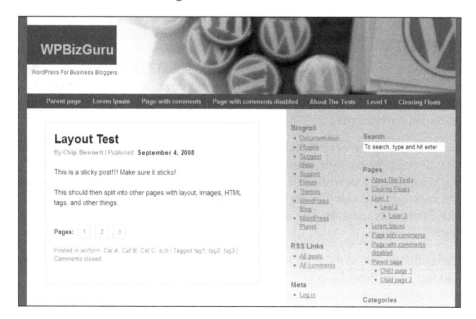

I admit, the WPBizGuru theme is unlikely to win any design awards, but that wasn't the point of the exercise. The point was to show you how easy it is to create a new child theme using the Thematic framework and come up with a unique, custom-made design just by editing the stylesheets. I had to keep things fairly simple to avoid the CSS code becoming too complicated and unwieldy. You could carry on tweaking the theme and see what you can come up with.

There's one final task to complete our new theme and that's to include a screenshot in the theme folder so that it appears in the **Manage Themes** tab in the WordPress dashboard. I've included a screenshot in the code bundle for this chapter, just copy it into your wpbizguru theme folder and you should see it in the **Manage Themes** tab:

# Summary

We've covered a lot of ground in this chapter. You should now know about some of the design principles to consider when working on your blog theme. These should give you the confidence to critically evaluate your existing blog design and maybe make some improvements.

We also went through a very brief introduction to HTML and CSS before setting up a local development environment. Finally, we worked through the process of applying a completely new design for our case study blog by using the Thematic theme framework. We saw how an attractive design can be achieved by just editing the child theme's stylesheets. The finished theme is included in the code bundle for this chapter.

In the next chapter, we will be looking at a variety of options for adding images and videos to our WordPress blog.

# 4
# Images and Videos

In this chapter, we are going to look at some advanced image handling techniques to ensure the images you use in your blog are displayed consistently and are easy to manage. We'll cover:

- Image theory basics
- Image editing
- How to alter the size and styling of thumbnails and images within posts
- How to create an image gallery in WordPress
- How to incorporate videos from third-party sites such as YouTube and Google Video
- How to add a favicon to our blog

## Image theory basics

The most common formats for web images are JPEG, GIF, and PNG. These are the three formats you're most likely to come across. JPEG and GIF have been around for a long time, while PNG is a relative newcomer. PNG is a far more versatile format than GIF and JPEG but you should be aware that some browsers (such as Internet Explorer 6 and older) have problems rendering PNG images correctly, particularly ones with transparent backgrounds.

Whichever file format you use, there are three important image measurements you need to be aware of. They are **dimensions**, **resolution**, and **file size**.

- **Dimensions**: This is simply the width and height of an image. Most image editing software allows you to express the dimensions of an image in a variety of units (for example centimeters, inches, or pixels). The most common and most useful unit in web design is pixels. The largest monitor screen size (or resolution) in common use at the moment is about 1280 by 1024 pixels, so there is little point in setting the dimensions of an image any higher than this, unless you want people to be able to print them at a reasonably high quality. Images intended for print should be placed in a separate folder for downloading.

- **Resolution**: The resolution of an image is measured in **pixels per inch (ppi)**. This is how much data is contained in each square inch of an image. The higher the ppi, the sharper the image will appear. However, computer monitors can only display around 72-100 pixels per inch so there's little point in having a resolution of more than 72 ppi for images on the Web. The only time when a higher resolution is necessary is when an image is intended to be printed, in which case, around 300 ppi is recommended.

- **File size**: The file size of an image is the amount of space it takes up on a hard disk and is measured in **kilobytes (KB)**, **megabytes (MB)**, or **gigabytes (GB)**. Crucially, the larger the dimensions and resolution of an image are, the bigger the file size. Large images take longer to download for your end user (which makes a web page slow to load), and they eat up the bandwidth allowance allocated by your web host. It's important to keep the dimensions and resolution of your images to the absolute minimum so that the file size is as small as possible. This is known as optimization.

# Optimization

To maximize usability and efficiency in terms of bandwidth, images for the Web need to be optimized. This simply means setting the resolution to 72 ppi and making sure that the dimensions are not larger than the area of the screen you want the images to occupy. Optimization is done using image editing software; there are many products available. The industry standard for design and web professionals is Adobe Photoshop (`http://www.adobe.com/photoshop`), however, it's very expensive and if you're only using it to optimize images for the Web, it's probably not worth the expense. There are cheaper alternatives but they don't come close to Photoshop in terms of features and performance. Luckily, there is an open source product, which does provide a viable alternative to Photoshop. It's called **The GIMP (The GNU Image Manipulation Program)** and many designers prefer it to Photoshop, not just for the economic advantage it offers (The GIMP is free, of course), but because of its impressive feature set.

We'll be using The GIMP to optimize our images later in this chapter, so let's download and install it now.

 **Installing 'The GIMP'**

Go to `http://www.gimp.org/downloads/` and download the GIMP installer for Windows XP SP2 or later (there are also versions available for Linux and Mac OS X). Run the installer and when it is finished, launch The GIMP.

# Images in WordPress posts

WordPress does a pretty good job of handling images that you upload via the Posts Editor in the admin area. For example, when you upload an image, WordPress automatically creates a thumbnail of the image. To get the best results from this feature, there are a few things to bear in mind.

# Thumbnail creation

First, you should note that even though WordPress creates a thumbnail of the image, the original full-size image will still be stored on your server. If the original image is particularly large (for example, wider than 1280 pixels), you need to decide whether you want your readers to be able to view it. If you do allow your readers to click the thumbnail and see the full-size image, it could be costly for you in terms of bandwidth and disk space. We will see how to prevent your readers from being able to open the full-size image shortly. But first, let's assume that you do want your readers to be able to see larger versions of the thumbnails.

Remember that the largest viewable size for computer monitors is about 1280 x 1024 pixels (admittedly, monitors are getting bigger all the time, but at the moment this is about the biggest size you need to worry about). Therefore, I recommend optimizing your images before you upload them to WordPress, so they are no bigger than this maximum monitor size. Let's try this out on the WPBizGuru case study.

In the code bundle for this chapter, you'll find an image called `dried_chillies.jpg`. Unzip it somewhere locally.

Now open up The GIMP and use **File | Open** to open **dried_chillies.jpg**. You'll notice that the image opens in a separate window. In the image window, select **Image | Scale Image**. In the **Scale Image** dialog, you'll see that the image dimensions (**Image Size**) are **3072 x 2304 pixels**:

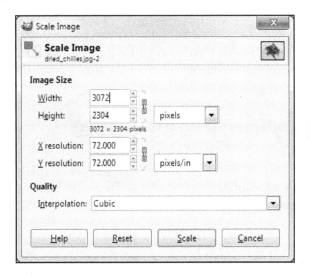

We need to make the width 1280 so that it fits nicely into our presumed maximum monitor size. Place your cursor in the **Width** box, delete **3072** and type **1280**. You can see that the resolution is already set to 72 ppi, which is perfect for web images. Click the **Scale** button and save the image (**File | Save**). In the **Save as JPEG** dialog box, move the **Quality** slider towards the left so that the number in the box is **75** then click **Save**. Having resized the image, the file size has reduced to about 103KB, from the original 1.19 MB — a nice improvement for download speeds and bandwidth economy.

The Quality slider is a useful optimization tool in The GIMP. If you have a very large JPEG image with a high resolution, as with our example, you can reduce the quality to maybe 60 or 75. This helps to reduce the file size. This is a feature you should experiment with and see how different quality settings affect the sharpness and file size of JPEG images. You're always looking for a trade-off between quality and file size.

Now let's upload the image to our test blog. You should already have the WPBizGuru blog we created in *Chapter 3, Designing your Blog* on your local test server.

1. Open the XAMPP control panel and start the servers (Apache and MySQL).

2. In your web browser, go to `http://localhost/wordpress/wp-login.php` and log in.

3. Create a new post and add a few paragraphs of 'Lorem ipsum' dummy text (you can get it for free at `http://www.lipsum.com/`). Place the cursor on a new line and click the **Add an Image** icon:

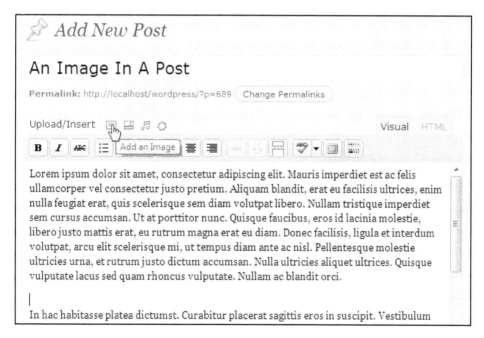

4.  The **Add an Image** window will open. Click the **Select Files** button:

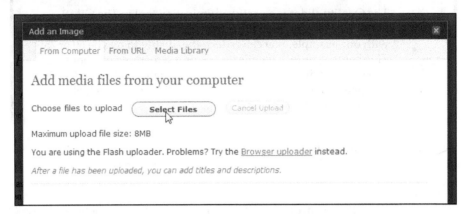

5.  Locate the **dried_chillies.jpg** image on your computer and upload it. Give the image a suitable **Title**, **Alternate Text**, **Caption**, and **Description**:

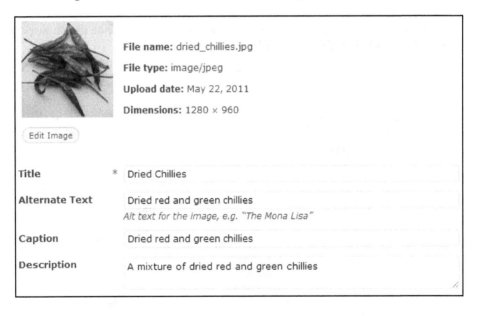

6.  For **Link URL** select **Post URL**, for **Alignment** select **None**, and for **Size** select **Thumbnail**. Then click the **Insert into Post** button:

If you want to prevent your readers from being able to view the original full-size image file, you have to select **None** for **Link URL**.

7.  Now publish the post. Notice that the caption is displayed below the image.

So, that's how we ensure that our images are optimized for WordPress. Use image editing software to scale the image width to 1280 pixels before uploading it to WordPress.

# Thumbnail size

As you can see from the previous exercise, the thumbnail image is rather small. By default WordPress creates thumbnails that are 150 x 150 pixels. That may be fine for your blog design. Some people align their images so that paragraph text wraps around them, in which case, 150 pixels is quite a good size. However, I prefer to place images between paragraphs and for this, I think larger images look better. We can achieve this by changing a couple of settings in WordPress.

In the WordPress admin area, select **Settings** | **Media**. In the **Image sizes** section, change the dimensions for **Medium size** to **450** and then click **Save Changes**:

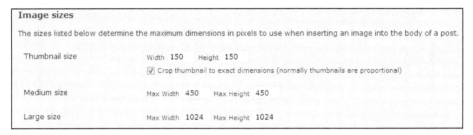

The change we just made won't affect the images that we have already uploaded, as WordPress has already resized the images using the old setting of 150 pixels. So, open up the post we created earlier and delete the image we placed there (to avoid confusion, you could also go to **Media** | **Library** and delete the original **Dried Chillies** image).

Once again, position your cursor between the two paragraphs of dummy text and click the **Add an Image** icon. Repeat the process of uploading the **dried_chillies.jpg** image, but this time, for **Size**, select **Medium** instead of **Thumbnail**:

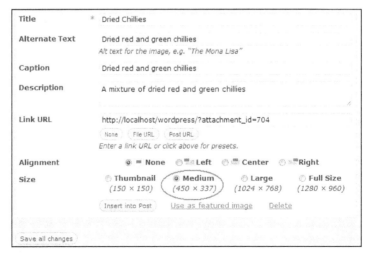

Even in the post editor, you'll notice that the image appears larger. When you view the blog, see how the medium thumbnail now fits nicely between the two paragraphs:

interdum volutpat, arcu elit scelerisque mi, ut tempus diam ante ac nisl. Pellentesque molestie ultricies urna, et rutrum justo dictum accumsan. Nulla ultricies aliquet ultrices. Quisque vulputate lacus sed quam rhoncus vulputate. Nullam ac blandit orci.

Dried red and green chillies

In hac habitasse platea dictumst. Curabitur placerat sagittis eros in suscipit. Vestibulum imperdiet, sapien quis congue malesuada, turpis tellus suscipit sem, cursus feugiat massa diam vel nibh. Cras non tortor

# Attachment size

You may recall that when we uploaded the image we chose **Post URL** for the **Link URL** menu. In WordPress, the page that this URL links to is known as an **Attachment Page** and the image is an **Attachment**. Click on the thumbnail in the blog and you will be taken to the Attachment Page. You'll notice something's wrong here. The image is way too big. It extends past the main content area and into the sidebars. We can fix this problem via the stylesheet.

Also notice on the attachment page that the image description appears below the image and there is a comment form. Readers can leave comments that relate specifically to the image. If you click on the image, the actual image file will open in your browser.

We only need to make a small change to the stylesheet, so we can use the Theme Editor within the WordPress admin area. Go back to the admin area and select **Appearance | Editor**, then select `default.css` from the list of stylesheets to the right of the editor area. Scroll down to the very bottom of the stylesheet, and add the following comment and CSS rule:

```
/* =Attachment Images
------------------------------------------------------------- */

div.entry-attachment img {
    max-width:450px;
}
```

Click **Update File** and view the attachment page in the blog (you may need to refresh your browser to see the changes). We've used CSS to set the maximum width for Attachment images to 450 pixels.

*« An Image In A Post*
# Dried Chillies
By admin | Published: **May 22, 2011**

A mixture of dried red and green chillies

# Styling images

We just changed the size by adding a rule to the stylesheet. So you've probably figured out that we can apply a whole load of other styles to our images. We'll run through a couple of simple examples to show how we can style images to enhance our blog design.

 It's worth noting that all we've done is change the **display size** of the image. The browser is still downloading the full size image and resizing it *on the fly*. In this case it's not too much of a problem because we already reduced the image file size using The GIMP, but if you were applying this *resizing on the fly* to a large image file, it could have implications for bandwidth and download size. It's best practice to always optimize the image as much as possible (using The GIMP) before you upload it to WordPress, and only use *resizing on the fly* for minor tweaks.

Let's begin by changing the border around images on Attachment Pages. Go back to the Theme Editor and locate the new CSS rule we just added. Change it to this:

```
div.entry-attachment img {
  max-width:450px;
  border:solid #bf5b04 2px;
}
```

Update the file, and view the attachment page and you'll see that the image now has a border color to match the text color of the entry meta text.

We can apply a different border style to the image within the post. Try adding the following rule:

```
div.entry-content img {
  border:solid black 1px;
  padding:5px;
}
```

Update the file and view the post we created and you'll see the new border:

**Setting up an image gallery**

We've looked at some advanced techniques for managing images within posts. However, if you would like to use a lot of images in your blog, you should consider using a standalone image gallery. Placing lots of images in a single post is not ideal. They can take up lots of space and the reader will be forced to do a lot of vertical scrolling to view the entire post. A better approach is to add a link within your post to a dedicated gallery page. A standalone gallery also allows you to categorize and group your images more efficiently.

Since version 2.5, WordPress includes a simple gallery feature. However, the functionality is very basic and you can achieve far better results using a gallery plugin, which is the approach we will use here. If you are interested in the gallery feature in WordPress, take a look at `http://codex.wordpress.org/Gallery_Shortcode`.

# NextGEN Gallery

One of the best third-party plugins for WordPress is **NextGEN Gallery**. It offers an easy-to-use gallery with lots of features. We'll install NextGEN Gallery for our WPBizGuru case study and take a look at some of the basic features.

Begin by installing the plugin in the usual way. Go to **Plugins** | **Add New**, search for **nextgen gallery** and click the **Install Now** link for **NextGEN Gallery** (make sure you install the correct plugin as there are several plugins with similar names).

We're now ready to start using the gallery but you'll need some images. For this demonstration, we'll set up two galleries and place them within an album (the difference between *gallery* and *album* will make sense shortly). For convenience, I've included two ZIP files in the code bundle (`gallery_imgs_1.zip` and `gallery_imgs_2.zip`) that contain some copyright-free images that you can use.

Of course, any images you have will do just as well.

**Images sources**

There are now dozens of great stock image libraries on the Web. Some provide images completely free of charge, others charge a fee. A couple of good ones are **stock.xchng** (`http://www.sxc.hu/`), which offers free and paid-for images and **Fotolia** (`http://www.fotolia.com`), which has paid-for images starting from just $1. These sites are great if you're looking for images to illustrate your blog posts. However, always be sure to check the license conditions for each image you download — the use of some is restricted.

Once you have activated the plugin, you will see a **Gallery** option in the admin area left-hand menu. Click on it and select **Add Gallery / Images**.

A Gallery is simply a collection of images. You can use just one gallery and place all of your images in it, but if you want to keep your images in some kind of order, it makes sense to set up several galleries, each containing related images. Groups of galleries such as this make up an Album.

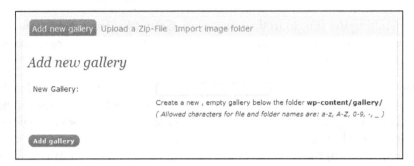

Type **Dried Chillies** in the **New Gallery** box and click **Add gallery**. You should see the following message:

Now we can import some images to the **Dried Chillies** gallery. There are several options available here. The first is to upload an entire ZIP file of images. The second is to use your FTP client to upload a folder of images to the gallery. And the third is to upload images one by one. We will use the first option, which should be the quickest. Click on the **Upload a Zip-File** tab. Use the **Choose File** button to locate **gallery_imgs_1.zip**, which you downloaded with the code for this chapter. From the **in to** drop-down box, select the **1 - Dried Chillies** gallery. Click on **Start upload**.

Once again, you should see a success message:

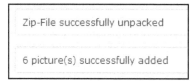

Now click **Manage Gallery** (in the **Gallery** menu in the left-hand navigation area). You should see our **Dried Chillies** gallery in the **Galleries** list. Click on it.

The page you are now looking at allows you to change the settings for the gallery. If you scroll down, you will also see the images we just uploaded into this gallery. There are several enhancements we can make to our gallery. The first thing we need to do is link the gallery to a page in our blog.

We need to add a description and assign a preview image for the gallery (you'll see the preview image in use when we place the gallery into an album). First click the **Add Page** button. Now type a suitable description in the **Description** box and in the **Preview image** drop-down box, select any one of the images. Click **Save Changes**.

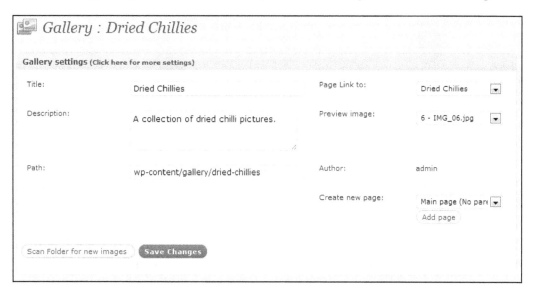

In the bottom half of the page we can change the settings for each image. For the time being, we'll just give the images some more meaningful titles. The title for each image appears in its **Alt tag**.

It's important to have sensible Alt tags for images to ensure maximum usability and accessibility for our readers. People who use screen readers and can't see the images rely on the Alt tags to make sense and understand the context of a web page. This is a basic principle of good usability and you should be sure to apply it in all your websites. Alt tags are also good for search engine optimization.

In the **Alt & Title Text / Description** column, enter a meaningful title for each image and then click **Save Changes**.

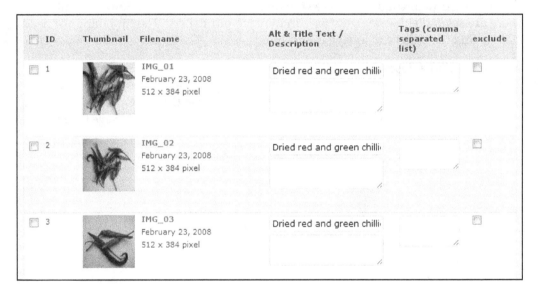

| | ID | Thumbnail | Filename | Alt & Title Text / Description | Tags (comma separated list) | exclude |
|---|---|---|---|---|---|---|
| | 1 | | IMG_01 February 23, 2008 512 x 384 pixel | Dried red and green chilli | | |
| | 2 | | IMG_02 February 23, 2008 512 x 384 pixel | Dried red and green chilli | | |
| | 3 | | IMG_03 February 23, 2008 512 x 384 pixel | Dried red and green chilli | | |

You could also add a description for each image, but for now we're done editing this gallery. We'll create our second gallery.

Click **Add Gallery / Images** and then the **Add new gallery** tab. Enter a name for the gallery — call it **Colorful Shapes**. Click the **Add Gallery** button. Use the **Upload a Zip-File** feature to upload the images in the **gallery_imgs_2.zip** archive, which came with this chapter's code. (Remember to select **2 - Colorful Shapes** in the **in to** drop-down box.)

Click **Manage Gallery** and choose our new gallery. Under **Gallery settings**, first click the **Add Page** button. Now give the gallery a description and choose a preview image, then click **Save Changes**.

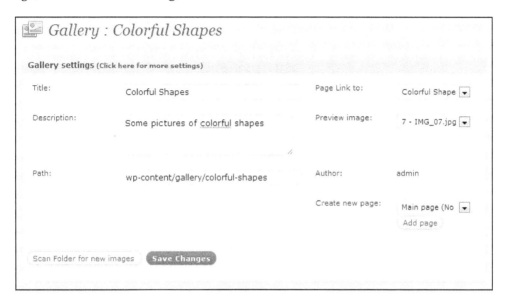

Give each image a new title. Save all your changes.

If you preview the blog now you'll see two new links in the main menu. These are the two pages that NextGEN gallery created for us to which we can link our galleries. (For the screenshot shown next, I sent a couple of other pages in the blog to *Draft* so that the menu fits on one line.)

Go ahead and click on one of these links and you'll see a gallery page:

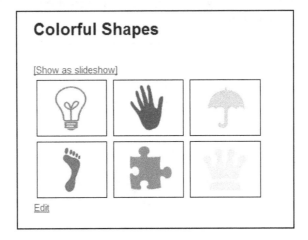

If you click on the thumbnails the full-size image will appear as an overlay in your browser window. You can also view the images as a slideshow.

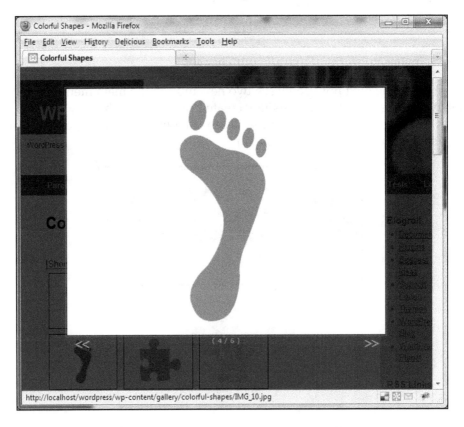

Pretty cool! But we don't want links to each gallery to appear in the main menu of our blog. A better option would be to have an **Image Gallery** link that takes us to a page that lists all of our galleries. We can set this up easily.

## Creating an image gallery page

Go back to WordPress admin. Click **Pages**. You should see the two gallery pages in the list. Click on the page title to edit one of them. In the **Publish** box on the right-hand side, choose to edit the **Visibility** settings, select **Private**, click **OK**, and then **Update** the page. Do the same for the other gallery page.

By setting both pages to **Private**, we have removed them from the blog's main menu.

Go to **Gallery | Album**. In the **Add new album** box type **Image Gallery** and click **Add**. You just created a new Album called *Image Gallery*.

Now choose **1 - Image Gallery** from the **Select album** drop-down box (if it isn't selected already). We want to place our **Dried Chillies** and **Colorful Shapes** galleries into the *Image Gallery* album we just created. You can see the two galleries listed in the **Select gallery** box (notice the preview images you selected earlier). If you place your cursor over one of the galleries, the cursor will become a cross-hair and you can drag the gallery into the Album box on the left-hand side.

Drag both galleries over and click **Update**.

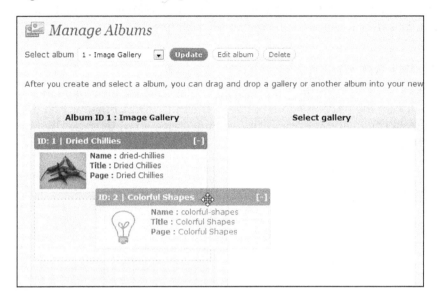

Now we need to create a page for our album and have it appear in the main menu for the blog. Make a note of the Album Page ID (in this case '1'). Go to **Pages | Add New** in the main WordPress admin area. Enter **Image Gallery** as the page title and type this tag in the page content area:

**[album id=1 template=extend]**

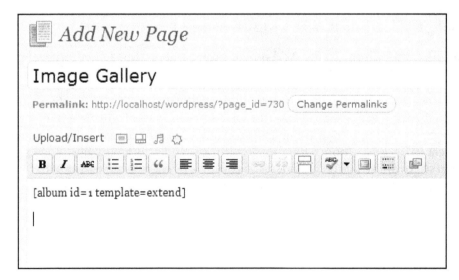

**Publish** the new page. Now view the blog and you'll see the **Image Gallery** link in the main menu. Follow this link and you will see our two albums:

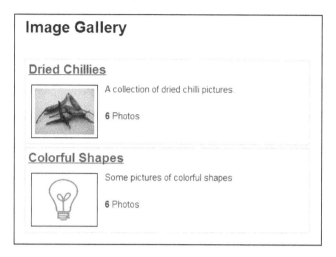

I think you'll agree that NextGEN Gallery is a pretty powerful plugin that allows you to easily create a gallery page. We've really only scratched the surface in terms of its functionality. Now you have the basics, it's up to you to experiment and see what it can do. There are support forums available at `http://wordpress.org/tags/nextgen-gallery?forum_id=10` and a full list of the NextGEN Gallery tags here: `http://wordpress.org/extend/plugins/nextgen-gallery/faq/`.

NextGEN Gallery also has its own stylesheet (see the **Style** option in the **Gallery** menu), so you can use CSS to change things such as the border colors and spacing between thumbnails.

Just one last exercise before we move on. Go to **Gallery | Options** and click the **Gallery** tab. In the **Number of images per page** box, type **4** and uncheck the **Integrate slideshow** box. Save your changes and view one of the gallery pages in the blog. You'll notice there are now a maximum of four thumbnails per page and the **Show as slideshow** option has gone. This is just one example of the many ways you can customize your new image galleries.

# Using video

In addition to images, video is also a great way to make your blog more engaging. You may want to shoot your own videos or use ones made by other people. If you have your own videos, it's possible to host them on your own web space and embed a media player in your blog posts to show them. However, this could be quite costly in terms of the bandwidth allowance from your web hosts as video files can be very large.

It's probably better (and easier) to upload your videos to a video sharing service such as **YouTube** or **Google Video** and use WordPress **Embeds** to display them.

Since WordPress 2.9, it's now far easier to embed videos, images, and other content into your WordPress blogs. See `http://codex.wordpress.org/Embeds` for more information.

This has a couple of benefits over hosting videos on your own web space. First, it saves your bandwidth. Second, it makes your videos available to a wider audience. Not only will your blog readers have access to them, but they will also be available to YouTube users. This could turn out to be a useful promotional tool for your blog as it may bring in new traffic from YouTube.

# Embedding a YouTube video

Create a new post; you can add some dummy *Lorem ipsum* text if you want. Now go over to YouTube and find a video you want to use (maybe your own).

All you need to do to embed the video is add the video's URL to your content area. The URL must be on its own line and not hyperlinked:

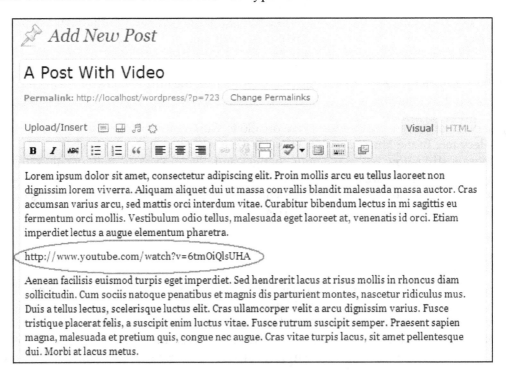

Now publish the new post and view your blog:

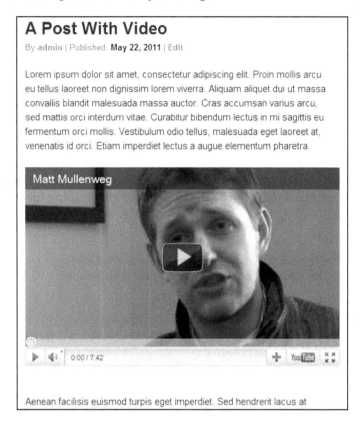

# Adding a favicon

The final image technique we'll look at will give your blog a really professional touch. It involves a special kind of image known as a **favicon**. This is the icon that you see in your browser address bar on many websites you visit. If a website is using a favicon, it will also be displayed in your browser's favorites folder next to the website link (hence the name, *fav*icon).

We'll go through the procedure for adding a favicon to your live blog, as there is little point in having one on your local development server (you may have noticed that XAMPP comes with its own favicon, anyway).

A favicon must be a square image of 16 pixels (that is, 16 x 16). You may be able to use your website logo or create a special square version of it. Another option is to make a completely new image—maybe using the initial letters of your blog. For WPBizGuru, I created a simple 'W' favicon. (I've included the WPBizGuru favicon in this chapter's code bundle.)

> You may wish to use a free favicon generator tool. There is a good one at http://tools.dynamicdrive.com/favicon/.

Once I had scaled the 'W' image down to 16 x 16 using The GIMP, I saved it as favicon.ico (note the special file extension). Next I used my FTP client to upload it into the root directory of my website (the root will be something like /public-html, /www, or /htdocs).

> The favicon.ico image must be in the root, which is not necessarily the directory where you'll have WordPress installed.

I then used my FTP client to download the functions.php file from the WPBizGuru child theme folder within /wp-content/themes/. I then edited the file locally, adding the following lines just before the closing </?> tag:

```
function childtheme_favicon() { ?>
  <link rel="shortcut icon" href="http://www.wpbizguru.com/favicon.
    ico">
<?php }

add_action('wp_head', 'childtheme_favicon');
```

Having saved the functions.php file, I FTPed it back to the WPBizGuru theme folder by overwriting the old version. And that's it—the favicon is now visible.

# Summary

In this chapter, we've looked at some advanced multimedia techniques. You now know how to prepare images for upload to your blog using an image editor such as The GIMP. You also know how to ensure that a thumbnail will be generated for every image you upload. We learned how to resize thumbnails so they fit our post area and how to add styles to images in WordPress using CSS.

We also installed a third-party gallery plugin—NextGEN Gallery—which we can use to create great-looking galleries containing multiple categories of images. We saw how easy it is to use WordPress Embeds to display video in posts. Finally, we looked at the process of adding a favicon to our blog to give it that professional look.

Although the majority of the work in this chapter was done in our local development environment, the techniques can be applied in exactly the same way to a live blog.

In the next chapter, we will focus on the content of your blog. We will discuss some copywriting tips to ensure that your content is engaging and keeps your readers coming back for more. We will also look at creating static pages and how to keep a backup of your content.

# 5
# Content is King

The title may seem like rather an old cliché now, but it still rings true—content *is* king. In this chapter, we will look at issues surrounding content creation, and discuss some techniques and methods to help you produce the best content you can. We've already looked at visual content, in the form of images and videos, but for many web users, blogging is still all about text—that's what we'll be focusing on here.

We will begin with some general writing tips for bloggers. Although you may be familiar with some of these already, it's as well to re-focus your attention on them and ensure that you are applying them as a part of your blogging routine. We then look at ways of organizing your content in a user-friendly way by using categories and tags. We will examine the apparently subtle differences between the two and ensure that you're using them correctly. We move on to apply categories and tags to the WPBizGuru case study.

Next, we will look at one of the most important pieces of *static* content on your blog—the *About* page. It's vital to get this right as it is so often the first port of call for new visitors to your blog. We will add an *About* page to WPBizGuru. Finally, we underline the importance of protecting your precious content by carrying out regular backups. You will learn how to back up both your WordPress site files and the all-important MySQL database, which drives your blog. This chapter includes:

- Blog writing tips
- How to use categories and tags correctly
- The importance of your *About* page
- Other types of static content

# Blog writing tips

The first thing to look at regarding content is the quality of your writing itself. Good writing takes practice. The best way to learn is to study the work of other good writers and bloggers, and by doing so, develop an ear for a good sentence. However, there are guidelines to bear in mind that apply specifically to blogs, and we'll look at some of these here.

# Killer headlines

Ask any newspaper sub-editor and he or she will tell you that writing good headlines is an art to be mastered. This is equally true for blogs. Your headlines are the post titles and it's very important to get them right.

Your headlines should be concise and to the point. You should try to convey the essence of the post in its title. Remember that blogs are often consumed quickly, and readers will use your post titles to decide if they want to carry on reading. People tend to scan through blogs, so the titles play a big part in helping them pick which posts they might be interested in.

Your post titles also have a part to play in search engine optimization (SEO will be covered in detail in the next chapter). Many search engines will use them to index your posts.

As more and more people are using RSS feeds to subscribe to blogs it becomes even more important to make your post titles as descriptive and informative as possible. Many RSS readers and aggregators only display the post title, so it's essential that you convey as much information as possible while keeping it short and snappy. For example, *Backing Up WordPress: A Tutorial* is a better post title than, *A new tutorial*.

# Length of posts

Try to keep your posts manageable in terms of their word count. It's difficult to be prescriptive about post lengths. There's no one-size-fits-all rule in blogging. You need to gauge the length of your posts based on your subject matter and target audience. There may be an element of experimentation to see how posts of different lengths are received by your readership. As with headlines, bear in mind that most people tend to read blogs fairly quickly and they may be put off by an overly long post. On the other hand, if you are blogging to demonstrate your expertise in specific matters, longer posts may be necessary to get your complex points across.

WordPress includes a useful word count feature at the bottom of the post editor.

An important factor in controlling the length of your posts is your writing skills. You will find that as you improve as a writer, you will be able to get your points across using fewer words. Good writing is all about making your point as quickly and concisely as possible. Inexperienced writers often feel the urge to embellish their sentences and use long, complicated phrases. This is usually unnecessary and when you read back that long sentence, you might see a few words that can be cut.

Editing your posts is an important process. At the very least you should always proofread them before clicking the **Publish** button. Better still; try to get into the habit of actively editing everything you write. If you know someone who is willing to act as an editor for you, that's great. It's always useful to get some feedback on your writing.

 If, after re-reading and editing your post, it still seems very long, it might be an idea to split the post in two and publish the second part a few days later.

# Post frequency

Again, there are no rules set in stone about how frequently you should post. You will probably know from your own experience of other blogs that this varies tremendously from blogger to blogger. Some bloggers post several times a day and others just once a week or less.

Figuring out the correct frequency of your posts is likely to take some trial and error. It will depend on your subject matter and how much you have to say about it. The length of your posts may also have a bearing on this. If you like to write short posts that make just one main point, you may find yourself posting quite regularly. Or, you may prefer to save up your thoughts and get them down in one longer post.

As a general rule of thumb, try to post at least once per week. Any less than this and there is a danger your readers will lose interest in your blog. However, it's extremely important not to post just for the sake of it. This is likely to annoy readers and they may very well delete your feed from their news reader. As with many issues in blogging, post frequency is a personal thing. You should aim to strike a balance between posting once in a blue moon and subjecting your readers to *verbal diarrhea*.

Almost as important as getting the post frequency right is fine-tuning the timing of your posts, that is, the time you publish them. Once again, you can achieve this by knowing your target audience. Who are they, and when are they most likely to sit down in front of their computers and read your blog? If most of your readers are office workers, then it makes sense to have your new posts ready for them when they switch on their workstations in the morning. Maybe your blog is aimed at stay-at-home moms, in which case a good time to post might be mid-morning when the kids have been dropped off at school, the supermarket run is over, and the first round of chores are done. If you blog about gigs, bars, and nightclubs in your local area, the readers may well include twenty-something professionals who access your blog on their iPhones while riding the subway home—a good time to post for them might be late afternoon.

# Links to other blogs

We'll examine this in more detail in *Chapter 8, Connecting with the Blogosphere*, but it's worth flagging up here, also. Links to other bloggers and websites are an important part of your content; they help to establish your place in the blogosphere. Blogging is all about linking to others and the resulting *conversations*.

Try to avoid over-using popular links that appear all over the Web, and instead introduce your readers to new websites and blogs that they may not have heard of. Admittedly, this is difficult nowadays with so many bloggers linking to each other's posts, but the more original you can be, the better. This may take quite a bit of research and trawling through the lower-ranked pages on search engines and indices, but it could be time well spent if your readers come to appreciate you as a source of new content beyond your own blog. Try to focus on finding blogs in your niche or key topic areas. However, don't just link to other blogs for the sake of it—make sure they are of real use to your readers.

# Establishing your tone and voice

Tone and voice are two concepts that professional writers are constantly aware of and are attempting to improve. An in-depth discussion isn't necessary here, but it's worth being aware of them. The concept of *tone* can seem rather esoteric to the non-professional writer but as you write more and more, it's something you will become increasingly aware of.

For our purposes, we could say the *tone* of a blog post is all about the way it feels or the way the blogger has pitched it. Some posts may seem very informal; others may be straight-laced, or appear overly complex and technical. Some may seem quite simplistic, while others come across as advanced material. These are all matters of tone. It can be quite subtle, but as far as most bloggers are concerned, it's usually a matter of formal or informal. How you pitch your writing boils down to understanding your target audience. Will they appreciate informal, first-person prose or should you keep it strictly third person, with no slang or casual language? On blogs, a conversational tone is often the most appropriate.

With regards to *voice*, this is what makes your writing distinctly yours. Writers who develop a distinct voice become instantly recognizable to readers who know them. It takes a lot of practice to develop and is not something you can consciously aim for; it just happens as you gain more experience. The only thing you can do to help it along is step back from your writing and ask yourself if any of your habits stand in the way of clarity.

While you read back your blog posts imagine yourself as one of your target readers and consider whether they would appreciate the language and style you've used. Employing the tone and voice well is all about getting inside their heads and producing content they can relate to.

 Developing a distinctive voice can also be an important aspect of your company's brand identity. Your marketing department may already have brand guidelines, which allude to the tone and voice that should be used while producing written communications. Or you may wish to develop guidelines yourself as a way of focusing your use of tone and voice.

# The structure of a post

This may not apply to very short posts that don't go further than a couple of brief paragraphs, but for anything longer, it's worth thinking about a structure. The classic form is *beginning*, *middle*, and *end*. Consider what your main point or argument is and get it down in the first paragraph. In the middle section, expand on it and back it up with secondary arguments. At the end reinforce it, and leave no doubt in the reader's mind what it is you've been trying to say.

As we've already mentioned, blogs are often read quickly or even just scanned through. Using this kind of structure, which most people are sub-consciously aware of, can help them extract your main points quickly and easily.

# Ending with a question

You may have already applied the *beginning*, *middle*, and *end* structure, but that's not necessarily the best place to end a post. Many bloggers finish with a question. This is a great way of soliciting comments. If it's an interesting or provocative question, it may persuade those readers who only scanned quickly through your post to go back and digest it in more detail, so that they can give an answer to your question and join the debate.

# A quick checklist

Based on the writing tips we've looked at, there are a few common themes that keep popping up. This checklist will help you to keep them in mind:

- Know your target audience and try to get inside their heads.
- Ask yourself if each post is truly relevant to your audience.
- Are you posting frequently enough (or too frequently)?
- Are your posts too long or too short?
- Make sure you include some links to other blogs and websites.
- Consider whether your tone and voice are appropriate for your target audience and how they could apply to your brand identity.
- Have you applied a structure to your post?
- Could you add a question at the end of your post?

Remember that the art of blog writing requires plenty of practice, but the points we have covered should help to get you on your way. The key is to constantly analyze your writing and ask yourself how it can be improved.

**A note about keywords**

We'll discuss the whole topic of SEO in the next chapter, but it's worth noting here that your writing has a big impact on search engine findability. This is what adds an extra dimension to writing for the Web. As well as all the usual considerations of style, tone, content, and so on, you also need to optimize your content for the search engines. This largely comes down to identifying your **keywords** and ensuring they're used with the right frequency—we'll discuss this in detail in *Chapter 6, Search Engine Optimization*. In the meantime, hold this thought.

# Categories and tags

It's very important to organize your content in a usable and logical way. Your readers will be frustrated if they cannot find what they're looking for. Their overall experience of your blog is greatly enhanced if you use clear signposts to your content. Luckily, WordPress makes this easy with the use of **Categories** and **Tags**.

## The difference between categories and tags

There can be some confusion about the differences between categories and tags, which can lead to them being used incorrectly. This is partly due to the fact that different bloggers use them in different ways. There is some debate about how they should be used, and some may argue that there are no hard and fast rules. However, I think it's important to establish in your mind some distinction between categories and tags. What follows is my method for using them.

Categories should be thought of as being part of the hierarchy of your blog's navigation. In a way, they are a bit like a filing system for your blog. Each post is *filed* in a category, giving your blog a hierarchical structure. Some people also think of categories as being the *table of contents* for a blog.

Tags supplement categories but they should not really be thought of as part of your blog's navigation. They are rather like an index in a book. You use an index to look up a keyword and it gives you a list of page references for that word. Similarly, when a reader clicks on one of your tags, they are given a list of references for that tag. Tags can also be thought of as keywords or search terms that readers (or potential readers) might associate with your posts.

Categories are a high-level way of organizing content, while tags are more granular or low-level. A category will contain many posts, whereas a tag may point to far fewer.

## Using categories

Bearing in mind that categories are a high-level method for organizing your content, you should keep the number of categories to a minimum. I would recommend not going above 12 categories, and in fact, for many blogs far fewer will be sufficient.

Remember that we are also using categories as part of our blog's navigation; they are not just a way of labeling posts. Your category list should be clearly displayed on each page of your blog so that it can be used as a navigation menu.

Each post should be placed in just one category. This is a controversial point, and you will see some bloggers place their posts in more than one category. However, this detracts from the idea of using categories as a navigational aid on your site or as a table of contents. A section in a book only appears under one chapter heading; it only occurs once within the book, so it is only listed once in the table of contents.

 You can set up your permalinks so that the category is part of the URL. For example: `http://blog.wpbizguru.com/tutorials/2011/05/29/a-tutorial-on-backing-up-wordPress/`. It's rather like the directory structure used in static HTML sites, where content is organized by placing each page in the relevant folder. *This is an important reason for placing your posts in just one category.* We will apply this to the WPBizGuru case study later in the chapter.

Avoid the use of sub-categories. If you keep the number of categories small, you shouldn't need any sub-categories. You must also constantly monitor your categories and how you are using them. If it turns out that one of your categories is only getting a few posts while all the others have dozens, you should consider merging the underused category into one (or more) of the others. A category with just one or two posts reflects badly on you, and many of your readers may doubt your expertise or enthusiasm.

# Using tags

We've mentioned that tags are a more granular way of organizing your content. You may only have a few categories, but you should use lots of tags. However, just because there are lots of them, you shouldn't be cavalier in the way you use them. Always use meaningful tags but try to keep them as short as possible. The best tags are just one word, although sometimes you will have to use more.

The whole point of tags is to use the same ones over and over. Do not create more than one tag with the same meaning. For example, if you were frequently writing about architecture you could have tags such as, *building, construction, development,* or a whole host of variations. The problem is that they are all too similar. It would be far better to use just one of these tags for posts on that subject. You should also be aware of any ambiguities in your tags, for example, *building* can mean *a structure of bricks and mortar* or *the act of constructing*. If you were to use it as a tag, you would need to be consistent and use it in just one meaning.

You can give more than one tag for a post; in fact, you will usually find you have to. The whole point of tagging is that readers can use it to find related posts, and this may be best achieved by using several tags per post.

# Applying tags and categories to WPBizGuru

Now, let's look at how we can apply this to our case-study blog. First, we'll consider the categories that are needed for the blog. Based on the subject matter of WPBizGuru, we can come up with a few broad topics that will be our categories:

- Tutorials
- Plugins
- Themes
- WordPress SEO
- Speaking and Events
- Web TV Appearances

This looks like a good list of categories to begin with—we can always add more, later. Now, start up your local development server and log in to the admin area of the WPBizGuru blog (`http://localhost/wordpress/wp-admin`). Select **Posts | Categories**. Begin by deleting all the old categories and then add the new ones.

Some of the category names contain several words, but you may wish to use just one word for the category slug. The slugs will be used by our permalinks, once we've re-configured them.

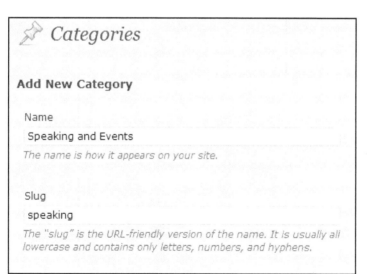

For the time being, leave the **Uncategorized** category—you can set one of the new ones as **Default** later.

Categories
- Plugins
- Speaking and Events
- Themes
- Tutorials
- Uncategorized
- Web TV Appearances
- WordPress SEO

Next, you need to go through each of the posts and assign them to a new category—remember, only one category per post. At the same time add a few tags for each post. Tags are placed in the **Post Tags** box, which is to the right of the main post editor. Since we're only using dummy content, it doesn't really matter which categories and tags you use for each post. As you add more tags, you'll notice that WordPress allows you to choose from the most used tags:

By default, the Thematic child theme we created for WPBizGuru displays tags within the meta information at the end of each post:

Posted in *Tutorials* | Tagged *blogging tips, google, plugin, tutorial, wordpress seo* | *1 Comment*

However, it's also useful to display your tags in a **tag cloud** within your sidebar. WordPress comes with its own tag cloud widget, but it's not very flexible. So, we'll use a third-party plugin, called **Ultimate Tag Cloud Widget** developed by Rickard Andersson of `http://www.0x539.se/`.

In your WordPress admin area, go to **Plugins | Add New**. Search for **ultimate tag cloud widget**, install the plugin in the usual way and activate it.

Go to **Appearance | Widgets**. Drag the **Ultimate Tag Cloud** widget into the **Primary Aside** between **Categories** and **Archive**.

The configuration options for the new widget should open automatically; if they don't, click the drop-down arrow.

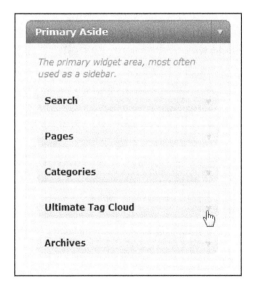

Here we can change a few settings for the tag cloud. Under **Data**, I changed the order to **Random**:

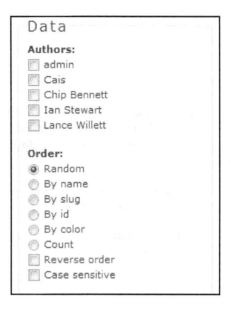

Under **Basic Appearance**, I changed the **Title** to **Blog Tags** and the **Coloring** to **Spanning between values From #B1B5B8 to #3D4245** (these are hexadecimal color values which I chose to match the theme colors):

Finally, under **Link CSS Styles | Normal Styles | Underline**, I selected **No**:

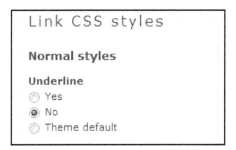

There are lots of other settings you can experiment with later, but we're done for now, so click **Save** and view the blog. You should see the tag cloud in the right-hand sidebar. Notice that the most-used tags appear larger, in the **#3D4245** color; there is a sliding scale of font sizes down to the least used tags, which are colored **#B1B5B8**. Also notice that we have removed the default underlining for hyperlinks. Clicking on one of the tags will show a list of all the posts that have been tagged with it.

You will see that there is a *tutorial* tag as well as a *Tutorials* category. This is because WPBizGuru knows that many of his readers visit the blog primarily to read his tutorials. This makes it as easy as possible to locate all his tutorials. Readers can either select the tag or the category.

Finally, we will update the permalinks so that the relevant category appears in the URL for each post. Whether you decide to implement this on your own blog is up to you. It has advantages and drawbacks. The advantage is that your category structure is reinforced in your post URLs and the drawback is that the URLs are slightly longer.

Select **Settings | Permalinks**. Under **Common settings**, select the **Custom Structure** radio button, and enter `/%category%/%year%/%monthnum%/%day%/%postname%/`.

Click **Save Changes**. Your permalinks will now be structured as the following:

```
http://blog.wpbizguru.com/tutorials/2011/05/08/ultimate-tag-cloud-
widget-tutorial.
```

Now we've dealt with categories and tags, we'll look at some of the static content you may wish to include in your blog.

# The About page

Your *About* page will be one of the very first points of contact with most new readers of your blog, so it's important to get it right. It's your chance to explain who you are and what you're doing with your blog. There are no hard and fast rules for writing the *About* page. A cursory visit to a random selection of blogs will reveal that there is no standard, as *About* pages come in all shapes and formats. However, there are a few similarities between most of them, and you would be well advised to include the following as a bare minimum.

## About you

This is the place for your potted résumé. Keep it brief and to the point, outlining the skills and experience that make you qualified to write your blog. Readers are more likely to trust what you write and come back for more if they know it's the words of someone 'in the know'. This might not necessarily include degrees and diplomas. Depending on your blog's subject matter and your own life experiences, you might not hold any relevant paper qualifications, but simply be a knowledgeable and committed *amateur*. As long as you can demonstrate that knowledge and commitment (both on your *About* page and in your posts), it should be enough to convince readers of your credentials.

It's also fairly common to include a photograph of yourself. If you do, try to pick a good one or even spend some money on getting your portrait taken professionally. Sometimes bloggers use an *alternative* image to represent themselves; maybe something like a gaming avatar, a caricature, or a graphic portrait.

If you have multiple authors on your blog, you should ensure that there is some information for all of them on your *About* page.

# About your blog

You should also give some information as to what your blog is about. Of course, this would be apparent from reading a few of your posts, but for new readers who may be in a hurry, it's worth including something on your *About* page. Think of this as being like the cover *blurb* on the back of a book. In effect, you're trying to sell your blog in a few short paragraphs. Try to stay focused on the blog's aims and think about how to get them across in as concise a way as possible.

This would also be a good place to include any complimentary reviews or quotes from other experts in your field, who have praised your blog. Maybe you could place a couple of these in block quotes on your *About* page.

# Anything to declare

Your *About* page is also a good place to declare any interests you have that might be viewed by some readers as compromising the objectivity of your blog. There's nothing wrong with using your blog to relentlessly promote your products or services, as long as you don't present it in a way that might mislead readers into thinking it's an independent, non-biased recommendation. If you blog about any professional or business interests make sure that your readers are clear that you have a stake in them. The same is true if you regularly blog about potentially partisan subjects such as politics or religion. Make sure your readers know where you're coming from and never pose as an impartial commentator if you have a vested interest in your subject matter.

# The WPBizGuru About page

Now, let's work through building the *About* page for WPBizGuru. Log in to the admin area of the WPBizGuru blog on your development server.

Select **Pages** | **Add New**. Give the page the title, **About**, and add some text (I've included the WPBizGuru *about* text in the **about.txt** file in the code bundle for this chapter; if you want to use that, you may). Tidy up the formatting by inserting the bullets and making the headings Level 3 (see `http://blog.wpbizguru.com/about/`). You can also upload an image, if you like.

To place the two quotes inside block quotes, highlight the text that belongs in the block quote, and click the **Blockquote** button in the toolbar:

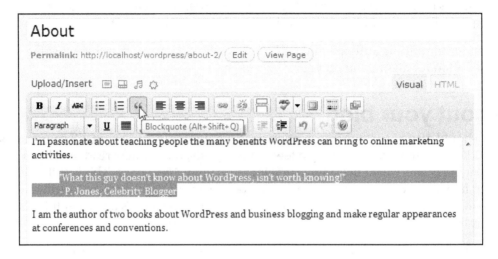

Enter a line break before the name of the quote speaker and make it bold:

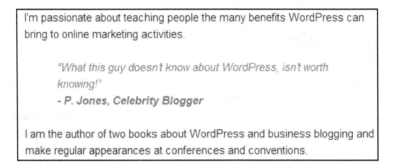

 Most bloggers don't allow comments on their *About* page. You can turn comments off by choosing to **Quick Edit** the page and unchecking the box.

# Other static content

Besides the *About* page there may be other static content that you should add to your blog. If you have another website as well as your blog, ask yourself whether you could bring that content into WordPress, so that all your web content is together in one place.

There are many other static pages that you may wish to add. For example, designers, photographers, and artists often have a portfolio page to display their work. Or you may wish to set up a page to showcase a handful of your bestselling products. If you've written a book you could add a book page with some blurb and a link to Amazon. As you know, WordPress is more than capable of handling static content alongside your dynamic blog posts.

# Backing up

Now you've put so much time and effort into creating great content, you need to make sure it's protected. To ensure your content is safe, you must back up your blog on a regular basis.

The frequency of your backups will depend on how often you post to your blog, but as a general rule of thumb it's a good idea to back up at least once a week. You never know when something might go wrong and when it does, it's usually beyond your control.

When considering your backup routine, remember there are two groups of data that make up your blog: the **site files** and the **database**. Both of these need to be backed up, but it may be that the site files don't need to be backed up as frequently as the database. The site files are basically everything from your original WordPress core installation. Much of this you won't have changed, so as long as you keep a copy of your version of WordPress somewhere on your PC, you should be able to use that as your backup site (just remember to back up your PC regularly, too!).

For most WordPress users, the only site files that change on a regular basis are the theme, plugins, and uploads, all of which are contained in the `wp-content` directory. The only file outside of this directory that you need to back up is `wp-config.php`. The `wp-config.php` file is unlikely to change after your blog has been installed, so it is probably only necessary to back up this file once, shortly after you first install your blog. So, regarding your site files, all you need to back up regularly is the `wp-content` directory.

# Backing up wp-content

Your web host will probably back up all the files on its servers on a daily basis. But you shouldn't rely on them. It's always quicker and easier to access your own backups than having to ask your web host for them. The safest way of backing up your site files is to use your FTP program to download the `wp-content` directory to a safe location on your computer.

The following screenshot shows the backup process for the WPBizGuru `wp-content` files using CuteFTP:

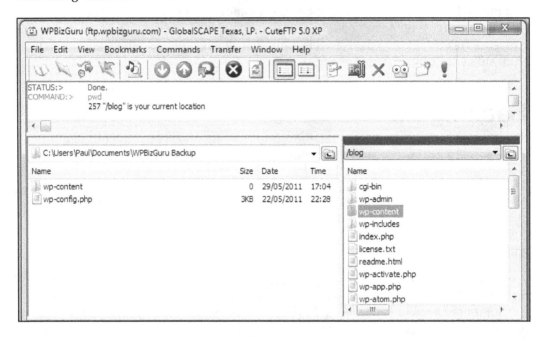

# Backing up the database using phpMyAdmin

While it's important to back up your site files, you'll only need that backup if you suffer a complete loss of data on your server. Thankfully, a complete data loss is fairly rare. If you should experience a data loss, it's far more common that it will involve the MySQL database that drives your blog. Remember, the database contains all the posts, pages, comments, and links from your blog.

Probably the easiest way of backing up your database is to use **phpMyAdmin**, so we'll run through this process here. This example uses version 3.3.9 of phpMyAdmin (other versions may vary).

1. Connect to phpMyAdmin on your server (if you're not sure how to do this, your web host will be able to give you instructions).

2. Select the database for your WordPress installation from the list on the left-hand side of the main phpMyAdmin page.

3. You will now see a page that lists all the tables in your WordPress installation.

4.  Click on the **Export** tab at the top of this page.

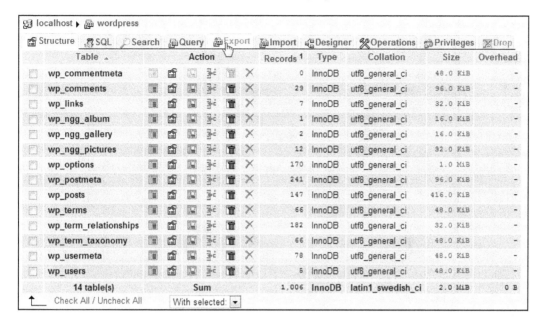

5.  On the next screen, select all the WordPress tables in the database. If WordPress is the only application using this database, you can just click **Select All**. If WordPress is sharing the database with other applications, you will need to go through the list and just select the WordPress tables. These will be the tables beginning with wp_ (or whatever table prefixes you chose when you installed WordPress).

6.  Ensure the **SQL** radio button (below the table list) is selected.

7. In the **Options** section, select the following:

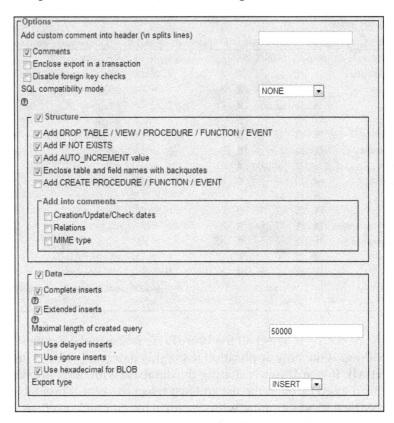

8. Choose to save the files as **"gzipped"**:

9. Click the **Go** button and choose to save the compressed file to disk. Save it using the default filename given by phpMyAdmin. The download and save procedure will vary depending on which browser you are using but it's the same process as downloading any file from a web page.

You now have a backed up copy of your database stored on your local computer.

# Restoring the database from a backup file

The circumstances that might surround a real-life data loss are many and varied. However, there are a couple of scenarios that are most common. First, the entire database is lost. In this case, when you log in to phpMyAdmin, your WordPress database will no longer appear in the list of databases. Second, one or more of the tables in your WordPress database has been lost or corrupted. In this case, the database will still appear in the database list within phpMyAdmin.

If you suspect the second scenario is the reason for your trouble and you cannot repair the tables or even identify which table is lost or corrupted, it's probably a good idea to remove the entire database and start again using your backup file. To remove the database, select it from the list in phpMyAdmin and then click the **Drop** tab.

At this point, whichever data loss scenario may have occurred, we're in the same situation. Your WordPress database no longer exists. The good news is you have a copy of all these tables.

The first step to restoring those tables is to create a new database to hold them. From the phpMyAdmin home page, create a new database, with exactly the same name as your old one.

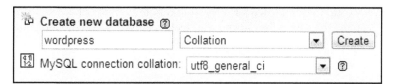

Once you've clicked **Create**, you'll be taken to your new database's phpMyAdmin home page. Click on the **Import** tab.

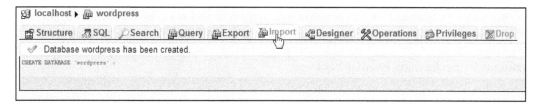

On the import page, click the **Browse** button and locate your database backup file on your computer. Leave all the other settings as they are and click the **Go** button at the bottom of the page. Depending on the size of your backup file, it may take a few minutes to upload. You should then see a success message.

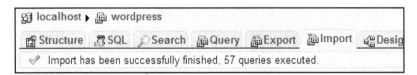

You have now restored your database as it was when you made the backup file, and your blog should be working again.

As you can see the process of backing up your WordPress database is fairly straightforward. However, to ensure you don't leave anything to chance, you might want to run through the procedure using the WPBizGuru blog on your local test server so you'll be completely comfortable, should the worst happen to your live blog.

**Back-up plugins**

As well as using phpMyAdmin to back up your blog, you could try a plugin that automates the process for you. There are several back-up plugins available; try searching at `http://wordpress.org/extend/plugins`. If you have a lot of content on your blog, phpMyAdmin may timeout while exporting your database (although this is very rare), in which case, a plugin may handle the export better. However, you should note that most back-up plugins have their own limitations and technical issues, so you should also know how to back up using phpMyAdmin.

# Summary

In this chapter, we've looked at all kinds of written content. We began with some general tips for writing your blog posts. We then looked at how to organize your content in a logical and usable way using categories and tags. We went through the process of setting up the categories and tags for WPBizGuru. We considered the importance of having a good *About* page. Finally, we saw how to protect your content by performing regular backups.

In the next chapter, we will look at the related subject of search engine optimization. You will see how content plays an important part in making your blog more visible to the search engines.

# 6
# Search Engine Optimization

Having put so much time and effort into making your blog look pretty and creating fabulous content, you would want people to find it. The most common way for this to happen is via search engines. For many people, a typical web browsing session begins with a visit to their favorite search engine, so you want to be sure your blog appears high up in the rankings. Unfortunately, having a great-looking blog with lots of interesting posts isn't enough. To get a good place in the rankings takes time, perseverance, and no small amount of knowledge.

The good news is that search engines love blogs. This fact, coupled with the techniques covered in this chapter, will go a long way to making your blog as findable as possible. **Search engine optimization (SEO)** is the art and science of getting your blog noticed by the search engines and ranked as high as possible. This chapter will cover the following:

- The principles of SEO and how search engines work
- How to choose and use your keywords
- The best permalink structures for SEO
- How to optimize your Title Tags and Meta Descriptions
- The importance of sitemaps; how to generate them and submit them
- The importance of inbound links and some ways of acquiring them
- A look at some of the most useful SEO tools

# The principles of SEO

SEO is a huge subject. There are thousands of professionals all over the world who earn their living by providing SEO services to website owners. The good SEO pros spend huge amounts of time and resources learning the skills of effective optimization. This goes to show that you could easily spend your entire life boning up on SEO—there's so much to learn. Obviously, you won't have anything like this amount of time to spend on your own SEO education. However, you can still do a lot to improve your blog's performance with the major search engines. The option to bring in a professional to really rocket through the rankings exists if your marketing budget allows. If you do decide to hire a professional, make sure you choose a reputable one who does not use unscrupulous tactics, which could harm you more than help you.

The good news is that WordPress has been made with SEO in mind. The software comes with many built-in SEO features. For example, you don't need to worry too much about the validity of the HTML on your blog. The WordPress developers have ensured their code is valid. This is a big help as search engines will rank sites with valid code higher than those that have been poorly put together. There is plenty of other stuff going on behind the scenes in your WordPress installation that will aid your search engine **findability**—WordPress developers have been very thoughtful. We'll be considering the aspects of SEO that are your responsibility. But first, a quick '101' on how search engines work.

# How search engines find stuff

Search engines use special programs called **robots** that automatically **crawl** the Web and send back information about the web pages to the search engines' servers. They navigate the Web by following all the links they find. This is how a search engine collects the data for its **index**. The index is a huge database of entries cross-referenced between keywords and relevant website pages. The search engines use special algorithms to determine the rank of the web pages held in their index. When a web user enters a search query, the engine returns a list of results. The order of the search results depends on the rank of the pages, as determined by the algorithm.

These algorithms are closely guarded secrets and the search engine companies are constantly updating them. The aim of the updates is to improve the relevancy of the search results. Because of the secrecy of the algorithms and the constant changes, it is very difficult for website owners to figure out the exact criteria used to rank pages. This prevents website owners from unfairly influencing the search rankings. However, by subscribing to the blogs or feeds of the major search engines, and using tools such as Google's Webmaster Tools (more on this later), you can keep abreast of major changes.

SEO professionals spend their lives trying to second-guess the search algorithms, but the search engine companies usually remain one step ahead. It's a game of cat and mouse, with the odds strongly skewed in favor of the search engines—they make the rules and can change them whenever they want.

Despite the ever-changing algorithms, there are certain principles of SEO that stay constant. These are what we will look at in this chapter.

 For the purposes of this chapter, we will be concentrating on techniques for the *traditional* search engines such as Google, Bing, Yahoo, and Ask. We will look at some of the blog-specific search engines, such as Technorati, in the next chapter.

# Keywords

Keywords are the search terms that people type into a search engine when they are looking for something on the Web. They can be single words or several words that make up a phrase. It's essential to know the keywords being used by people who are looking for the type of content on your blog. You then need to ensure that you're using those keywords correctly. Let's look at a few strategies for finding and using keywords effectively.

# Choosing your keywords

You should spend some time building up a list of your blog's keywords. The first step is to be clear in your mind about what your blog's content is about. What are the main themes you are writing about? If you worked through the planning exercises in *Chapter 2, Introducing our Case Study – WPBizGuru*, you should already have a fairly good idea of this.

Once you are clear about the main theme(s) of your blog, try a quick brainstorming exercise. You can do this alone or enlist the help of colleagues and friends. Put yourself in the shoes of someone looking for the kind of information you publish on your blog. What words or phrases are they likely to type into a search engine? We could run this exercise for `WPBizGuru.com`. People looking for the kind of content on WPBizGuru, may use the following keywords:

- WordPress expert
- WordPress tutorials
- WordPress advice
- WordPress tips

- Learn WordPress

- WordPress consultant

- WordPress help

- Install WordPress

- WordPress training

- Using WordPress

- WordPress book

- WordPress how to

OK, that's just a small handful of the more obvious keywords that took me about 60 seconds to come up with. If I spent longer, I'm sure I could come up with a list of 50 or more words and phrases. The more people you enlist into your keyword brainstorming, the more you are likely to come up with.

Once you have a fairly good list, you can use keyword software to help you find even more. There are literally hundreds of keyword tools out there. Some are free, some are paid for, and they have a range of features. You can start with some of the tools provided by the search engines themselves. For example, Google provides a keyword selector tool for its advertising (AdWords) customers, but you can all use it to research your keywords for SEO. Go to `https://adwords.google.com/select/KeywordToolExternal` and enter a keyword or phrase into the search box.

Enter the security code and click **Search** and you will be presented with a list of related keywords:

| Keyword ideas (100) | | | |
|---|---|---|---|
| Keyword | Competition | Global Monthly Searches ⓘ | Local Monthly Searches ⓘ |
| wordpress tips | | 40,500 | 9,900 |
| wordpress how to | | 450,000 | 165,000 |
| learn wordpress | | 12,100 | 4,400 |
| wordpress tips and tricks | | 1,600 | 390 |
| wordpress seo tips | | 1,900 | 720 |
| wordpress classes | | 6,600 | 2,400 |
| wordpress course | | 6,600 | 1,900 |
| wordpress tutorial video | | 4,400 | 1,300 |
| learn how to use wordpress | | 390 | 260 |
| wordpress more | | 40,500 | 14,800 |
| seo tips for wordpress | | 1,900 | 720 |
| wordpress tips tricks | | 1,600 | 390 |

OK, so it's a pretty long list; not all of the keywords will be relevant to your blog. The preceding screenshot shows just the first few suggestions for one keyword, **wordpress tips** (the whole list runs into dozens). So you can see that if you were to use this tool for all the keywords in your original brainstorming list, you could easily end up with a very long list. This might seem like a good idea, but when we discuss using your keywords, shortly, you'll see that you don't actually want too many. When you're working on your list, try to be selective and keep the list manageable. Use your judgment to pick the important keywords and also look at the **Global Monthly Searches** and **Local Monthly Searches** columns in the Google list. These tell you how often each keyword is actually being used by people searching in Google worldwide (Global) and in your own country (Local). Focus on the most popular ones.

There's no point in my giving you a recommended number of keywords for your list, as this will depend on the type of content in your blog. If your blog covers a fairly narrow subject area, you won't need as many keywords as you would if it covered a broader subject, or even a range of subjects. Once you've read the next section on using keywords, you'll also have a better idea of how many you need.

# Using your keywords

Once you've drawn up your list of keywords you need to make sure you're using them correctly. This basically boils down to the number of times you place keywords in each post. This is known as **keyword density**. As with many other aspects of SEO they are no definitive rules. You will see lots of varied advice from different web experts. The fact of the matter is, no one can be certain about the optimum keyword density, because the search algorithms are kept secret. Many SEO experts have used trial and error in an attempt to gauge the best keyword density. Some have arrived at what are probably fairly arbitrary figures. It would be pointless for me to recommend a specific keyword density. Instead, here are a few general tips for using your keywords:

1. Be selective with your keywords. You'll never be able to include your entire keyword list in each and every post you publish. Try to focus on two or three keywords or keyword phrases, which seem most relevant for each post you write.

2. Whenever possible, try to include at least one keyword in the post title.

3. Try to repeat a couple of the most relevant keywords twice in the first two paragraphs of the post. From then on, aim at using a keyword at least once in every paragraph.

5. Keywords aren't just for your posts. Try to use a selection of your most relevant keywords in your *About* pages and any other static pages in your blog. You should also use keywords in your tags and categories.

6. If you can, use keywords in your image Alt Tags. The Alt Tag is the *title* of your image. Search engines index these Alt Tags; this gives you another way to provide them with more keyword-rich content. The following screenshot shows an example of keywords in an Alt Tag on the WPBizGuru blog:

## Using WordPress For Your Business Blog

By admin | Published: **April 11, 2011** | Edit

If you're planning to set up a blog for your business, you should definitely consider WordPress as your preferred platform. WordPress offers a whole host of powerful benefits that make it the number one choice of millions of bloggers around the world. Here are just a few of the benefits WordPress offers:

**Keyword stuffing**

When writing content for your blog, be aware of **keyword stuffing**. Always write for humans first and search engines second. If your content reads clumsily, because you have tried to shoe-horn in too many keywords, you're putting the search engines before your human readers and that's a bad thing. You need to use your judgment to avoid keyword stuffing and to keep your writing natural.

# Permalinks

We looked at permalinks briefly in the last chapter with regards to structuring your URLs to reflect your blog's categories. Permalinks are also very important for SEO. The default permalink structure in WordPress is `http://blog.wpbizguru.com/?p=123`. This format isn't very search engine friendly. It's far better to have the post title appear in the permalink URL. Again, this is another way of getting more of your keywords into the search engine's index.

In *Chapter 5, Content is King*, we discussed changing the permalink structure to something like `http://blog.wpbizguru.com/tutorials/2011/05/29/a-tutorial-on-backing-up-wordPress/`. This is better as it includes the post title. However, the optimal permalink structure, in terms of SEO, has the post title as close to your blog's domain name as possible, for example, `http://blog.wpbizguru.com/a-tutorial-on-backing-up-wordPress/`.

This structure is the very best for SEO, but it can sometimes cause problems when you try to access some of the WordPress admin pages. If you're really keen on SEO, and are happy to work around any problems accessing admin pages, then go with this structure. However, I would prefer to use a second-best SEO structure, which includes the post's category: `http://blog.wpbizguru.com/tutorials/a-tutorial-on-backing-up-wordPress/`. This is still a good permalink structure for SEO and avoids any possible pitfalls in accessing your admin pages. This structure will be even more beneficial if your categories are also keywords.

When you change your permalink structure, WordPress will automatically redirect all the old URLs to the new ones. This is important because if you have a well-established blog, the search engines will already have indexed your pages using your old permalink URLs. These URLs will remain in the search engine's index for quite some time, so until the index is updated, all your links on search engine results pages will be broken. This will also be true for any of your links that appear on other websites or as browser bookmarks.

WordPress's automatic redirection will work for most common server configurations, but some web hosting companies may have server settings that prevent WordPress from doing the job automatically. When you change your permalinks, you should check that the old ones are redirecting properly (simply type one of your old permalinks into your browser address bar). If you are getting 404 errors from your old permalinks, something is wrong. In these cases I recommend you install a plugin to take control of the redirects — there are several available, for example, **Redirection** (`http://wordpress.org/extend/plugins/redirection/`).

To switch to the new SEO-friendly permalinks on your own blog and the WPBizGuru case study, select **Settings** | **Permalinks** and enter the new permalink structure (`/%category%/%postname%/`) in the **Custom structure box**, then click **Save Changes**.

**Common settings**

| | |
|---|---|
| ○ Default | `http://localhost/wordpress/?p=123` |
| ○ Day and name | `http://localhost/wordpress/2011/06/06/sample-post/` |
| ○ Month and name | `http://localhost/wordpress/2011/06/sample-post/` |
| ○ Numeric | `http://localhost/wordpress/archives/123` |
| ⦿ Custom Structure | `/%category%/%postname%/` |

**Optional**

If you like, you may enter custom structures for your category and tag URLs here. For example, using `topics` as your category base would make your category links like `http://example.org/topics/uncategorized/` . If you leave these blank the defaults will be used.

Category base

Tag base

[ Save Changes ]

# Title tags

Many experts claim that `<Title>` tags are one of the most important aspects of SEO. The `<Title>` tag is displayed in the browser title bar, but it is also one of the first things a search engine sees when it indexes your blog. The `<Title>` tag on your home page is particularly important for SEO.

It's worth spending some time considering your `<Title>` tags and ensuring they are as search engine friendly as possible (while remaining readable and useful to humans). Here are a few guidelines to bear in mind about `<Title>` tags:

1. Ensure they include keywords that are relevant to the post.
2. Ensure the keyword or keyword phrase is as close to the start of the tag as possible.
3. Try to keep your home page `<Title>` tag at around 50-60 characters in length.

4. Capitalize the first letter in each word of the tag.

5. Don't use the keyword phrase more than once in your title.

6. Include the blog title in the `<Title>` tag on each page.

As you may have noticed, the default `<Title>` tags in WordPress are not perfect for SEO—the preceding screenshot shows that the default WPBizGuru title is not using all the guidelines I just outlined. However, there is an excellent plugin we can use to customize our titles (so they are working as hard as possible for SEO). The plugin is **All in One SEO Pack** (`http://wordpress.org/extend/plugins/all-in-one-seo-pack/`). We'll work through configuring the plugin for our WPBizGuru case study. Login to your case study blog then install and activate the plugin in the usual way.

We'll begin by optimizing the home page title. As you can see, by default, WordPress uses the blog title followed by the blog description in the home page `<Title>` tag. The blog title and description are great for our blog's branding. *WordPress for Business Bloggers* is a good tagline for the blog and it looks nice in the blog header. You may have a company slogan or tagline that you want to keep in your header, which is great for your branding but not necessarily so great for SEO. We can fix this using our new plugin.

Under **Settings**, select **All in One SEO**. Here, we can make the necessary changes to our page titles. First, we need to come up with a good home page title using the guidelines I outlined earlier. How about:

**WordPress Advice, Tips And Tutorials | WPBizGuru.com**

This seems to follow our guidelines: It's the right length (52 characters); each word begins with a capital letter; the keywords are close to the start. So, we can insert this in the **Home Title** box. I've also added a brief site description (keep it short; I recommend no more than two lines as they appear in the box) and some of my main generic keywords (again, be brief here, no more than 10 of your most popular keywords). Select **Enabled** for **Plugin Status** and click the **Update Options** button when you're done.

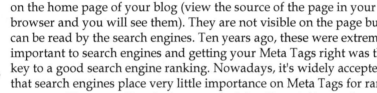

**A note about Meta Tags**

The **Home Description** and **Home Keywords** will be added to your blog's **Meta Tags**. These appear within the `<header></header>` tags on the home page of your blog (view the source of the page in your browser and you will see them). They are not visible on the page but they can be read by the search engines. Ten years ago, these were extremely important to search engines and getting your Meta Tags right was the key to a good search engine ranking. Nowadays, it's widely accepted that search engines place very little importance on Meta Tags for ranking purposes. However, Google does use the Meta Description as the snippet in the search results pages, which gives you the opportunity to provide a relevant and concise description of your blog to potential visitors as they view the search results. A good description may encourage people to click on your blog rather than another website.

We now have a search engine friendly home page title…

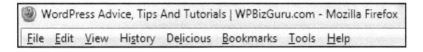

…while keeping the blog title and blog tagline in our header, for branding purposes:

As for the other pages on your blog, the default settings for **All In One SEO Pack** do a pretty good job of making them search engine friendly. For example, you should already be using keywords in your post title, so it's fine to carry on using post titles for the `<Title>` tags, as per the default settings. It may not always be possible to keep within the 50-60 characters length with your post titles, but as long as you are using your keywords wisely, it should be fine. One thing to remember is to use a capital letter at the start of each word in your post title:

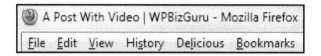

So, for the remaining page titles, you could stick with the defaults. However, I decided to make a couple of small changes. The first is to replace `%blog_ti-tle%`
with `WPBizGuru.com`. This is more for branding than SEO; it means your blog's
web address (including the `.com`) appears in the clickable link in the search engine results pages.

The second change is to update the **Page Title Format** so that it's now **WordPress Advice, Tips And Tutorials | %page_title% | WPBizGuru.com** (once again, remember to click the **Update Options** button):

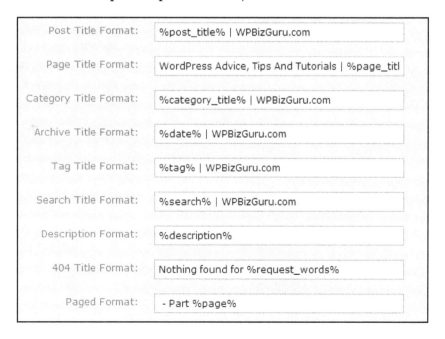

So, the title for our *About* page now looks like this (notice that it contains the keywords from the home page title, instead of just saying *About*):

So, with the help of the **All in One SEO Pack** plugin, you now have search engine friendly titles for all the pages in your blog. We'll now look at another important element of SEO, which is **Sitemaps**.

# Sitemaps

A sitemap is an overview of all the posts and pages in your blog laid out on a single page. Not only is it great for improving your blog's usability, it is also good for SEO. When the search engine robots are crawling through your site they will use the sitemap to find all your pages. By providing a sitemap you are making it easier for them to crawl your blog because there will always be a link pointing to each of your posts. Again, we will use a third-party plugin to create a sitemap for WPBizGuru.

The plugin is called **Simple Sitemap** (http://wordpress.org/extend/plugins/simple-sitemap/). Go ahead and install it in the usual way in your case study blog, then activate it.

Now create a new page (**Pages | Add New**). Give it the title **Sitemap**. Click on the **HTML** tab and add [simple-sitemap]. **Publish** the page.

Now view the site. The **Sitemap** page will have been added to the menu and it should look like this:

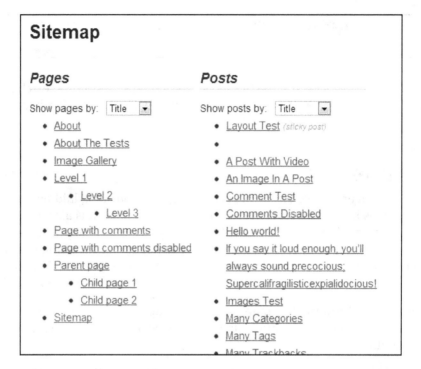

## Adding a Google Sitemap

A **Google Sitemap** is a sitemap in a special XML format that helps Google to crawl your site more efficiently. It is also recognized by other search engines such as Yahoo, Bing, and Ask.

Again, there's a great plugin that we can use. It's called **Google XML Sitemaps** by Arne Brachhold (`http://wordpress.org/extend/plugins/google-sitemap-generator/`).

Once you've installed and activated it, select **XML-Sitemap** under **Settings** in your admin area. At the top of the page, click the link to generate the sitemap for the first time (you don't need to change any of the settings). You should see a success message. You can view the sitemap you just created at `http://localhost/wordpress/sitemap.xml`.

## XML Sitemap

This is a XML Sitemap which is supposed to be processed by search engines like Google, MSN Search and YAHOO.

It was generated using the Blogging-Software WordPress and the Google Sitemap Generator Plugin by Arne Brachhold.

You can find more information about XML sitemaps on sitemaps.org and Google's list of sitemap programs.

| URL | Priority | Change Frequency | LastChange (GMT) |
|---|---|---|---|
| http://localhost/wordpress/ | 100% | Daily | 2011-06-08 17:30 |
| http://localhost/wordpress/sitemap/ | 60% | Weekly | 2011-06-08 17:30 |
| http://localhost/wordpress/about-2/ | 60% | Weekly | 2011-05-29 15:45 |
| http://localhost/wordpress/uncategorized/many-trackbacks/ | 20% | Monthly | 2011-05-29 14:01 |
| http://localhost/wordpress/uncategorized/comments-disabled/ | 20% | Monthly | 2011-05-29 14:00 |
| http://localhost/wordpress/uncategorized/comment-test/ | 70% | Monthly | 2011-05-29 13:59 |

# Inbound links

Having plenty of good quality inbound links to your blog will improve your ranking in the search engines. Google started life as a student project to rank the importance of websites based on the number of incoming links; link popularity is still at the heart of Google's ranking process.

But for many people, link building seems like a daunting task. How do you get other people to link to you? It's actually not as difficult as it first seems—once you get into it, you'll see there are plenty of strategies to use. The point is to stick at it and treat link building as an integral part of your blogging routine.

You can check how many inbound links Google has found for your blog by using the **link:** command. Enter **link:http://www.packtpub.com** into the Google search box to see all the inbound links for the Packt website. You can do the same for your blog.

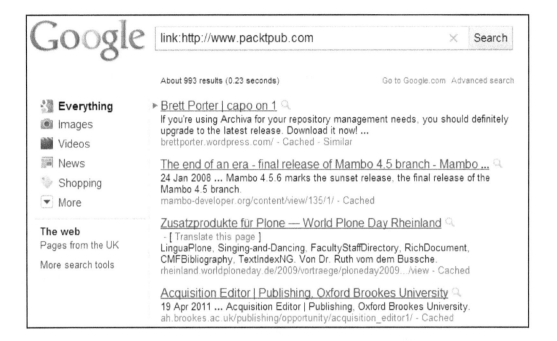

Many of the techniques for building links, such as using social bookmarking, social networking, and getting listed in the blog search engines, will be covered in the next chapter. There will be some more discussed in *Chapter 8, Connecting with the Blogosphere*. But there is a more *organic* technique that we'll discuss here.

It's often referred to by SEO pros as **link baiting**. It's basically creating content that other bloggers and webmasters just can't resist linking to. Obviously, you should always be trying to create interesting and exciting content, but every now and then it pays to come up with a killer post that is intended purely to attract links. There are several methods to achieve this. Here are a few suggestions to get you thinking:

1. Write something controversial that other people will just have to disagree with. Be careful not to upset anyone and don't be offensive, but come up with something that goes against the grain and makes your opinion on an issue stand out.

2. Disagree with a renowned expert. A post title such as, *Seth Godin Is Plain Wrong About XYZ*, backed up with a reasoned argument, could attract plenty of attention and encourage backlinks to the post.

3. Provide a really useful resource. This could be something like a *Top 10* list or a how-to guide.

4. Run a contest, competition, or some other event that is likely to attract attention.

5. Give away a useful *freebie*. For example, a PDF e-book, a piece of software (that you own the rights to), or a free sample of one of your products.

6. Create and give away an *infographic*. Infographics have become popular over the last few years. As their name suggests, they present some kind of statistical data or other factual information in a fun, eye-catching way. For an example of great infographic about SEO take a look at `http://searchengineland.com/seotable`.

These are the kind of posts that are likely to attract attention and links back to your blog. Try brainstorming a few ideas along these lines and you'll be surprised how many you come up with.

As well as link baiting you can also simply ask other people to link to you. This is a fairly straightforward approach, but you need to be careful not to come across as a spammer. It may be worth restricting this to people you know or people who regularly leave comments on your blog. Some people may be annoyed about receiving an e-mail out of the blue requesting a backlink, so exercise some discretion here. Definitely don't send out a **broadcast** e-mail to lots of addresses requesting links.

**Warning**

Don't be tempted to buy inbound links. There are many unscrupulous dealers on the Web who will sell you quantities of inbound links. Google and the other search engines regard this practice as *cheating* and severely frown upon anyone involved. *If you buy links, you stand a very good chance of being banned from the search engines.*

# Robots.txt optimization

A `robots.txt` file is read by search engine robots when they crawl your blog. You can use it to tell them which pages should be indexed. There are a couple of reasons why using a `robots.txt` file is good for SEO. First, Google and other search engines recommend you use one and it's generally a good idea to do what they say. Second, it can help you to cut down on duplicated content.

Search engines do not like duplicated content (that is, the same content appearing at two different URLs within a website) because they suspect it might be spam. One minor drawback with WordPress is that it can create a lot of duplicate content. For example, `http://blog.wpbizguru.com/category/tutorials` points to exactly the same content as `http://blog.wpbizguru.com/tutorials`. Also, the same content is repeated on different pages. For example, most of the posts listed at `http://blog.wpbizguru.com/category/tutorials` are also listed on `http://blog.wpbizguru.com/tag/tutorial`. We can tell the search engines to ignore any duplicate content by giving instructions in the `robots.txt` file. Here is the `robots.txt` file for WPBizGuru:

```
Sitemap: http://blog.wpbizguru.com/sitemap.xml

User-agent: *
Disallow: /cgi-bin
Disallow: /wp-admin
Disallow: /wp-includes
Disallow: /wp-content/plugins
Disallow: /wp-content/cache
Disallow: /wp-content/themes
Disallow: /trackback
Disallow: /feed
Disallow: /comments
Disallow: /category/*
Allow: /wp-content/uploads/
```

The first line is a big signpost to your Google Sitemap. `User-agent: *` means that the file is intended for all robots to read. It is possible to target the different search engine robots with specific instructions, for example, `User-agent: Googlebot` would just apply to the Google robot; however, you don't need to do this with your blog.

The lines that begin with `Disallow:` tell the robots not to visit those files and folders. This is how you tell them to ignore certain parts of your site. For example, we don't need any of the content in the `wp-` directories to be indexed because it's mainly just PHP code. The one exception is `/wp-content/uploads/`, so we have used `Allow: /wp-content/uploads/` to tell the robots they *should* visit that directory because there may be images in there that should be indexed. `Disallow: /category/*` should cure the duplicate content problem we outlined previously.

You can use a simple text editor (for example, Notepad) to create your `robots.txt` file (you can go to `http://blog.wpbizguru.com/robots.txt` and use that file as a starting point). Then it's simply a matter of using your FTP client to upload it to the **root** directory of your blog.

# Using excerpts on the home page

Another way to cut down on duplicated content is to display just excerpts of the posts on your home page instead of showing them in full. Obviously, each post is displayed in full on its own single post page, so having them in full on the home page may be regarded as duplicate content by the search engines. In fact, it's not just the home page, as the posts slip down to pages 2, 3, 4, and so on; they are still displayed in full to the search engine spiders.

Using excerpts is not only a great SEO strategy; it is also becoming popular amongst bloggers in its own right. Some people prefer it as it makes the home page more concise and there is less vertical scrolling required to get an overview of all the posts. It makes it easier for readers to scan the posts and pick the ones they are really interested in. Also, forcing readers to click through to the single post page means they see the comments in full for each post and so may be more inclined to make a contribution to the discussion.

It should still be OK to display the most recent post in full as it can take up to a week for a new post to be indexed by the search engines. By then, the post will have moved down the list and become excerpted, thus removing the risk of duplicate content.

I'm noticing home page excerpts more and more. I did a very quick (and un-scientific) survey of the current top-10 blogs on `technorati.com` and seven of them used excerpts on their home page (these are big names like Gizmodo, Gawker, TechCrunch, and so on).

However, there will always be some traditionalists who prefer to see the full posts on the home page. You need to balance the SEO and usability benefits against the possibility of alienating some of your readers. Personally, I think the benefits of using excerpts outweigh any drawbacks, so we'll go ahead and set them up on WPBizGuru.

You could go through and edit each post adding a `<!--more-->` tag where appropriate. However, there is a plugin we can use that will do this automatically. It's called **Excerpt Editor** (`http://wordpress.org/extend/plugins/excerpt-editor/`). Install, and activate it in the usual way on your local development server.

Select the plugin (**Tools | Excerpt Editor**). First, select **Auto-Generate** from the menu and enter the following settings:

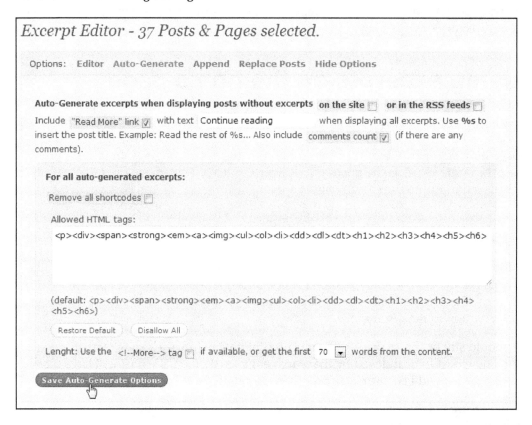

Click **Save Auto-Generate Options**. Now select **Replace Posts** from the menu and enter the following settings:

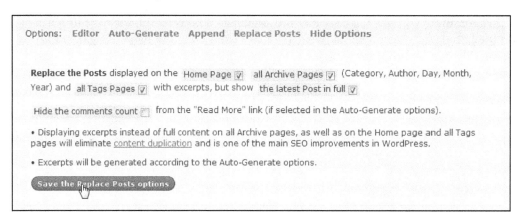

Click **Save the Replace Posts** options and view your home page. You will see that the latest post is shown in full but all the others have been excerpted and now have a **Continue reading** link. The same thing has been applied on all the Archive pages (Category, Author, Day, Month, and Year).

## An Image In A Post

By admin | Published: **May 22, 2011** | Edit

Lorem ipsum dolor sit amet, consectetur adipiscing elit. Mauris imperdiet est ac felis ullamcorper vel consectetur justo pretium. Aliquam blandit, erat eu facilisis ultrices, enim nulla feugiat erat, quis scelerisque sem diam volutpat libero. Nullam tristique imperdiet sem cursus accumsan. Ut at porttitor nunc. Quisque faucibus, eros id lacinia molestie, libero justo mattis erat, eu rutrum magna erat eu diam. Donec facilisis, ligula et interdum volutpat, arcu elit scelerisque mi... Continue reading

Posted in *Themes* | Tagged *blogging tips, image, plugin, wordpress advice* | *Leave a comment* | *Edit*

The default settings in the plugin mean that the first 70 words are used in the excerpts. On the **Auto-Generate** page of the plugin, you can change the number of words included in the excerpts. Or, if you don't like having the post cut-off in the middle of a sentence, you can use the **Editor** to select each post and then manually set the content you want to appear in the excerpt.

Having set the **Auto-Generate** options, every new post you publish will be excerpted accordingly. Simply deactivate the plugin if you ever want to revert to full posts.

# Search engine submissions

We've now highlighted some of the most important SEO strategies. Once you've spent some time implementing these on your blog, it's time to submit it to the search engines.

# The big four

If your blog has been around for some time, then most likely it has already been crawled and indexed by the big four search engines (Google, Yahoo!, Bing, and Ask). You can check if they already have it indexed by searching for your home page URL in each of the big four. If you get results in return, they already have it and there is no need to submit it.

If there are no results returned for your URL, it means the search engines have not found it yet. In which case, you can submit it to Google, Yahoo, and Bing (Ask does not have a facility for submitting your URL). If your blog is new, make sure there is a fair amount of content to be indexed—I suggest you wait until you have at least ten posts before submitting. At the time of writing, the submission pages for Google, Yahoo, and Bing are as follows (the URLs for these pages have changed in the past, so you may have to search for them):

- Google: `http://www.google.com/addurl/`
- Yahoo: `https://siteexplorer.search.yahoo.com/submit`
- Bing: `http://www.bing.com/webmaster/SubmitSitePage.aspx`

For Google and Bing, it's simply a case of entering your home page URL. At Yahoo you can also add the URL for your main RSS feed. Yahoo also offers a range of paid-for submission services that guarantee quicker indexing, which you might like to consider.

# DMOZ.org

**DMOZ**, or the **Open Directory Project**, is the most important directory on the Web. Its content is licensed in a similar fashion to open source software, so it is widely syndicated. In fact, almost all of the major search engines use its directory in some way or another. Many experts argue that DMOZ is no longer very important, but there is still evidence that having your site accepted by DMOZ can have a positive impact on your search engine rankings. Therefore, I would recommend that you submit your blog to DMOZ. Go to `http://www.dmoz.org/add.html` for full details about submitting.

# Minor search engines and directories

Along with the big four search engines and DMOZ, there are thousands of other minor search engines and directories out there. Some of these are general, while others operate within a specific niche. For an idea of the sheer quantity take a look at the list at `http://www.searchengineguide.com/searchengines.html`.

Not all of these are worth bothering with as they don't attract very much traffic. However, it's worth doing some research into the ones that serve your particular niche. By looking around a bit, you will identify those that appear to be well used and popular. Ways of spotting decent directories are to look at the number of websites they have listed and check out their ranking at Alexa.com (`http://www.alexa.com/site/ds/top_500`). If they have plenty of websites listed and a decent Alexa ranking, they are probably worth submitting your URL to. Remember, the more good-quality inbound links you can get, the better your ranking will be on Google and the other majors.

If you intend to submit to the smaller search engines and directories, it will be more productive if you log what you're doing. Set aside some time each month to research and submit to the minor search engines. Use a spreadsheet to log which ones you are submitting to and follow up by seeing how much traffic (if any) you are receiving from them. You'll find out how to monitor your traffic sources in *Chapter 9, Analyzing Your Blog Stats.*

# SEO software and tools

There are many tools and applications that claim to help you optimize your site and/or submit it to the search engines. These vary greatly in their usefulness and value for money. If you decide you need some automated help with your SEO (and there's no denying, some of these tools can save hours) I recommend you research the market carefully before you part with any of your marketing budget. SEO products and services are big business and there are plenty of charlatans out there who have jumped on the bandwagon just to make a quick buck. Having said that, there are some excellent tools from reputable vendors. We will look at some of the better ones in the following pages (I also regularly review SEO tools on my blog at `http://blog.paulthewlis.com/seo-tools`).

# Web CEO

This is one I strongly suggest you take a look at. **Web CEO** (`http://www.webceo.com`) is probably the most complete tool of its kind, and it comes highly recommended by many online marketers and SEO pros. It can help you with several aspects of SEO, including:

- Keyword research
- Optimizing your content
- Submitting to the minor search engines and directories
- Building inbound links

Although it's a paid-for product, there is a free version with plenty of useful features. I suggest you download it, if only to submit your blog to the dozens of minor search engines it supports. The free version allows you to automatically submit your URL to over 100 search engines. It's also very useful for doing keyword research (similar to the Google tool we discussed earlier in this chapter).

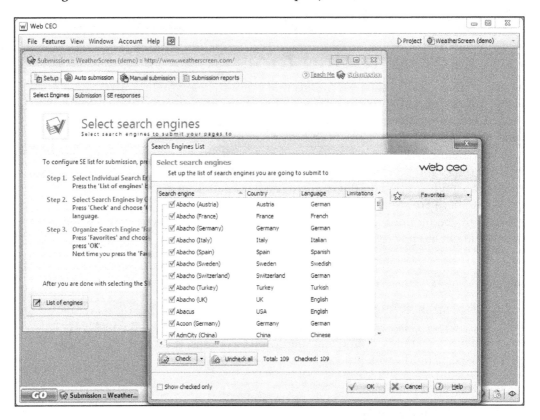

# Google webmaster tools

This collection of tools is indispensable for SEO. It provides you with the information you need to fine-tune your blog to make it more Google-friendly. It gives you some insight into how Google views and ranks your pages, which is a great way of learning about SEO in more detail. Google Webmaster Tools is completely free to use.

It's easy to get started. You just need to sign up for a Google account (if you don't already have one). Then go to `http://www.google.com/webmasters/tools/`, login, and submit your blog's URL. Before you can access any detailed information about your blog, you need to verify that you are the site owner. One of the verification methods is to add a Meta Tag to your home page (you'll find it under the **Alternate methods** tab on the **Verify ownership** page).

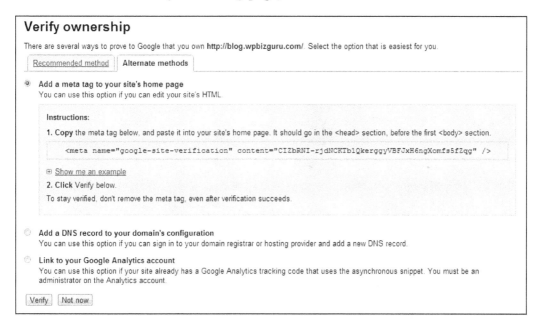

We can use our **All in One SEO** plugin to do this. In your WordPress admin area, go to the plugin page, and copy and paste the Meta Tag that Google gives you into the **Additional Home Headers** box, then click **Update Options**:

Now go back to Google Webmaster Tools and click the **Verify** button. If verification is successful, you will be taken to the Dashboard:

Google Webmaster Tools is very intuitive with good help files and documentation, so I won't go into detailed instructions here. Use the menu to see what tools are on offer, and read the recommendations Google gives you. For example, under **Your site on the web** you can see the top search queries in which your blog appears—this is very useful for your keyword research. You can also use the **Links to your site** option to see which websites are linking to you.

If your blog is new, some of the data may not be available yet. Keep checking over the coming days and weeks—the data will appear as Google re-indexes your blog. You can see in **Crawl stats** the last time Googlebot visited you.

The first recommendation for WPBizGuru is to add a sitemap. Since we've already created a Google Sitemap, it's simply a matter of telling Google the URL:

# Firefox SEO extensions

There are several extensions for the Firefox browser that have been developed to help with SEO. My favorite is **SEOQuake** (`https://addons.mozilla.org/en-US/firefox/addon/seoquake-seo-extension/`). Its main benefit is to help you evaluate your SEO efforts and track your blog's progress in the major search engines. At a glance you can see a variety of useful SEO parameters such as Google Page Rank, Alexa Ranking, Yahoo, and Google links data, Del.icio.us and Digg links, and more. Keeping track of this kind of data is really useful to determine how successful your SEO work has been.

The following is a screenshot from the Google results page showing SEOQuake data for `http://www.packtpub.com`:

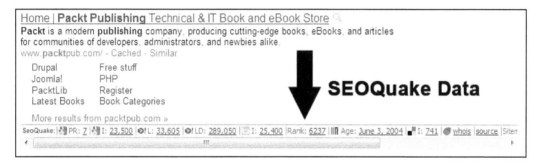

# Seeing results

SEO should always be seen as an ongoing process. If you've just applied the strategies from this chapter to your blog, don't expect to see big improvements in your search engine rankings overnight. The search engine bots crawl the Web relatively infrequently, so it will take time for your SEO work to have a visible impact. It will also take time to build links and tweak your keyword list until it is just right. SEO is not a one-off activity; it's something you should do on a regular basis. Adopt an organized approach and keep records of the SEO work you do and carefully monitor your progress through the rankings. If you put in the effort, you will see results over time.

# Summary

In this chapter, we have examined some of the most important SEO strategies and how to apply them. We also looked at submitting your blog to the search engines, and introduced some tools and software to make life easier. If you've followed these guidelines, your blog should already be on its way up the search engine rankings.

Next, we'll look at a whole host of other promotion techniques to boost your blog's popularity and send your traffic figures even higher.

# 7
# Supercharged Promotion

You can't rely solely on search engines to spread the word about your blog. In order to supercharge your promotion campaign, you need to get creative.

Promoting your blog and steadily growing your traffic volume is a long, hard job. In fact, it's never ending. A large part of your time should be spent on your promotional work. Indeed, you'll probably need to spend much more time on this than actually writing posts. The key to success is getting to know how the blogosphere works and learning about the tools, websites, and social networks that can help you along the way.

In this chapter, we will examine some of the options available to build up your promotional arsenal. It's by no means an exhaustive reference, but it should get you going. Hopefully, the tips and tricks here will get you thinking more creatively about your promotion work. This chapter includes:

- RSS syndication and WordPress feeds
- How FeedBurner can enhance your RSS feeds
- Using specialist blog indexes and search engines
- Promoting your blog via social networks, such as Facebook, Twitter, and LinkedIn
- Making the most of social bookmarking

## Syndication

One of the most powerful promotional tools available to bloggers is RSS. It's a specification that allows your visitors to *subscribe* to your content using feed-reading software and then receive your latest posts and comments without having to visit your blog. Your new content automatically appears in their **feed reader**.

RSS and blogging have always been intimately related. RSS has been available for many years, but no one really found a mass application for it until blogging arrived on the scene. The two are a perfect match. RSS is just what bloggers need to keep their readers updated with the latest content from their blogs. Pretty much all blogging software (including WordPress) has native support for RSS syndication.

Some may argue that the uptake of RSS by the Web surfing masses has been a relatively *slow burn*. It's true that it's taken several years for RSS to become mainstream, and there are still many Web surfers who are yet to appreciate its benefits, but take-up remains steady. It will continue to grow as the world's most popular web browsers now ship with integrated feed readers, while more and more high profile websites (for example Yahoo!, Facebook, BBC, and so on) promote RSS to their users. The following screenshots show the built-in feed readers in Firefox 4 (left) and Internet Explorer 9 (right).

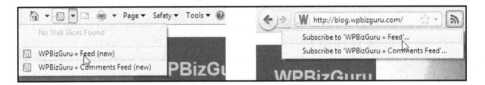

# WordPress feeds

There are several different formats of RSS feeds, such as RSS 0.91, RSS 1.0, RSS 2.0, and Atom. The differences between these are in the XML code that makes them work. WordPress supports all of these different formats, which means anyone can subscribe to your feed.

WordPress has an excellent built-in feed generator, which makes your main posts feed auto-discoverable. So, virtually all RSS feed readers and the most popular web browsers will automatically detect your main feed just from your blog's URL. For example, Google Reader will find the WPBizGuru feed just from the main URL:

There are specific URLs for accessing each of the different feed formats:

- `http://blog.wpbizguru.com/wp-rss.php` – RDF/RSS1.0 feed
- `http://blog.wpbizguru.com/wp-rss2.php` – RSS 2.0 feed
- `http://blog.wpbizguru.com/wp-atom.php` – Atom feed

However, because WPBizGuru is using **custom permalinks**, the URLs are much simpler:

- `http://blog.wpbizguru.com/feed` – The main posts feed
- `http://blog.wpbizguru.com/comments/feed` – The comments feed
- `http://blog.wpbizguru.com/category/tutorials/feed` – The *Tutorials* category feed (this uses the tutorials slug, but you can substitute it with the slug for any category)
- `http://blog.wpbizguru.com/tag/tutorial/feed` – The *tutorial* tag feed (again, you can substitute **tutorial** for any tag)

In fact, if you add **/feed** to the end of any URL on the blog, you will see the feed for that page.

# Excerpts or full posts?

WordPress provides you with an option either to display an excerpt or the entire post in your RSS feed. There are advantages and disadvantages to both and, as with the debate in *Chapter 6, Search Engine Optimization* over full posts or excerpts on the home page, it's largely a matter of personal choice.

Full posts may be more useful for your subscribers as they won't have to leave their feed readers to see your content in full. It can be annoying having to click through from the feed reader in order to see the whole post. The downside for you is that it may lose traffic to your blog (if people are reading your posts in their feed readers, they won't be visiting your pages). This is really only a problem if you rely on adverts for revenue (more on this in *Chapter 10, Monetizing your Blog*). A decrease in traffic will probably mean less ad revenues. However, the small amount of revenue you lose may be a price worth paying. At the end of the day, the whole point of your blog is to have it read by as many people as possible. Whether they do that at your blog's URL or in their feed readers doesn't really matter.

I prefer to display full posts in the RSS feed because of the extra convenience it offers to subscribers. However, you can change the settings for this under **Settings | Reading** in the WordPress admin area. You can also change the number of posts to be shown in the feed.

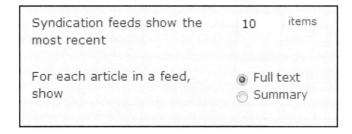

# FeedBurner

As we've just seen, WordPress does a pretty good job of handling RSS syndication. However, there's a third-party service that offers better functionality.

**FeedBurner** (http://feedburner.google.com) provides a great range of feed management tools, and since it was acquired by Google, it's completely free to use. It works particularly well with the **FeedBurner FeedSmith Extended** plugin (http://wordpress.org/extend/plugins/feedburner-setting/). FeedBurner gives the following advantages to your RSS feeds:

- The **PingShot** tool automatically updates (or pings) a wide range of search engines, indices, and aggregators as soon as it detects new content in your feed.

- There is a sophisticated e-mail subscription system which allows people to receive your RSS feed by e-mail. This system is great for people who are still slow to adopt RSS, or just prefer receiving their subscription by e-mail.

- You have the ability to add interactive links into your feed. For example, at the end of each post you can add links that allow users to e-mail the content direct to their friends or add it to social bookmarking sites such as Delicious.

- FeedBurner automatically serves the correct format of your feed (RSS 1.0, Atom, RDF, or whatever) to the reader.

- There is a whole host of analytical tools so that you can tell how many people are subscribing to your feed (more on this in *Chapter 9, Analyzing Your Blog Stats*).

- The **FeedBurner FeedSmith Extended** plugin ensures that all the analytic and feed forwarding features offered by FeedBurner work in WordPress without you having to configure them.

There is an official FeedBurner plugin maintained by Google, called **FeedSmith**. However, I'm recommending the **FeedBurner FeedSmith Extended** plugin, which takes the official plugin and adds some useful functionality such as the ability to redirect category and tag feeds.

# Setting up FeedBurner

We'll run through the process of setting up FeedBurner and take a look at some of its most useful features by applying it to the WPBizGuru blog. As FeedBurner requires a publicly accessible URL in order to work properly, we can't set it up for our local development server, but you can work through the following example on your own live blog.

Begin by installing and activating the **FeedBurner FeedSmith Extended** plugin in the usual way.

You need a Google account to use FeedBurner so if you don't already have one, you can create one at `https://www.google.com/accounts/NewAccount`. Now go to `http://feedburner.google.com` and log in using your Google account details. Enter the URL for your blog in the **Burn a feed right this instant** box and click **Next**:

Select the Posts feed for your blog (we'll do the Comments feed shortly) and click on **Next**.

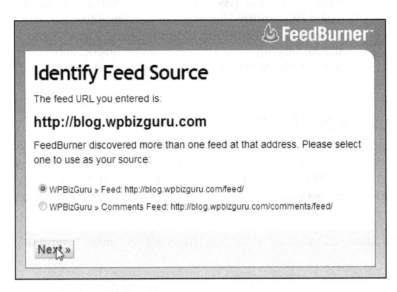

On the next screen, you can change the **Feed Title** and **Feed Address**, but the defaults should be fine. Click **Next**.

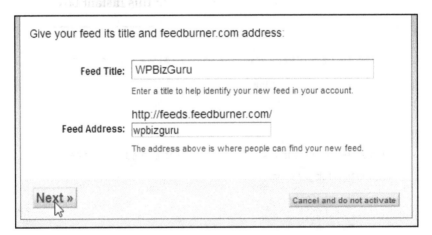

On the next page, you should see a success message. Before we return to WordPress, we'll activate the FeedBurner Stats tools. At the bottom of the success page, click on **Next**. On the next page, check all the boxes and click on **Next**.

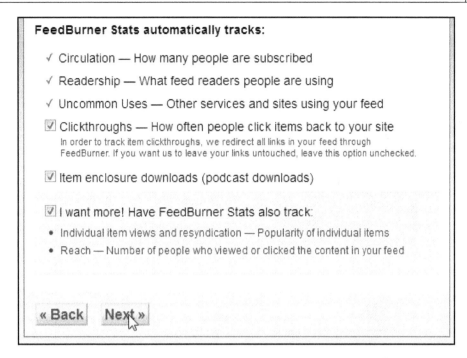

The sign-up process is now complete and you will be taken to your FeedBurner dashboard page.

Now, return to the FeedBurner FeedSmith Extended plugin page in your WordPress admin area and enter your FeedBurner feed URL into the appropriate box (the URL will be something like `http://feeds.feedburner.com/wpbizguru`) and click **Save**:

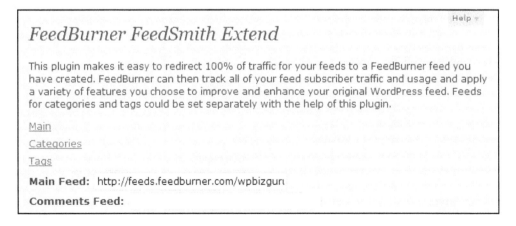

Now, we'll set up our Comments feed. Back in FeedBurner, click on **My Feeds** and, once again, enter your blog's URL in the **Burn a feed right this instant** box and click **Next**. This time, on the next screen select the comments feed and click **Next**.

Work through the remaining steps as we did for the Posts feed.

Return to the FeedBurner FeedSmith Extended plugin and enter your FeedBurner comments feed URL:

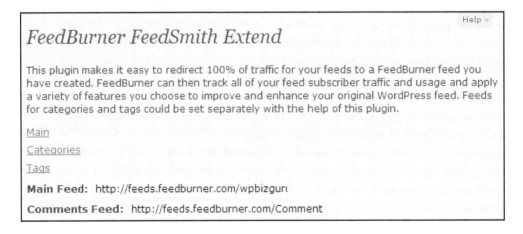

Click on **Save**.

On the plugin page, you will have noticed that you can also set up FeedBurner feeds for all your categories and tags. This isn't essential, but if you would like to do so, it's a similar process that we used for the main feed and the comments feed. In FeedBurner, go to **My Feeds** to set up a new feed and enter the full URL to the category feed, for example, `http://blog.wpbizguru.com/category/tutorials/feed/` (instead of just the URL for your blog home page). Go through the set-up process as before and enter the URL of the FeedBurner feed next to the relevant category on the plugin page. Click **Save**.

Tutorials   Feed: http://feeds.feedburner.com/Wpbizgur

We have now set up our FeedBurner feeds and configured the FeedBurner FeedSmith Extended plugin. Next we'll take a quick look at some of FeedBurner's most important features.

# Using FeedBurner

First, you need to check that your new FeedBurner feed is working. Enter the WordPress URL for your blog's main feed, for example, `http://blog.wpbizguru.com/feed`. The FeedBurner FeedSmith Extended plugin will work its magic and you should now be forwarded to your new FeedBurner feed:

If you're not forwarded to FeedBurner, you may need to regenerate your feed—simply choose any post to edit and click **Update** (you don't need to make any changes to the post). The feed will now be regenerated and the plugin will forward the feed URL to FeedBurner.

Now, let's take a look at the FeedBurner admin area. You probably still have it open in a browser window, but if not, you can log in at `http://feedburner.google.com` using your Google account.

You'll notice five tabs near the top of the dashboard (**Analyze**, **Optimize**, **Publicize**, **Monetize**, and **Troubleshootize**), which enable you to access all of FeedBurner's features. You need to first activate **SmartFeed** so that your feed has maximum compatibility with the widest range of feed readers and browsers. Click on the **Optimize** tab and then choose **SmartFeed** from the left-hand menu. It's then simply a matter of clicking the **Activate** button to set up this feature.

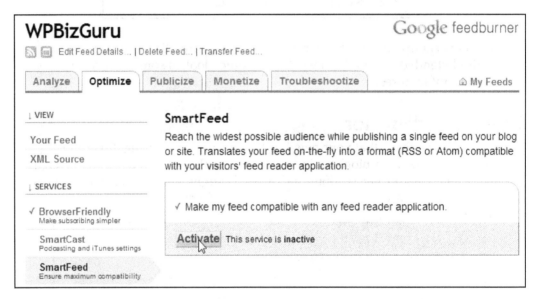

Another cool feature is **FeedFlare**. This allows you to add some interactive links to the bottom of each post in your feed. Click on **FeedFlare** in the left-hand menu to set it up. You're presented with a list of services to add to your feed and there are many more available by clicking the **Browse the Catalog** link.

I wouldn't go overboard by selecting too many as they will clutter up your feed (maybe choose three or four to begin with). Remember to click the **Activate** button at the bottom of the page once you have selected your services. For WPBizGuru, I've chosen **Email This**, **Add to del.icio.us**, **Digg This!**, and **Share on Facebook**.

This is how they look in the feed:

You can take your time to examine most of the other features under the **Optimize** tab as they are mostly self-explanatory. The only other one I will flag up here is the **Title/Description Burner**, which enables you to turn your feed's title and description into something more interesting, and that matches the branding of your blog:

As we move on to the **Publicize** tab, we will see the FeedBurner features that will really help supercharge your blog promotion.

**Email Subscriptions** is easy to set up. It allows you to provide an alternative method for your readers to subscribe to your RSS feed. Once you have activated the service, you add a small subscription form to your blog where readers can sign up. Your subscribers will receive an e-mail containing your new posts once a day. Obviously, they will only receive an e-mail if you add new posts every day. No e-mails are sent on days that you don't post.

You have full access to the e-mail addresses of all the subscribers and you can export them for use in other applications. We'll run through the process of setting this up using the WPBizGuru blog *on our local development server*.

Under the **Publicize** tab, choose **Email Subscriptions** from the left-hand menu and click the **Activate** button. You will then be taken to a page that contains the HTML code for the sign-up form.

Open up Notepad++ (or a text editor of your choice), then copy and paste the **Subscription Form Code** from FeedBurner into a new Notepad++ document. Select **View | Word Wrap**.

The code is rather messy so we'll tidy it up before inserting it into our WordPress sidebar. Add a few line breaks so that the code is laid out as it appears in the following screenshot:

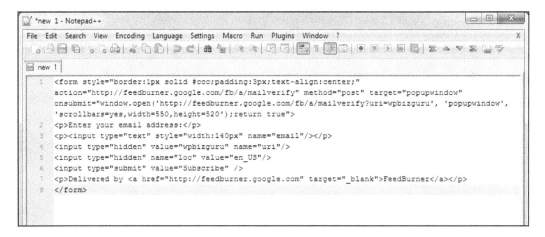

 We'll use a feature in WordPress called **Text Widgets** to insert the subscription form. Text Widgets allow you to add your own code into an *empty* widget.

In your local WordPress admin area, go to **Appearance | Widgets**. We'll place the e-mail subscription form in the Secondary Aside and move the RSS Links above it. Drag a Text widget from the Available Widgets panel to the top of the **Secondary Aside** then drag the **RSS Links** widget to the slot above it:

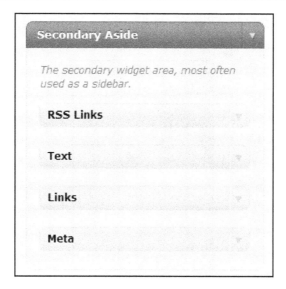

Open up the **Text** widget, go back to Notepad++ and copy all of the subscription form code, then paste it into the widget textbox. Click **Save** to save and close the textbox.

I also changed the title in the **RSS Links** widget to **RSS Feeds**:

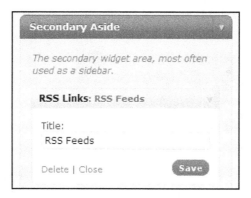

Click the **Save** button.

If you preview the blog, you will see that the sign-up form appears in the RSS section of the sidebar:

The form doesn't look too bad, but the sign-up instructions aren't very informative and it could use a bit of tidying up. We need to edit the code to achieve this. Here is the subscription form code after it's been edited (this is included in the code bundle for this chapter (`email_form.txt`), which you can download from the Packt website):

```
<form style="border:0px;"
  action="http://feedburner.google.com/fb/a/mailverify" method="post"
  target="popupwindow"
  onsubmit="window.open('http://feedburner.google.com/fb/a
    /mailverify?uri=wpbizguru', 'popupwindow',
    'scrollbars=yes,width=550,height=520');return true">
  <p>To receive our main feed by email, type your email address and
    hit enter:</p>
  <input type="text" style="width:100px" name="email"/>
  <input type="hidden" value="wpbizguru" name="uri"/>
  <input type="hidden" name="loc" value="en_US"/>
</form>
```

Go back to the **Text** widget and replace the original subscription form code with the improved, edited version. Save your changes. The form looks a bit better now:

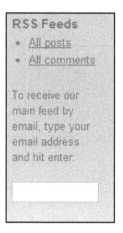

When a user enters their e-mail address, a FeedBurner pop-up will open for them to complete the sign-up process. They will then receive an e-mail containing a confirmation link, which they must click to start their subscription. This protects you from any unwanted sign-ups and prevents spammers from hijacking your form.

Once you have added the sign-up form to your blog, you can change some of the other settings for e-mail subscriptions from the FeedBurner dashboard. For example, if you select **Email Branding** in the left-hand menu, you can change the subject line for your e-mails and also add a logo:

**Email Branding**

HTML Email Appearance

Email Subject/Title: | WPBizGuru - Latest Updates

This line will appear as both the Subject of update emails and as the main title in the body of the message.

HOT TIP
Use ${latestItemTitle} to insert your latest post's title into the Subject/Title of email.

☐ Change Subject when an email has 2 or more items

Logo URL: | http://blog.wpbizguru.com/logo.jpg

You should now have a pretty good idea of what FeedBurner can do for your blog. Spend some time exploring all the services on offer. We will be discussing the **PingShot** feature in the next section on blog indexes and search engines.

# Blog indexes and search engines

In *Chapter 6, Search Engine Optimization*, we discussed methods of optimizing your blog for the major search engines. However, there's a whole host of other search engines and indexes that are specifically for blogs. One of the most popular of these is Technorati (`http://www.technorati.com`). These search engines represent another great way of promoting your blog by getting it in front of another group of web searchers.

## Ping-O-Matic

Luckily, WordPress makes it easy to get listed on the most popular blog indexes and search engines. These search engines compile their indexes from blogs **pinging** them.

**Ping** is a mechanism by which blogs notify external servers (in this case, the search engines) that their content has been updated.

By default, WordPress is automatically set up to ping your new content to the most popular blog search engines via a service called **Ping-O-Matic**. You can see the settings for this under **Settings | Writing**:

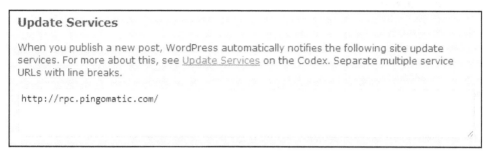

# FeedBurner's Pingshot

Ping-O-Matic covers most of the blog search engines, but we can also use FeedBurner's pinging service, **Pingshot**, to add even more. Log in to your FeedBurner account. Choose to manage your main content feed (as opposed to the comments feed), click the **Publicize** tab in the dashboard and then **Pingshot** from the left-hand menu.

On the Pingshot page, it's simply a matter of clicking the **Activate** button.

# Technorati

WordPress will automatically ping your blog updates to Technorati via Ping-O-Matic. However, you should also sign up to Technorati to claim your blog and set up a profile. You can sign up using the **Join** link on the Technorati home page. Once you've signed up, you can edit your profile and claim your blogs.

From the **My Profile** page you can upload a photo, add a bio, and claim your blog:

In order to claim your blog, you need to enter some details about it and then go through a process to verify that you are the rightful owner. Technorati will e-mail you a claim token which you then need to place in a new blog post (Technorati gives full instructions and guides you through the process):

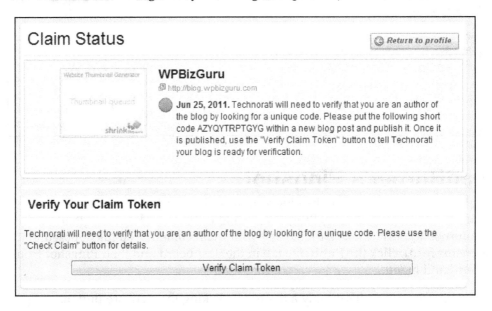

When you have set up your profile, people who find your blog on Technorati will get a little bit more information about you (see the WPBizGuru profile page at `http://technorati.com/blogs/blog.wpbizguru.com`):

# Minor blog indexes

We've covered most of the major blog search engines by setting up our automatic pings. However, there are plenty of minor blog indexes that don't use the pinging system. These have less traffic, but it may still be worth submitting your URL to them. I won't give a list of these here as many of them cover specific niches. You can find them by searching on Google. A couple of examples are: `http://www.poweredbywp.com/`, which lists blogs that run on WordPress, and `http://www.britblog.com/`, which covers British bloggers.

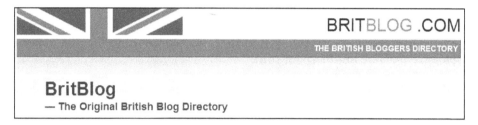

# Using social networks

In recent years, the social networking phenomenon has swept the Web. Sites such as Facebook, Twitter, and LinkedIn now have millions of users worldwide. Businesses have been hard at work figuring out how to leverage the power of social networks in their marketing activities. Social networks can be useful to you as a business blogger, but it will very much depend on your type of business and you need to know what you are getting into.

Social networks will probably be more useful to you if your business is quite personal in nature. For example, if you are a sole trader, consultant, or freelancer, your personal profile page on Facebook can be a useful place to help build your brand and find new prospects. If, however, you run a larger company and have a more *corporate* identity, social networking can be more difficult to harness. However, there are more and more social networks that are aimed specifically at business users, the best known being LinkedIn.

The main thing to bear in mind with social networks is that most people tend to use them in a *social* context, rather than a *business* context. People use Facebook to stay connected with their friends, see photos of last weekend's parties, talk about vacations, weddings, sports, and so on. This means the content tends to be very informal. This is why social networks are not necessarily a great place to do business. If you frequently post risqué images of your wild weekend escapades, it's probably a good idea to keep your business totally separate.

However, if you're a little more restrained about what you post on Facebook and the tone of your profile page is a good match with the tone of your blog, there may be an opportunity for some cross-promotion. But remember that many Facebook users don't like business encroaching onto the network. If you use a *hard sell* approach, you're likely to lose a lot of friends.

# Facebook

If you use Facebook, you could try publishing your blog posts to your Facebook profile. This could be a useful technique for driving some traffic to your blog posts. Remember, however, not to overload your Facebook profile with too much business-related content (keep things informal and bear in mind that the majority of people on Facebook are there for fun).

If you have a slightly larger business or feel that your personal profile isn't an appropriate place for content from your business blog, you can set up a **Facebook Page**. To set one up, click on the **Create a Page** link in the Facebook footer. The set up process is straightforward—just follow the on-screen prompts.

Probably the easiest way to publish your blog posts to your Facebook account is to use a Facebook app called **RSS Graffiti**. As you've probably guessed from its name, RSS Graffiti periodically checks the RSS feeds you specify and posts any new entries it finds to your Facebook wall. So, if you specify the posts feed for your blog, the app will publish your blog posts on your wall.

To set this up, login to your Facebook account, go to the app page (http://apps.facebook.com/rssgraffiti/) and authorize access for the app:

Next, click on the **Add Feed** button. Enter the URL of your blog's posts feed into the **Feed URL** box and click the link to preview it:

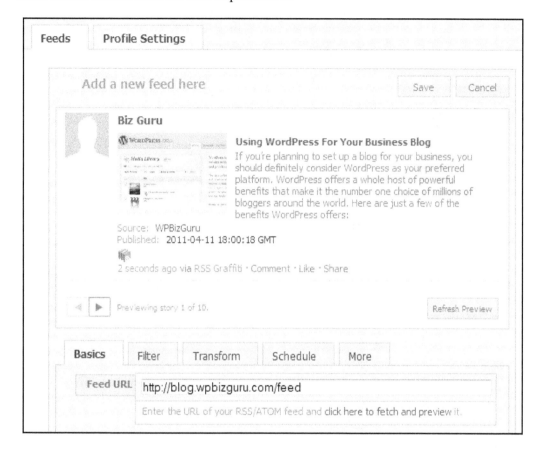

When you add a new feed, by default the app will only publish posts it finds after the time you added the feed. If you want historic posts to be published, you need to click on the **Filter** tab and change the **Time Filtering Options**. Your blog posts should now be published on your Facebook Wall:

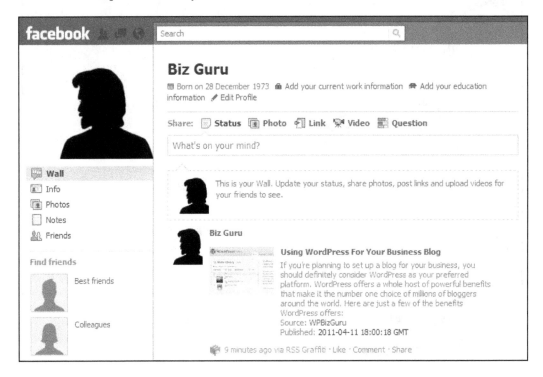

# LinkedIn

For many business bloggers, **LinkedIn** (http://www.linkedin.com/) may be a more useful social network than Facebook. It's targeted more towards commercial users and is all about business networking. If you don't already have one, I suggest you create a LinkedIn account and a company page.

When you create a LinkedIn profile, you can add the URLs of up to three websites — you should make one of these your blog. You can also display your blog posts in your LinkedIn updates by installing the **WordPress LinkedIn App** (http://learn.linkedin.com/apps/wordpress/). Installing and configuring the WordPress app is very simple. Log in to your LinkedIn account and choose **Profile | Edit Profile**. Find the **Applications** section and click **Add an application**. On the apps page, click on the WordPress app and then choose to add the application:

You then just need to enter the URL of your blog and the app will start displaying your blog posts in your LinkedIn updates (the following screenshot shows the WordPress app in my personal LinkedIn account):

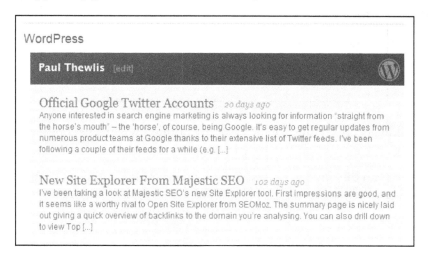

# Using Twitter

**Twitter** (`http://www.twitter.com`) is a micro-blogging platform available via the Web, IM, and mobile devices. It allows you to publish short, quick-fire messages called **Tweets**, up to 140 characters in length, aimed at answering a simple question: *What's happening?* You can invite people to follow your Tweets and in turn, you follow theirs. It's a very social medium, which is one of its major attractions to bloggers.

So, what can it do for your blog? Well, as with many Web 2.0 applications, people are still figuring out exactly how they can use it to best effect. At its simplest level, it's just a way of keeping in touch with your friends, family, and colleagues. But it could be used as another channel to publicize your blog.

The most obvious way of putting it to work on your blog is to supplement your RSS feed. Each time you publish a new post, you can announce it via Twitter:

All your followers on Twitter will be instantly notified when a new post is published on your blog.

Likewise, you can display your latest Tweets on your blog, either as posts or in a sidebar widget (we'll do this later with the aid of a couple of plugins).

Twitter is great for breaking news fast. If you're unable to write a full blog post, you can tweet it and follow-up with a full post later. You could also tweet previews or teasers for your posts. If you are attending a conference or event, you can use Twitter to update your blog with the latest news from the event in real time using your cell phone or PDA.

Twitter is a great way to get instant feedback, which makes it a useful research tool. The following screenshot shows that WPBizGuru tweeted the question, *What's your favorite WordPress Plugin?*. His followers have started tweeting their replies:

Once you have signed up to Twitter, you will find that you attract new followers relatively quickly, which makes it a great networking tool. Having a presence on Twitter adds to your online brand and could bring your blog and your business to the attention of a whole new audience.

# Setting up Twitter in WordPress

It's easy to integrate Twitter into your WordPress blog thanks to a couple of cool plugins. The first one we'll look at automatically tweets your new blog posts. It's called **WP to Twitter** (`http://wordpress.org/extend/plugins/wp-to-twitter/`), and we'll run through the process of setting it up for the WPBizGuru case study. The plugin needs to be installed on a publicly accessible web server, so won't work on our local development server. You can follow along with these instructions on your own live blog.

The plugin can use your favorite URL shortening service to shorten the URLs of your blog posts. If you don't have an account with a URL shortening service, I recommend you sign up to one of those supported by the plugin, so you can follow along with the tutorial. I'll be using bit.ly (`http://bit.ly`). You will, of course, also need a Twitter account for the plugin to work.

Install and activate the plugin in the usual way and then go to the settings page: **Settings | WP -> Twitter**. To begin, you need to register your blog as an application with Twitter. To do this, click the link on the plugin's settings page and follow the instructions:

1. **Register this site as an application on** Twitter's application registration page

- If you're not currently logged in, use the Twitter username and password which you want associated with this site
- Your Application's Name will be what shows up after "via" in your twitter stream. Your application name cannot include the word "Twitter." Use the name of your web site.
- Your Application Description can be whatever you want.
- Application Type should be set on **Browser**
- The Callback URL should be **http://blog.wpbizguru.com**
- Default Access type must be set to **Read & Write** (this is NOT the default)

*Once you have registered your site as an application, you will be provided with a consumer key and a consumer secret.*

To help you with registering an application with Twitter, the following screenshot shows the settings I entered for WPBizGuru:

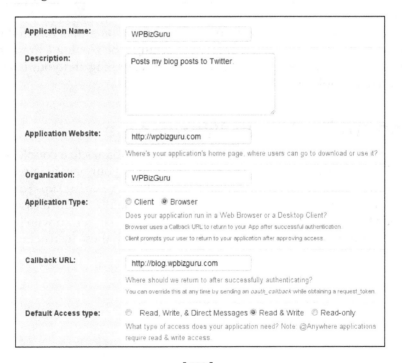

Once you've finished registering, you'll be taken to your application's settings page at Twitter. Under the **OAuth 1.0a Settings** section, you'll find your **consumer key** and **consumer secret**. Copy these and paste them into the relevant boxes on the plugin settings page:

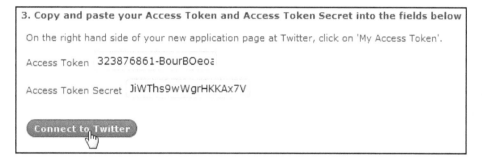

On the right-hand side of your new application page at Twitter, click on **My Access Token**, and paste the **Access Token** and **Access Token Secret** into the boxes on the plugin settings page and click **Connect to Twitter**:

3. Copy and paste your Access Token and Access Token Secret into the fields below

On the right hand side of your new application page at Twitter, click on 'My Access Token'.

Access Token   323876861-BourBOeo

Access Token Secret   JiWThs9wWgrHKKAx7V

Connect to Twitter

You should see a success message telling you that WP to Twitter is now connected to Twitter. Now we'll run through some of the other settings for the plugin.

Under **Basic Settings**, I changed the **Text for new post updates** to **New blog post: #title# #url#** and I unchecked **Update when post is edited**. I selected Bit.ly as the short URL service. When you're happy with the basic settings, click **Save WP -> Twitter Options**.

Finally, you need to enter the API key for your URL shortening service. For Bit.ly, you can find the API key on the account settings page (`https://bitly.com/a/account`). Copy and paste the API key into the appropriate box in the plugin settings and click the **Save Bit.ly API Key** button:

Your blog should now be set up to update your Twitter account every time a new post is published:

Now we'll look at another plugin for Twitter. It's called **Twitter Goodies** (http://wordpress.org/extend/plugins/twitter-goodies/) and it allows you to place a widget on your blog which displays your latest tweets. Again, we'll run through the set up process for WPBizGuru.

First, install and activate the plugin, then go to the settings page: **Settings | Twitter Goodies**. Scroll down to the **Twitter Goodies Profile Widget Options**. Enter a **Widget Title**, your **Twitter Username**, and set the **Widget Height** and **Widget Width** (to fit the WPBizGuru theme, I've set the height to **300** and the width to **190**). Click **Update Options**.

| 2) Twitter Goodies Profile Widget Options | | |
|---|---|---|
| Widget Title | WPBizGuru's Tweets | |
| Twitter Username | wpbizguru | (for Twitter Goodies Widget) |
| Widget Height | 300 | |
| Widget Width | 190 | |

Now go to **Appearance | Widgets** and drag the **Twitter Goodies – Profile Widget** into your sidebar of choice (for the WPBizGuru blog I used the **Primary Aside**):

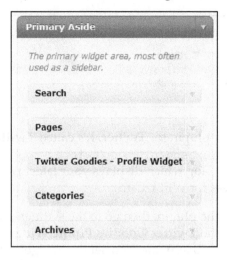

Refresh your blog and you will see the widget is displaying your latest tweets:

If you don't like the widget's color scheme, you can go back to the plugin's settings page and adjust it.

# Social bookmarking

Websites such as Digg, Delicious, StumbleUpon, and Reddit list URLs or *bookmarks* that have been submitted by Web users all over the world. The idea is that if somebody comes across an article or blog post they like, they can submit it as a bookmark and, in doing so, recommend it to other people. The more people who bookmark a particular blog post or article, the higher up the listing pages it will appear. Having one of your posts appear on the front page of Digg or one of the other social bookmarking sites, could send an avalanche of traffic to your blog.

Google has recently launched a bookmarking service called **Google +1**. By clicking on the Google +1 button, which may appear on a web page or in Google search results, you are giving that web page your seal of approval or recommendation. Your +1's are shown to your social connections in your Google profile and the aggregated +1's for a particular web page or website may also be shown in Google search results. Google +1's may even help to improve a website's search rankings. At the time of writing, Google +1 is fairly new, but already it's showing the potential of being a very important bookmarking service, not least because of the possible SEO benefits of receiving lots of +1's.

# Adding links

Before we discuss some tips and tricks to improve your chances of getting your posts bookmarked, we need to make it as easy as possible for your readers to do so. Luckily there is a service called **AddThis**, which makes it easy to add all the major social bookmarking links at the end of each of your posts. Readers just click on these links to bookmark your post or e-mail it to their friends. AddThis includes the Google +1 button and provides a WordPress plugin (`http://wordpress.org/extend/plugins/addthis/`), which makes integration with your blog a cinch. AddThis also provides excellent analytics features, which help you to see how often your blog's content is being bookmarked. We'll install the plugin on the WPBizGuru case study blog.

First you need to register for a free account with AddThis at `https://www.addthis.com/register`. On the registration confirmation screen, click the link to get a Profile ID and make a note of it—you'll need this to make the analytics features work in the plugin:

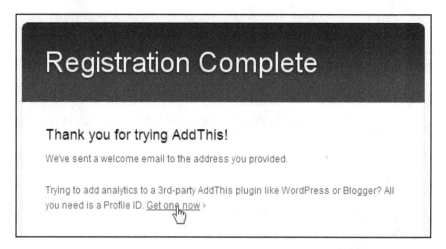

Next, install and activate the AddThis plugin in the usual way and go to the settings page at **Settings | AddThis**. Enter your profile ID, username, and password, and then click **Save Changes:**

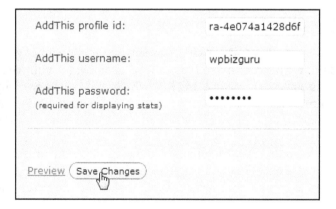

To display the Google +1 button above each post in your blog, click **additional style options**, select the Google +1 option, and click **Save Changes**.

We've now added the AddThis buttons at the beginning and end of each of our posts:

When a user clicks on one of the buttons, they are presented with a neat widget that lets them share via their social bookmarking accounts:

# Bookmarking tips

Simply adding the bookmarking links to your blog posts isn't quite enough to get a good placement in the bookmark listings. In fact, getting anywhere near the front page of the big bookmarking sites such as Digg and Delicious is quite a challenge. If you're serious about social bookmarking as a promotion tool, be warned that it takes time and perseverance to crack it.

The good news is that the big bookmarking sites are just the tip of the iceberg. There are hundreds of smaller sites, many aimed towards a specific niche, which may be much easier to break into. The volume of traffic on these smaller sites may not be as great, but it is likely to be better quality if the niche fits your blog.

You should start by researching these websites. Monitor them for several days and see what kind of posts regularly appear on their front pages. You will soon realize that different sites appeal to different users and this is reflected in the content that gets bookmarked. There is a good list of social bookmarking sites at `http://traffikd.com/social-media-websites/`. Research a selection of these and see which are likely to work well with your content. Choose no more than half a dozen upon which to target your efforts.

You should also focus your efforts on selected posts. There is no point trying to get each and every post you publish into a good position on the bookmarking sites. Wait until you have a really special post that you think will do well on the sites you are targeting.

You should register with the bookmarking sites you are targeting and start bookmarking other people's content. This grows your profile and enables you to build up a group of friends. Networking with other users is the key element of social media. If possible, try to befriend high-profile users on the sites and bookmark their content. Eventually they may notice you and bookmark one of your posts. On some networks (for example, Digg), these *power users* carry more weight than regular users. It's a real boost to have them bookmark your content as they have so many friends who follow their bookmarks and vote them up (it's a snowball effect).

When you have written a good post that you think has a chance on the bookmarking sites, ask your friends and colleagues to bookmark it. On the larger sites you need at least 15 votes before an article even gets noticed. Take some time to come up with a really catchy title for the post.

Examples of the types of posts that might do well include:

- Top-10 lists
- How-to's and *Ultimate guides*

- Posts offering free resources and gifts
- Controversial or funny articles about famous personalities
- Interesting or amusing videos

As you can see, these are similar to some of the link-baiting ideas we discussed in *Chapter 6, Search Engine Optimization*.

On the big bookmarking sites, you are not only competing with other bloggers but with some of the biggest media organizations in the world. Therefore, high quality content is a must. If you combine that with diligent research into the networks you're targeting and take time to build up your profile, you could have some great success with social bookmarking.

**Beware the 'Digg Effect'**

It's fantastic to have a big success on Digg or Delicious and get one of your posts at the top of the list. However, the tidal wave of traffic it could bring may totally overload your blog's server and bring it to a complete stop. This is known as the 'Digg Effect'. If you're lucky enough to do well on the social bookmarking networks, make sure your blog can cope with the strain (we look at ways of managing high traffic in *Chapter 11, Managing Growth*).

# Summary

In this chapter, we've looked at some of the more advanced techniques for promoting your blog and growing traffic. We began by examining the RSS capabilities of WordPress and how they can be enhanced with FeedBurner. We discussed how to use blog search engines such as Technorati, as well as a variety of social media such as Facebook, LinkedIn, and Twitter. We also examined the benefits of social bookmarking, using services such as Digg, Delicious, and Google +1.

In the next chapter, we stay on the theme of promotion and traffic-building by examining how your interaction in the blogosphere can create a mutually beneficial relationship with other bloggers.

# *8*
# Connecting with the Blogosphere

Blogging should never be regarded as a solitary activity. As a blogger, you are part of the *social web*. You should always regard your blog as a piece of something bigger — the blogosphere. Interaction with other blogs will be a linchpin in your success. In this chapter we will cover:

- Defining the blogosphere
- Why it's so important to be connected
- Methods you can employ to connect with the blogosphere, including using your blogroll, RSS feeds, comments, and contact forms

## Defining the blogosphere

Wikipedia gives this definition (`http://en.wikipedia.org/wiki/Blogosphere`):

> The **blogosphere** *is made up of all blogs and their interconnections. The term implies that blogs exist together as a connected community (or as a collection of connected communities) or as a social network in which everyday authors can publish their opinions.*

The key idea is **connectivity**. The Wikipedia definition is concerned with the connectivity between blogs, which is something we will be exploring here. However, I would also widen this definition to include the connectivity between blogs and their readers. They are as much a part of the blogosphere as the bloggers themselves. The readers are the *glue* that holds together all the connections in the blogosphere. This is particularly true of the avid blog readers, who probably subscribe to, and regularly read, dozens of different blogs. Readers often discover new blogs thanks to the links that bloggers make to each other. So, as well as connecting with other bloggers, we'll also be looking at ways of connecting with your regular readers.

# Why it's so important to be connected

The social element of blogs and the connectedness of the blogosphere is a defining characteristic of blogging as a communication platform. It is how blogging began and how it has evolved into what it is today. Blogs feed off each other and are dependent on each other for their existence. Readers are tuned into this sense of connectedness and have come to expect it from the blogs they follow. The relationships between blogs are an intrinsic part of the reader experience (this is how they link to new content and become habitual consumers of the blogging medium).

You need to be part of this in order to truly call yourself a blogger. A blog isn't a blog unless it's a fully connected part of the blogosphere. No blog is an island.

# How to engage with the blogosphere

You shouldn't view other bloggers as a threat or competition — in fact, they are your friends. Blogging is about mutually beneficial relationships.

Having said that, bloggers are notoriously distrustful and skeptical about any approaches they receive from traditional PR or marketing professionals. If you're going to make friends in the blogosphere you need to engage bloggers on their own terms. Most successful bloggers become a target for PR pros. To them, a blog is just another media outlet to pitch their message to. However, too many people in the PR industry don't understand how to connect with the blogosphere. Bloggers will take a very dim view of approaches made via press releases or unsolicited e-mails from PR firms. They will (rightly) regard this kind of communication as spam. One blogger has become so annoyed by the constant barrage of PR spam that he has set up a wiki, which lists the PR companies who have spammed him (`http://prspammers.pbwiki.com/`).

If you're involved with business blogging, you may well be a PR pro and may have experienced this kind of response from angry bloggers. However, the majority of people reading this are not PR pros — so what has this got to do with you, the average business blogger? Well, the fact that you're blogging for a business, particularly if it's a corporate entity, places you in a group alongside PR and marketing pros in the eyes of many bloggers. They're almost as distrustful of *corporate* blogging as they are of PR spammers. These are the people you need to befriend, so how do you get them on your side?

Well, we've already established that press releases and unsolicited e-mails are out. The best way to engage with other bloggers is on their blogs. You need to take the time to read their posts, leave comments, and write posts that link back to them. Here is an outline strategy for becoming a more connected blogger:

- Research the blogs in your market niche or specific arena. Take time to identify the key players. Analyze their content and try to figure out what their readers like.

- Come up with a list of bloggers you intend to target for relationship-building. You can start small, just five would be enough to get you going (you can always expand your list as time goes by).

- Begin leaving comments at your target blogs. Try to make them as relevant and *on topic* as possible. You need to genuinely engage with the issues they raise. It's very important that you don't come across as a comment spammer.

- Write posts on your own blog that expand on the topics raised by those on your target list. Link back to their posts.

- Continue doing this consistently and regularly; soon some of the bloggers you are targeting will notice you. They will begin to comment on your blog and write posts about the issues you are raising.

- Keep expanding your list of target blogs and keep working on this strategy for building new relationships. Sites such as Technorati (`http://technorati.com`) and Google Blog Search (`http://www.google.com/blogsearch`) are great places to find relevant blogs.

In the rest of this chapter, we will examine some of the practical steps you need to take to make this strategy work and improve your connectedness with the blogosphere.

**Link building**

We touched on the idea of link building in *Chapter 6, Search Engine Optimization*, where I gave you a fairly organic method of encouraging other people to link to you. Hopefully, you can understand how your blossoming relationships with other bloggers will be a great help in your link-building efforts. This is a more proactive approach to building links, but it is just as useful for search engine optimization.

# The blogroll

A blogroll is a list of links to other blogs that you read and wish to recommend to your readers. It's a great way to declare that you belong to the blogosphere. It can also be great for generating traffic. How can that be the case when it's you sending traffic to other blogs? Well, the benefit comes to you from something called **link reciprocity**.

Bloggers are pretty keen when it comes to checking their stats and tracking their referrals (more details on this in the next chapter). When they notice a blog (that is, yours) sending traffic their way, they will most likely check it out. If they like what they see, there's a very good chance they will add you to their own blogroll, and you get the chance of receiving traffic from them. Even if you don't make it onto their blogroll, you will certainly be on their *radar*, and they may link to you in one of their posts.

# Managing your blogroll

Some bloggers adopt the policy to blogroll anyone who blogrolls them. This may be a useful approach, particularly when your blog is in its infancy. However, you may have to be a little more selective as your popularity grows. Excessively long blogrolls can look messy and may be detrimental to SEO. Having a fairly indiscriminate list of blogs also defeats the object of the blogroll. The idea is to recommend blogs that you like and think will be of use to your readers. The closer they are to your own topic or area of interest, the more relevant the links will be to your readers. Having a load of dull or dormant blogs in your blogroll may reflect badly on you. As your blogroll grows, you need to be selective. You may also find it useful to organize the links in your blogroll under categories. Not only will this make it easier for you to manage the blogroll, it will also be much more usable for your readers.

## Adding categories and links

Adding categories is straightforward—we'll run through the process for WPBizGuru. Log into the admin area and go to **Links | Link Categories** and enter the details of your new category, then click the **Add New Link Category** button:

Now you have added new categories, you can add and remove links. Click on **Links** in the admin area left-hand menu:

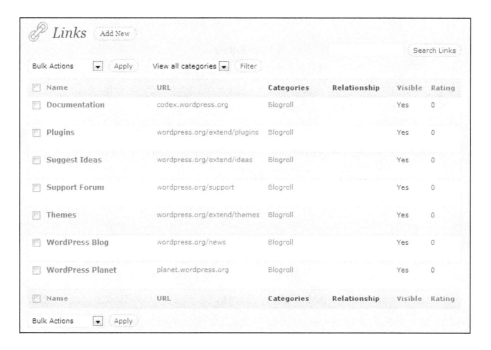

Let's begin by deleting the links that were included in the default installation of WordPress. Simply check the boxes next to the links you want to delete, choose **Delete** from the **Bulk Actions** drop-down, and click the **Apply** button.

To add links, click on **Add New**. Enter the name of the link in the **Name** box and the URL in the **Web Address** box. The text you enter in the **Description** box will be shown when someone hovers the cursor over the link in the blogroll. You can also select whether the link should be visible or not (invisible links remain in the database, but don't appear in the blogroll — they are like your own private bookmarks):

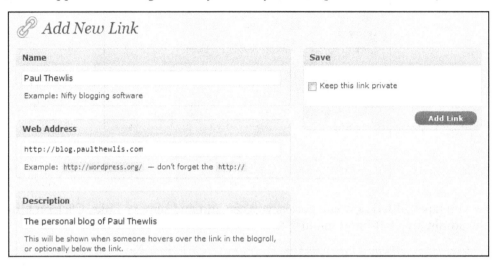

On the second half of the page, choose the category you want the link to appear in. You should also select a target for your link, which tells the user's browser how the link should be opened:

- **_blank** opens the link in a new window.
- **_top** opens the link in the top frame, if your blog is using frames.
- **_none** opens the link in the same browser window.

I always select **_none** and leave the user to decide whether they want to open the link in a new window (by right-clicking it).

The other options on the **Add Links** page are not as important, and you don't have to use them. The **Link Relationship (XFN)** option allows you to define your relationship to the person you are linking to. It is used by some web applications such as RSS feed readers and search engines. The options under **Advanced** allow you to:

- Add an image to the link (this is displayed next to the link in some themes)
- Include the RSS feed for the blog you are linking to (again, used by some themes)

- Add notes (these are not displayed in your blog, they are just for your own reference)
- Give a rating for the link (some themes display the highest rated links first)

Once you have finished, click the **Add Link** button and view the blog to see your new blogroll. In the following screenshot, you can see the new categories and links I have added to WPBizGuru:

**Blogroll SEO issues**

There is some evidence that Google and other search engines take a dim view of lists of text links published site-wide (that is, the same list of links on every page). Their reasoning is that these text links could have been purchased for the purpose of link-building. If you're worried about this, you can use a plugin to add the 'nofollow' attribute to your blogroll. An example of such a plugin is **Nofollow Blogroll SEO** (http://wordpress.org/extend/plugins/nofollow-blogroll-seo/).

# Feeding off the blogosphere

Blogrolls have been around for a long time. Many people regard them as a standard feature on any blog. I tend to agree with that point of view. Generally, I find blogrolls useful and they give me an extra insight into the mind of the blogger by showing me his or her favorite links. However, more and more blogs are choosing not to display a blogroll. Probably the main reason for this decision is the difficulty in maintaining a long list of links and the *politics* that may arise as decisions have to be made about which to add and which to remove. There is also the SEO issue I mentioned previously.

As an alternative (or even in addition) to a blogroll, some bloggers now include headlines from other blogs using the RSS feeds from those blogs. Usually they only do this for a handful of their most favorite blogs, maybe no more than five—far fewer than the number of links that normally appears in a blogroll. This is easier to manage as the number of links is smaller, but it still demonstrates the blogger's connectedness to the blogosphere.

>  If you run more than one blog, you can use this method to display the latest headlines from your other blog(s).

There is a widget in WordPress that makes it easy to set this up—we'll run through it for WPBizGuru. In the admin area, go to **Appearance | Widgets**. We'll set up two RSS widgets. From the **Available Widgets** list, drag two instances of the **RSS** widget into the **Primary Aside** sidebar:

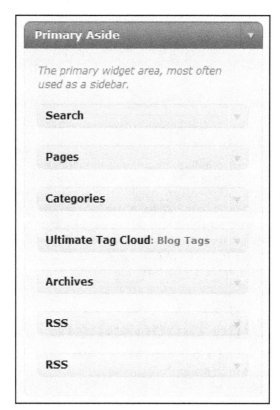

Open up the first **RSS** widget for editing and enter the RSS feed URL for the blog you want to link to, a title for the feed, and the number of posts you wish to display. Leave the checkboxes empty, as we just want to display the headlines for the items in the feed. Click the **Save** button:

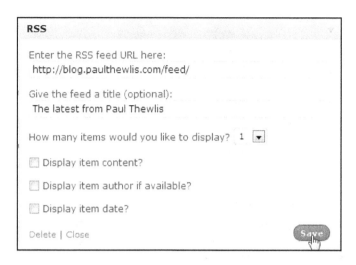

Repeat the configuration process for the second **RSS** widget by entering the details for the second blog you would like to link to.

If you view the blog, you will see the latest posts being pulled from the blogs you linked to:

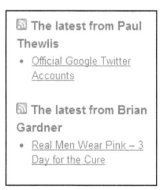

# The importance of comments

Comments are probably one of the most important elements of blogging. They allow a high level of interactivity and really connect the blogger to his or her readership. It's all about being part of a **conversation**; a principle that forms the bedrock of the live Web.

The conversational dimension of comments allows the business blogger to open a dialog with their customers, stakeholders, investors, or whomever their blog is aimed at. Comments also provide a great connection with the rest of the blogosphere. A good blogger should also be an active commenter on other people's blogs. Again, it demonstrates being part of an ongoing and far-reaching conversation. Commenting on other people's blogs also offers an opportunity for you to present yourself to their readership, which may entice new readers to your own blog.

# Fishing for comments

There are several strategies that can be employed to increase the chances of people leaving comments for your posts. The first is simply to ensure that your content is engaging, interesting, and raises some tangible issues or opinions. A dull post that doesn't really say anything of interest is not going to inspire commenters.

The second is a technique we mentioned in *Chapter 5, Content is King*—ask questions. There's no more direct and straightforward approach for soliciting some kind of response than asking a question. Make the questions quite direct and focused so that they are easy to answer in a fairly short comment. If the question is too complicated or ethereal, it will be unlikely to inspire readers to hit the comment button.

Another approach is to set tasks or assignments for your readers. Of course, this should not be anything too difficult or time consuming, but something fun or interesting. It may not be appropriate for all types of blogs. However, many bloggers who are experts or *gurus* in their field use their blogs to impart knowledge to their readers; they're teachers. For example, WPBizGuru may write a post about a new theme framework for WordPress. He could then ask his readers to send links to examples of child themes they have created using the new framework. This approach could spark a lively thread of comments as readers submit links and critique each others' themes. Another example could be asking your readers to come up with the slogan for your next advertising campaign. You could even run this type of thing as a contest, rewarding the best suggestion with a prize.

Another approach to encourage comments and feedback is to involve your readers in the research and development of new products and services. Get them involved in the early days of Research and Development (R&D). Not only does this encourage interactivity on your blog, it's a great form of market research. Your readers are likely to be potential customers for your product or service, so if they have been involved in the development of your products they may well feel a sense of *ownership* for them, which is likely to reflect positively in your sales figures.

# Managing the conversation

You should assume the role of facilitator or moderator in any discussions that arise in the comments section of your blog. This means being active in the comment threads. Don't think that just because you did all the work in writing the original post, you can hand it over to your readers and let them run with it. You should always try to steer the debate in the direction you would like it to go.

This involves responding to comments as much as possible. By doing so, you demonstrate that you are listening to the people who take the time to leave comments, which will encourage them and others, to respond some more. Obviously, your time restraints may make it difficult to give in-depth responses to every comment, but do ensure you set aside some time to get involved. At the very least try to engage with new commenters, those who are frequent contributors, and those who leave negative comments (more on this later). Remember, it's a conversation.

# Moderation

Some staunch *old-school* bloggers may balk at the notion of moderating or censoring comments. They may argue that it stifles the debate and erodes the free-speech ethos of social media. These may be worthy values for a personal blogger, but for any business, reputation management is extremely important. No profit-making organization can allow complete openness on what is, essentially, its own communication channel.

WordPress gives you the tools to moderate comments on your blog. I suggest you use these and ensure you have a system in place that allows you to control what's published. You can set this up in the WordPress admin area by going to **Settings | Discussion**. I recommend that you approve every comment. This can be done by checking the appropriate boxes in the top half of the page:

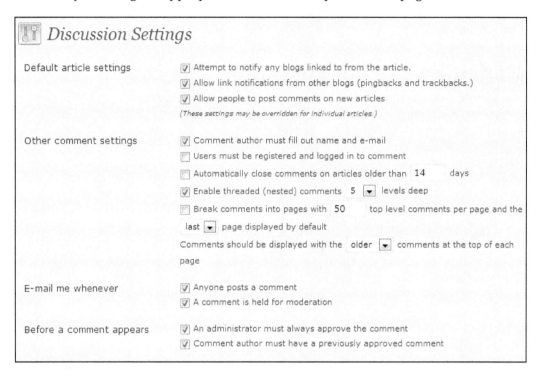

With the settings shown previously, you will receive an e-mail every time someone leaves a comment and the comment will not be published until you have approved it. Approving every comment will obviously take more time, but it does give you complete control over what appears on your blog. As your blog becomes more popular and more comments are being left, you may consider reducing your workload by lowering the moderation level for comments. For example, remove the requirement for an administrator to always approve each comment, but keep the requirement that the comment author must have a previously approved comment. Continue monitoring your comments and see if this level of moderation works for you. However, unless you *really* can't find the time to moderate every comment, I would recommend keeping the moderation levels at their highest setting.

I also recommend displaying a **comments policy** on your blog. This clearly lays out the *rules of engagement* for commenters. It may also help readers who are staunchly *anti-moderation* to understand why, as a business, you need to moderate comments. Remember, you may be held legally responsible for any content that appears on your blog. This means there is a certain amount of risk, which any business must seek to mitigate. Making this clear in your comments policy may help readers understand why you moderate all comments. I have placed a sample comments policy on WPBizGuru. It's a static page under the **About** section: `http://blog.wpbizguru.com/about/comments-policy/`.

## Comments Policy

  Share

We welcome comments from our readers and value your contributions. We do moderate all comments to ensure our legal obligations as a responsible publisher are met. We reserve the right to edit or remove any comment that we believe is inappropriate. We will not publish any of the following:

- Potentially libelous comments
- Obscene or sexually explicit comments
- Hateful or mean-spirited comments
- Plagiarized material or material that violates intellectual property rights
- Commercial promotions or spam
- Comments that are off topic or that link to material that is off topic
- Comments that violate any law

We ask for your co-operation by ensuring any comments you post meet the above guidelines.

# Dealing with negative comments

At some point you're going to come across a certain amount of negativity from commenters. This may take the form of constructive criticism and reasoned argument against your post, or it may be random insults and seemingly off-topic **flaming**.

If you're not familiar with the term, this is how Wikipedia defines flaming:

> **Flaming**, *also known as* **bashing**, *is hostile and insulting interaction between Internet users. [...] It is frequently the result of the discussion of heated real-world issues such as politics, sports, religion, and philosophy, or of issues that polarize subpopulations, but can also be provoked by seemingly trivial differences.*
>
> *Deliberate flaming, as opposed to flaming as a result of emotional discussions, is carried out by individuals known as* **flamers**, *who are specifically motivated to incite flaming. These users specialize in flaming and target specific aspects of a controversial conversation, and are usually more subtle than their counterparts. Their counterparts are known as* **trolls** *who are less "professional" and write obvious and blunt remarks to incite a flame war, as opposed to the more subtle, yet precise flamers.*

Dealing with flame comments is simple—hit **Delete**; don't give them the time of day. You should also block persistent offenders by using the **Comment Blacklist** at the bottom of the **Discussion Settings** page:

| Comment Blacklist | When a comment contains any of these words in its content, name, URL, e-mail, or IP, it will be marked as spam. One word or IP per line. It will match inside words, so "press" will match "WordPress". |
| --- | --- |
| | `jollyroger@hatemail.com`<br>`125.10.80.650`<br>`http://WeHateWP.com` |

Dealing with constructive criticism is a slightly more delicate issue. The fact is that this kind of *negativity* could actually be a good thing. Not only does it bring your shortcomings to your attention, but the fact that it's happening on your territory (that is, your blog) and on your terms makes it easier for you to deal with.

Resist the temptation to delete comments that contain this kind of constructive criticism, instead adopt a cool, calm, and honest approach to answer the issues straightforwardly. Reassure your readers that you have taken the comments on board and either present your argument to show that the comments are not true, or if they are true, explain how you are going to put things right. It's important not to be combative or aloof as this may make matters worse.

The beauty of blogging is that it provides you with a platform to turn these potentially *negative* opinions into something positive. You have the ability to demonstrate to your readers and customers that you are listening to their constructive criticism and you are constantly working to put things right.

If you have successfully built up and nurtured a loyal community of readers on your blog, you may find that they do some of the work of answering constructive criticism for you. If this is the case, it may not always be necessary for you to immediately jump in on a negative comment. See if any commenter comes to your defense. If they do, there is probably no need to get involved.

# Trackbacks

Trackbacks provide a simple way for bloggers to comment on each others' posts via their own blogs. In WordPress, you can leave a trackback to another blogger's post simply by including the permalink for their post in your own post. We have already set up the automatic pinging feature that makes this happen, on the **Discussion Settings** page (highlighted in the following screenshot):

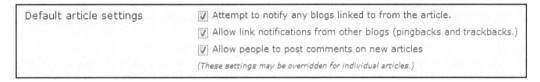

So let's imagine WPBizGuru wants to comment on another blogger's post by using a trackback. The permalink for the post he wants to comment on is: `http://blog.paulthewlis.com/seo/official-google-twitter-accounts/`.

So, WPBizGuru writes a new post and includes the permalink:

A trackback will be sent to the blog he or she is linking to, which will appear in the comments for the post:

Likewise, if someone links to a WPBizGuru post from their blog, the trackback will appear in the comments (of course, because of the moderation settings, WPBizGuru has to approve the comment first):

Readers can view the post by clicking on the link that appears in the trackback.

# Comment and trackback spam

Sadly, we live in a world plagued by spam. Blogs are now a target for spammers, as the comment and trackback facilities that feature on most blogs provide spammers with a mechanism to get their message published.

The developers of WordPress have worked hard to free their users from the frustration and inconvenience of spam by providing a service called **Akismet**. The Akismet plugin is provided by default in all WordPress installations. If you haven't done so already, you should activate Akismet now.

In the WordPress admin area, go to **Plugins** and activate **Akismet**. WordPress will tell you that the plugin has been activated, but you need to enter your Akismet API key:

To get an API key, go to `http://akismet.com` and sign up for an account. Akismet is free for personal blogs (although you are invited to make a donation, if you wish); for commercial blogs, choose the appropriate plan. Once you have signed up, you will receive an e-mail containing your API key.

Now copy the API key and go back to your blog's admin area.

Click on the **enter your Akismet API key** link. You will be taken to the **Akismet Configuration** page, where you need to enter your API key:

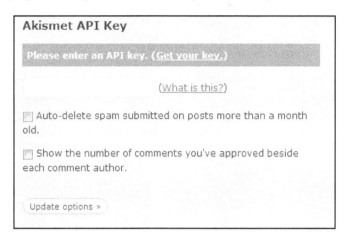

Akismet is now activated; it will automatically intercept comments it believes to be spam and they will be placed in the **Spam** section on the **Comments** page in your dashboard.

If any genuine comments have been intercepted, you can release them by clicking the **Not Spam** link below each comment. Likewise, if a spam comment gets through, mark it as spam by clicking the **Spam** link.

Akismet learns from its users, so by *de-spamming* genuine comments (and vice versa), you're helping it to get smarter and doing the whole WordPress community a favor.

By moderating all comments and using Akismet, you shouldn't have the problem of spam comments appearing on your blog. However, if you get to the enviable position of receiving hundreds of comments per day, you may not be able to moderate them all and decide to loosen your moderation settings. If this is the case, you will find that Akismet does a pretty good job. But if you do notice a large amount of spam comments slipping through the net, there are some even tougher anti-spam precautions you can take.

For example, you may decide to add a **Captcha** to your comments form. Captcha is an anti-spam technology that requires a random code, or the answer to a math question, to be entered before a form can be submitted. If a code is used, it is displayed as an image, so it cannot be read by non-human users. This prevents spam bots from using the form. Captcha is an effective anti-spam technology, but it does have drawbacks. It can cause accessibility issues for users who have vision impairment, and users who choose to browse with images turned off in their browser will not be able to see the code image. If a math question is used, it solves some of the accessibility issues (because it can be read by a screen reader), but because it can be read by non-humans, it may be slightly less effective. Because of these issues, you should consider carefully whether or not to use Captcha. It should be a last resort only to be used if spam is a real problem for you.

If you feel that you really must use Captcha on your comment form, there is a plugin called **SI CAPTCHA Anti-Spam** (`http://wordpress.org/extend/plugins/si-captcha-for-wordpress/`). To set it up, install and activate the plugin in the usual way. You will now have a Captcha image at the end of your comment form:

On the SI CAPTCHA Anti-Spam settings page, you can choose which forms you want Captcha to be used on. For example, you may not want Captcha on the WordPress login form or the lost password form; just uncheck these on the settings page to remove them.

# Installing a contact form

Comments provide a great platform for a public discussion on your blog. However, some readers may prefer to contact you privately. You could simply provide an e-mail address on your **About** page or on a dedicated **Contact** page, but you can present a far more professional image for your blog by providing a contact form. It also provides an easy and obvious way of making yourself contactable by other bloggers and the wider blogosphere, enforcing your image as a *connected* blogger who is open to feedback and discussion.

# Using the Contact Form 7 plugin

We'll set up a contact form for WPBizGuru. To do this we'll use an excellent plugin called **Contact Form 7** (`http://wordpress.org/extend/plugins/contact-form-7/`). First, install and activate the plugin in the usual way.

There is a default form already set up, which we can use as the basis to create our own. Select **Contact | Edit** in the left-hand menu of the WordPress admin area to view the default form. You will see the default form, **Contact form 1**:

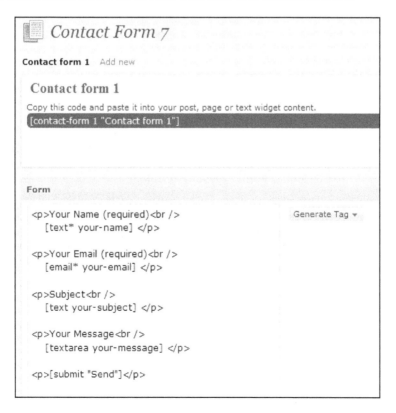

The plugin uses custom tags to generate the contact form. You can see the tags in the square brackets in the **Form** area. There are several other tags available. We won't be using them all here, but you can learn about them in the documentation at the plugin's website (`http://contactform7.com/docs/`).

The default form settings should be fine for your first simple contact form. You just need to check that the e-mail address in the **Mail** section is correct; this is the e-mail address where the completed forms will be sent to. By default the plugin uses the WordPress admin e-mail address, but you can use any e-mail address you like:

 Remember, that we do not have e-mail set up on our local development server, so the form will not actually work on our local case study blog. However, this step is important when you install Contact Form 7 on your live blog.

Our basic contact form is now ready for us to embed in a new page. Click on **Pages | Add New** to create a new WordPress page. I've called the new page **Contact**. In the first part of the page I've put a selection of contact methods. Directly below that I've added the embed tag for our contact form – `[contact-form 1 "Contact form 1"]`. I've chosen **About** as the parent of the **Contact** page:

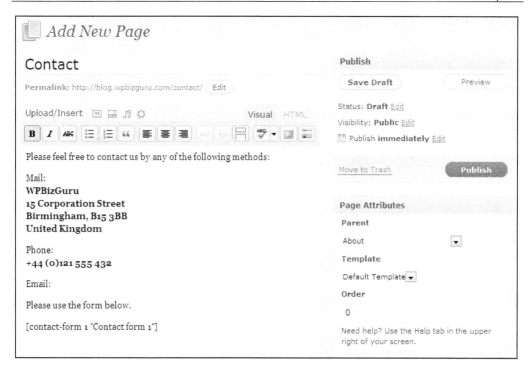

It's important to include *bricks and mortar* contact details whenever possible. This gives your blog a higher level of legitimacy. Research has shown that web users are far more trusting of websites that display real-world contact details. Displaying a physical address will also allow you to leverage the mapping tools on search engines such as Yahoo!, Bing, and Google.

If you are uncomfortable sharing real-world contact details, you could consider using a Google Voice number (`http://www.google.com/voice`) and/or setting up a PO Box for mail.

Now click the **Publish** button and view the blog:

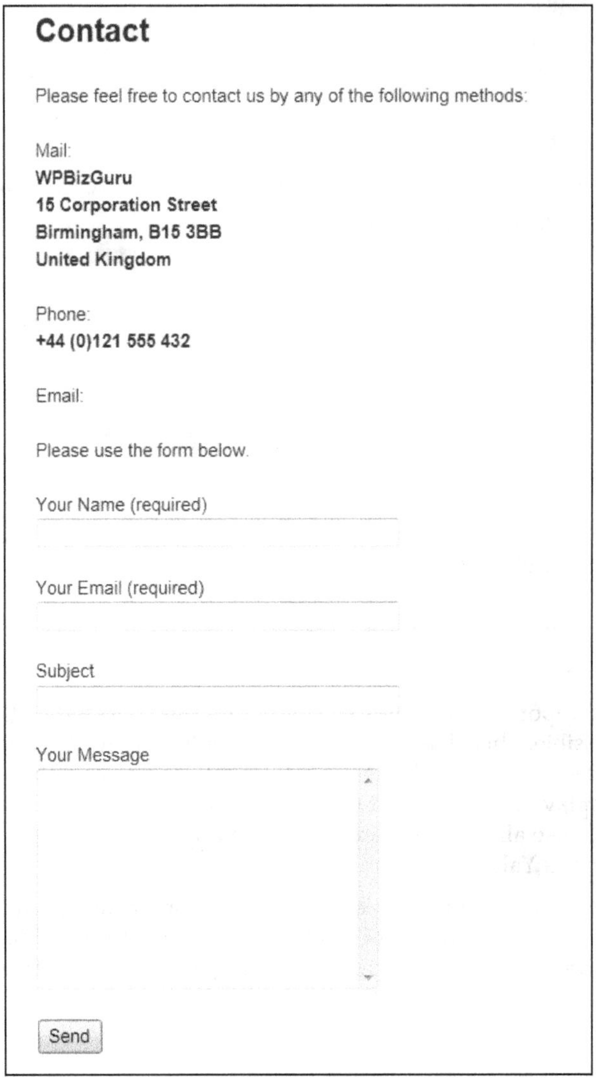

## Contact

Please feel free to contact us by any of the following methods:

Mail:
**WPBizGuru**
**15 Corporation Street**
**Birmingham, B15 3BB**
**United Kingdom**

Phone:
**+44 (0)121 555 432**

Email:

Please use the form below.

Your Name (required)

Your Email (required)

Subject

Your Message

Send

# Preventing contact form spam

We saw earlier in the chapter that comment forms can cause a spam problem. Unfortunately, the same is true for contact forms. Spam bots trawl the web looking for unprotected forms and then use them to send spam. There's a chance they could find the contact form on your blog.

Luckily, Contact Form 7 provides a couple of features to help prevent spamming via your contact form. You can use a Captcha image (this requires another plugin) or a verification question. As we discussed earlier, Captcha images can cause accessibility and usability issues. However, the verification question approach is less prone to accessibility problems. The person using the contact form is asked a very simple question; they cannot submit the form unless they answer it correctly. The questions are so easy that no human user is likely to get them wrong, but a spam bot is unlikely to get the answer right as it's not smart enough to understand the question.

No anti-spam protection can be guaranteed 100% effective. The verification question method is fairly sound, but spammers are constantly improving their techniques and re-programming their evil bots. Some people suggest that it may be possible to program a spam bot and increase its chances of answering verification questions correctly. So far this doesn't seem to have caused any major problems, but it's always a possibility that your spam guards could be breached. Sadly, that's the world we live in.

If your contact form begins to generate large amounts of spam, you can add one of the security measures provided by Contact Form 7. We'll run through the process of setting up the verification questions.

Go back to the configuration page for **Contact form 1** in your WordPress admin area. We will use the **Generate Tag** feature to create the tag for the verification question. Choose **Quiz** from the **Generate Tag** drop-down.

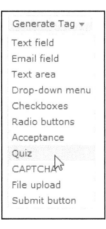

In the **Quizzes** text area, enter some simple math questions, with each one on a new line — you can add as many as you like. The syntax to use is **12+48=? | 60** — that is, the question, followed by a pipe **|**, followed by the answer. When you're done entering questions, click anywhere outside the **Quizzes** text area and the tag will be generated:

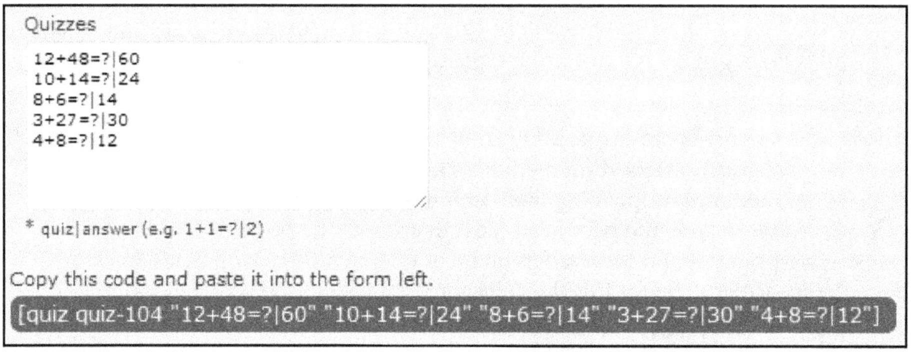

```
Quizzes

 12+48=?|60
 10+14=?|24
 8+6=?|14
 3+27=?|30
 4+8=?|12



* quiz|answer (e.g. 1+1=?|2)

Copy this code and paste it into the form left.
[quiz quiz-104 "12+48=?|60" "10+14=?|24" "8+6=?|14" "3+27=?|30" "4+8=?|12"]
```

Copy the generated code and paste it into the form, along with some explanatory text for the form user. I've highlighted the code in the following screenshot:

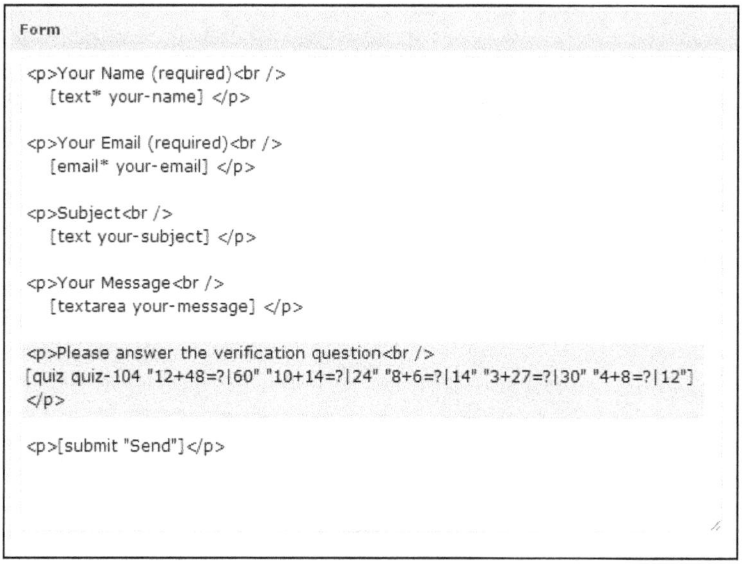

```
Form

<p>Your Name (required)<br />
   [text* your-name] </p>

<p>Your Email (required)<br />
   [email* your-email] </p>

<p>Subject<br />
   [text your-subject] </p>

<p>Your Message <br />
   [textarea your-message] </p>

<p>Please answer the verification question<br />
[quiz quiz-104 "12+48=?|60" "10+14=?|24" "8+6=?|14" "3+27=?|30" "4+8=?|12"]
</p>

<p>[submit "Send"]</p>
```

Click the **Save** button. Now when anyone uses the contact form, they must answer the verification question before they can submit it:

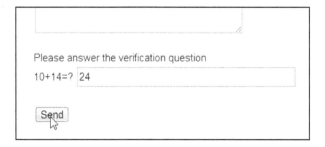

# Summary

In this chapter, we discussed the importance of connecting with the blogosphere. We began by defining what the blogosphere is and why you need to be an active part of it. We then discussed a simple strategy for engaging with other bloggers. We also looked at the practical steps you need to take in becoming a well-connected blogger, including managing your blogroll, using RSS feeds to display content from other blogs, how to manage comments, and how to make yourself as approachable as possible by using a contact form.

In the next chapter, we will look at the important subject of web analytics. You will learn how to measure the success of your blog by analyzing the visitor data.

# *9*
# Analyzing your Blog Stats

How do you know if anyone's reading your blog? Is the time and effort you put in showing any results? These are some questions you should be able to answer. The whole point of blogging is to help your business, so you need to be sure you're reaching your target audience. In this chapter, we will look at statistics that are essential for measuring your success and the tools that can help you gather them. We'll cover:

- The key performance indicators (KPIs) you should be monitoring
- How to use WordPress.com Stats
- An overview of Google Analytics
- Using FeedBurner stats
- Checking your Alexa rankings

## Key performance indicators

As with any other aspect of business, measuring the performance of your blog is the key to understanding its value and success. There are many different metrics that can inform you about the progress of your blog. Some bloggers look at many indicators and aggregate them to give a very detailed analysis of their blog. Others prefer to focus on a smaller set of metrics.

The information you choose to measure the success of your blog will be largely dependent on your blogging goals, which you decided in *Chapter 2, Introducing Our Case Study – WPBizGuru*. For example, if you see your blog as a vehicle for building your company brand, then the number of unique visitors may be relevant. If the main aim of your blog is to improve communications and open a dialog with your existing customer base, then the number of comments may be more important to you.

Broadly speaking, there are five groups of **KPIs (key performance indicators)** that can be applied to a blog:

- Traffic
- Subscribers
- Number (and quality) of comments and feedback
- Search engine results
- Inbound links

In this section, we'll take a look at each of these in turn before moving on to examine the tools we can use to measure them.

# Traffic

Raw traffic is probably one of the simplest metrics for measuring the success of any website, including your blog. However, even this seemingly simple indicator has several facets, as there are different ways of measuring it. Different people will prefer different methods.

# Hits

These days, **hits** are pretty much obsolete as a method of measuring traffic. A *hit* is a request sent to a web server for a file. In the early days of the Web, hits were regarded as an important statistic. However, as web analytics became more sophisticated, people began to realize that server hits are a fairly meaningless way of measuring traffic. This is because a web page can contain several links to files on the server. For example, if a page has six images, there will be seven hits on the server when the page is requested (one for the page itself, and then one for each of the images). So you could increase your hits simply by adding more images to the page!

The term *hits* has slipped into common usage over the years; people use it (wrongly) when they are talking about traffic in general.

# Unique visitors

The number of **unique visitors** is one of the most important metrics for measuring a blog's traffic. It is particularly favored by potential advertisers, so if you ever decide to sell advertising on your blog, you will need to have this statistic available. It's basically the number of different people who visit a website.

It can be difficult to measure unique visitors. The only way any website owner could be certain about the number of unique visitors would be to have every visitor register for a user account and log in each time they use the site. Obviously, this isn't practical! Unfortunately, each of the two main ways of measuring unique visitors has pitfalls.

The first approach is to log the IP address of each visitor. Every device that connects to the internet has an IP address, but the accuracy of this approach can't be guaranteed. This is because some ISPs and company networks issue their users with dynamic IP addresses. This means that each time a user connects to the internet they have a different IP address. In this situation, the same person visiting a website at different times would be counted as a different unique visitor each time. A second problem arises because users on some large networks are all connected to the internet via the *same* IP address. So, if there were 20 people on such a network, all accessing the same website independently, it would only be counted as one unique visitor.

The second approach for measuring unique visitors is to use **cookies**. A cookie is a snippet of text, usually containing a unique reference code, which is saved by the user's browser when they visit a website. Each web page that uses this approach also contains a small piece of JavaScript (usually in the page footer), which detects the cookie (or installs it, if it's the user's first visit) and sends information back to the analytics software. This avoids the problems that may arise with the IP address logging approach, but has its own limitations. The problem is that some people delete cookies or choose not to accept them, as they believe they pose a security and/or privacy threat. They may also disable JavaScript in their browsers for similar reasons.

## Visits

Hopefully, each unique visitor will visit your blog more than once. This is measured simply as **visits**. It is a more reliable statistic than unique visitors because it is easier to measure. However, most analytics software packages add a little more depth to the measurement of visits than simply the headline number. For example, it's also useful to know how long each visit lasted. This gives you a good indication of how well your readers are engaging with your content, and whether or not they find it interesting. Obviously, if a visit only lasts a few seconds, you know the visitor was not impressed and clicked away from your blog very quickly.

Different analytics software has different ways of defining what a visit is. A **visit** is usually classed as a continuous series of page views, uninterrupted by any period of inactivity.

# Page views

**Page views** are the total number of pages read by all your visitors. Basically, this statistic tells you how many of your blog's pages have been opened on a daily, weekly, or monthly basis. It's also useful to know the average page views per visit. This tells you how many pages, on average, a visitor looks at each time they visit your blog. It gives a good indication of how engaged users are and how *sticky* your content is. Low average page views show that visitors soon get bored of your content and are not motivated to read another post.

You should also pay attention to the number of views for individual pages. From this data, you can identify which of your posts are popular with your readership. This helps you to create content that your readers are more likely to enjoy.

# Subscribers

Blogging adds another dimension to web analytics—it's not just about traffic to web pages. As most of the blog content is syndicated via RSS feeds, bloggers need to measure how many subscribers they have.

Subscriber data seems particularly important when you consider who your subscribers are. Quite simply, they're your biggest fans, your loyal supporters (the people who are waiting for your next post). They have taken the effort to subscribe to your blog and in doing so, are making it clear they are interested in what you're saying on a long-term basis. These people are far more valuable than the casual readers who just stop by your blog now and again, or those who may only ever visit once. As we discussed in *Chapter 7, Supercharged Promotion*, subscription is extremely important in blogging. Therefore, it's essential you know the levels of subscription for your blog. As you already know, there are two types of subscription: **RSS** and **email**.

# RSS subscriptions

RSS feeds are notoriously difficult to track and measure. However, **FeedBurner** provides statistics about how many people are subscribed to your feed. This is one of the main attractions of FeedBurner and has made it very popular with bloggers. The problem is that counting the number of feed readers is not an exact science. This means you are likely to see anomalies and inconsistencies in your FeedBurner stats. Even so, the stats are better than nothing and will at least give you a good indication of the progress of your feed subscriptions, even if the numbers are not exact.

# E-mail subscriptions

Measuring the number of people who are subscribing to your feed by e-mail can be done much more accurately than for RSS readers. It's simply a matter of counting up the e-mail addresses in your subscription list. Again, FeedBurner is a useful tool for providing e-mail subscription options to your readers (as we saw in *Chapter 7, Supercharged Promotion*). We will be looking at FeedBurner stats in more detail later in this chapter.

# Comments and feedback

The number of comments that your blog receives is another statistic that helps you measure your success. Watching the number of commenters increase as your blog gains popularity is not only satisfying, but should be regarded as a key indicator of your performance.

However, along with the simple number of comments, it's also important to consider the quality of the comments that people are leaving. Carefully considered, on-topic comments that, in themselves, are good content for your blog are far more valuable than short one-liners that don't really say very much. You will receive many comments that simply say, 'Great post! ☺'. They're nice to have, but they have most likely been left so that the commenter gets a link back to his or her own blog.

Along with the comments, you should also take note and count the amount of feedback you receive by e-mail or through your contact form. Again, as these increase in volume, it will give a fairly good indication that your blog is becoming more widely read and is making an impact in the blogosphere. As with comments, you should also take note of the quality of the feedback you receive and whether it is negative or positive.

# Search engine results

Another important performance indicator is how well you rank in the search engines for certain keywords. Along with your regular web analytics, this is something that you should constantly monitor. We touched on this topic in *Chapter 6, Search Engine Optimization*, but I raise it again here to remind you that monitoring your SEO performance should be a routine part of your blog analysis.

# Inbound links

Again, we mentioned this in *Chapter 6, Search Engine Optimization*, but as with search engine results, it's something you need to constantly monitor and treat as part of your web stats analysis. Having plenty of inbound links is not only good for your search engine rankings, but it also demonstrates how well you are connecting with the blogosphere. There are several ways you can measure how many inbound links there are to your blog.

The first is simply to count the number of trackbacks coming into your blog. Remember, a trackback is a link from another blogger when they refer to one of your posts.

You can also use search engines to check your incoming links. By typing `links:blog.wpbizguru.com` into Google, you will see a list of all the incoming links that Google has indexed for WPBizGuru. You can do this for any domain. Your Google Page Rank is also largely based on incoming links, so periodically checking it can give a good indication of your blog's performance. To check the Page Rank for any web page, you can use the SEOQuake Firefox plugin that we installed in *Chapter 6, Search Engine Optimization* or download the **Google Toolbar** from `http://toolbar.google.com`. The following screenshot shows the Google Page Rank for `http://www.packtpub.com` using the Google Toolbar:

Technorati provides another way of monitoring your incoming links. Each blog listed on Technorati has something they call **authority**. The authority of a blog is based on the number of incoming links to that blog—the more incoming links the blog has, the higher the authority. The following screenshot shows the authority for `http://scobleizer.com`:

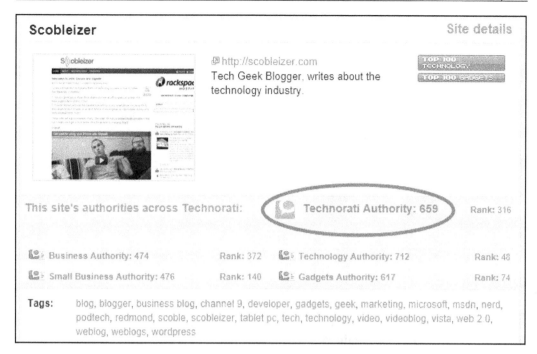

# Web analytics tools

Now you know the kind of things you need to be monitoring, let's take a look at some of the tools that can help you do this.

There are dozens of web analytics tools available. They have varying degrees of complexity and widely varying costs—some of the high-end solutions require expensive licenses. However, the good news for bloggers is that there are some great solutions that don't cost a penny. Here, we'll take a look at two: WordPress.com Stats and Google Analytics.

# WordPress.com Stats

The hosted version of WordPress includes a great stats system. Many self-hosted WordPress users were green with envy when they saw what WordPress.com bloggers got to play with. So the WordPress.org community (specifically, Andy Skelton) came up with a plugin that makes WordPress.com Stats available to anyone with a self-hosted blog. The plugin is now available as part of Jetpack (`http://jetpack.me`).

To get started, install and activate the Jetpack plugin in the usual way (`http://wordpress.org/extend/plugins/jetpack/`). Note that there's no point installing this on your WPBizGuru local development server as no one else can visit that blog except you.

You need to connect Jetpack to WordPress.com in order to make the plugin work. To do this click on the **Connect to WordPress.com** button and follow the instructions—you'll need to create a free account at WordPress.com.

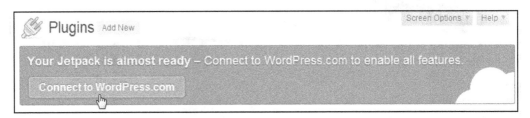

Once you've connected to WordPress.com, you'll be forwarded to the Jetpack admin page on your blog. Click the **Configure** button for **WordPress.com Stats** and then **Save configuration**, leaving the default options as they are. You should now see **Site Stats** under **Jetpack** in the main WordPress left-hand admin menu—click on it to view your stats page.

 When you first install the plugin, it will take a while for any stats to come through, so for the time being your stats page probably has a message telling you to wait patiently.

The beauty of the WordPress.com Stats system is its simplicity. It doesn't over-complicate things by providing too much information. In fact, for many bloggers WordPress.com Stats provides all the information they need (or want) to know. I'll run through a few of the major features.

 At the time of writing, WPBizGuru was still *in development* and had not been released as a live blog. This means that visitor numbers you see in the following screenshots are very small, but they still illustrate how WordPress.com Stats work.

At the top of the stats page you will notice a large bar chart, which gives you an overview of page visits by **Days**, **Weeks**, or **Months**:

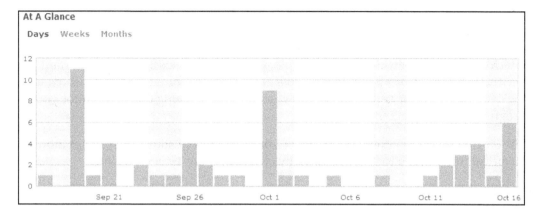

The bars on the chart are clickable. When you click on one, you will be shown more details for that particular day:

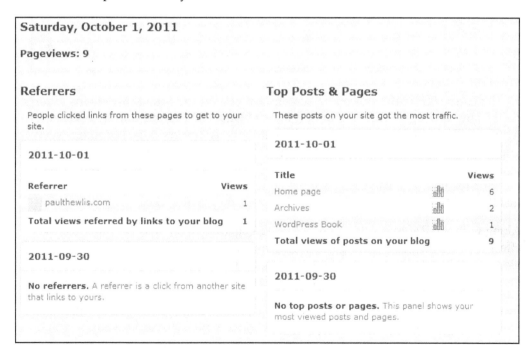

Back on the main **Stats** page, below the bar chart, you will see more information about your blog. One of the good things about WordPress.com Stats is that everything appears on one page.

The first stat you can see is **Referrers**. This tells you where your visitors are coming from. It's extremely important to know who your best referrers are as this tells you which of your relationships with other bloggers and websites are most important. As we discussed in *Chapter 8, Connecting with the Blogosphere*, building relationships with the rest of the blogosphere is the key to your success, so being able to monitor your progress in this respect is very useful.

The dashboard gives you an overview of your most recent stats. You can get more historical information for each statistic by clicking on the **This week** link:

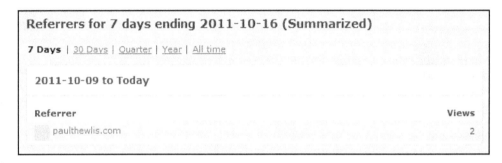

As you can see from the preceding screenshot, you are able to view data for different periods by clicking on the time period links (**7 Days**, **30 Days**, **Quarter**, **Year**, and **All time**). Back on the main Stats page, next to the **Referrers** data, is another very important piece of information for bloggers. **Top Posts & Pages** informs you of the most popular content on your blog. This will really help you to tailor your posts for your readers. You can easily see which posts work well and which don't, and therefore give them more of the kind of content they really like.

Along with the **Referrers** data, **Top Posts & Pages** can also help you monitor the effect of other bloggers linking to one of your posts. For example, if a well-known blogger decides to link to one of your posts, there is a good chance you will see an increase in the number of people viewing that post on the day he or she links to you.

**Search Engine Terms** tell you what people are searching for in order to find your blog via the search engines. This is very useful for your keyword research, which we discussed in *Chapter 6, Search Engine Optimization*. Hopefully, as time goes by, you will see patterns emerging in the search-engine terms people are using. This will tell you the best keywords to use in your posts and post titles.

**Clicks** tell you which links to external blogs and websites are most popular on your blog. This is useful information for building up a profile of your readers. It helps you to understand what they find interesting, and the types of blogs and websites they want to visit. This will help you to create content your readers are likely to enjoy and engage with. It also allows you to monitor the blogs and websites they are visiting. By doing so, you may be able to identify opportunities for cross-promotion. You're sending traffic to them, so it may be that they could send traffic to you.

# Google Analytics

For many bloggers WordPress.com Stats provide all the information they need. However, if you want to analyze your blog in more detail then you might want to use Google Analytics.

 Google Analytics works perfectly well alongside WordPress.com Stats, so you can have both installed at the same time.

Google Analytics is a free service, which provides some pretty powerful features. To get started with Google Analytics you need a Google account. If you don't already have a Google account, click the **Sign in** link in the top right-hand corner of the Google home page, then follow the **Create an account now** link. Once you have a Google account, go to `http://www.google.com/analytics/`, click the **Access Analytics** button and sign in with your Google account details.

On the next page, click the **Sign Up** button:

On the following page, enter the details for your blog and click **Continue**:

On the next page, enter your contact information, and then on the final page, accept the terms and conditions and click **Create New Account**.

You will then be taken to a page that contains your Google Analytics tracking code:

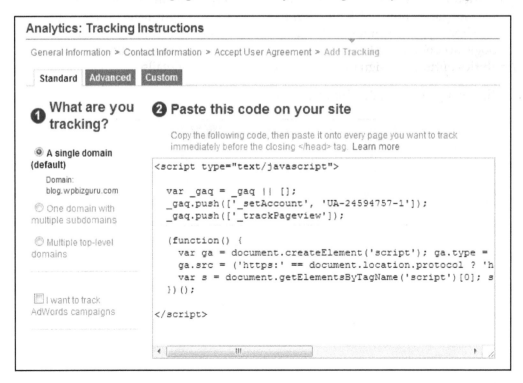

You could copy-and-paste the code into the header of your blog's theme in order to set up Google Analytics tracking. However, we'll use a plugin that uses the Google Analytics API to automatically install the tracking code in your blog. The plugin is called **Google Analytics for WordPress** (`http://wordpress.org/extend/plugins/google-analytics-for-wordpress/`). Open a new tab or browser window to go to your blog's admin area, then install and activate the plugin in the usual way. You will see a message that invites you to select which Analytics profile to track. Go ahead and click on the link:

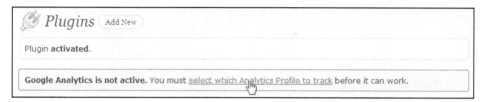

Click on the button to authenticate with Google:

You will be forwarded to the Google website where you need to grant permission for your blog to access your Analytics account:

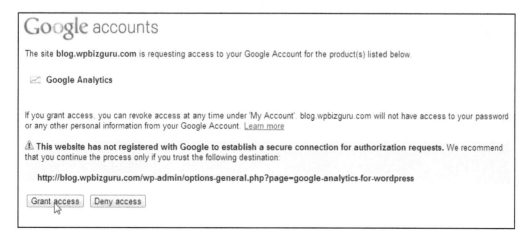

You will then be taken back to the plugin page where you need to select the **Account** and **Profile** for your Google Analytics, and then click the **Update Google Analytics Settings** button:

You now have Google Analytics installed on your WordPress blog. Unfortunately, it will take up to 24 hours before any data is available in your Google Analytics account. You may want to return to the next section tomorrow, when you have some data to look at.

# Using Google Analytics

You can log in to Google Analytics at `http://www.google.com/analytics`. The first page you see shows a list of all the websites you are tracking.

 You can track several websites using the same Google Analytics account. So if you have other websites besides your blog, you can add them too.

 At the time of writing, Google was rolling out a new version of Analytics, which can be accessed by clicking the link in the top right-hand corner of the page. All the following screenshots and menu references are taken from the new version.

# Getting started

Click on the profile you would like to view and you will be taken to the **My Site** page.

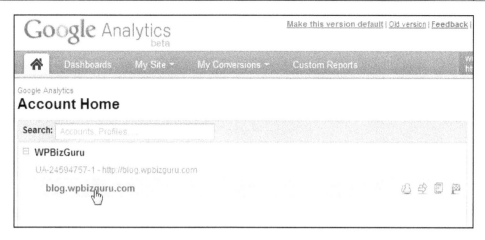

From here you can access all the data for your blog. By default, you will see a general overview of the headline numbers, while the menu on the left-hand side gives you options to drill down deeper. As you can see, there are quite a lot more features than in WordPress.com Stats; we'll run through some of the more useful ones for bloggers.

The top half of the page shows a graph and some of the most important statistics:

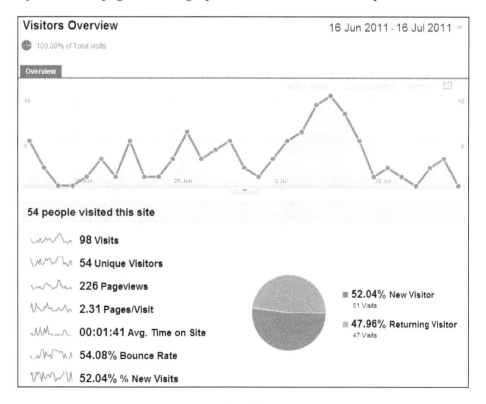

By default, the graph shows visits but you can have it display different metrics by clicking the drop-down arrow next to **Visits**:

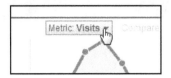

You can then choose which data you want to view:

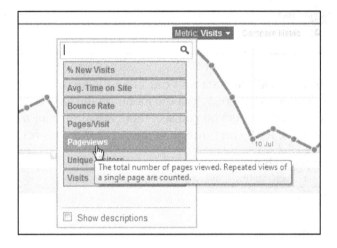

And then compare with another metric, if you like, by clicking the **Compare Metric** drop-down:

You can also select the date range you want to display by clicking on the date:

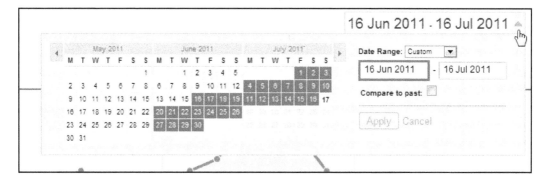

Most of the stats displayed under the graph are self-explanatory, with one exception: **Bounce Rate**. The bounce rate is the percentage of total visits whereby visitors left your blog from the same page they entered — that is to say, it was the only page they visited. A high bounce rate means that visitors are not clicking around your blog; they're leaving virtually straight away. You can lower the bounce rate by making sure that your content (particularly on the home page) is engaging and tailored to the readers you are targeting.

## Visitors

The **Visitors** menu gives you more detailed information about who is visiting your site. Click on **Visitors** to expand the menu and you will see the categories of data that are available, for example, **Demographics**, **Behavior**, and **Technology**.

Click on **Demographics** in the left-hand menu and then **Location**. You will now see a map which shows the locations of your visitors:

You can hover over individual countries to see the number of visitors from there.

This is an interesting feature that gives you geographic data about the visitors to your site. It could be very useful in helping you to tailor your content for the countries from which you receive the most visitors. For example, you may be a blogger-based in the UK and notice that the majority of your readers are from the US. Maybe you should consider adapting your writing so that you are using US spelling. Or consider including cultural references that an American audience is more likely to appreciate. Of course, you need to monitor this carefully. Maybe your US readers like your blog precisely because of the quirky British spellings and its UK cultural bias—changing things might drive them away.

Below the map there is a tabulated break down of the map data. If you click on a country name you are presented with a larger scale map of that country. In the table below the country map, you are presented with data by state, province, or city. Again, clicking on one of the place names will drill down more finely until you come to the most precise location available. The following screenshot shows there was one visitor from San Antonio, TX:

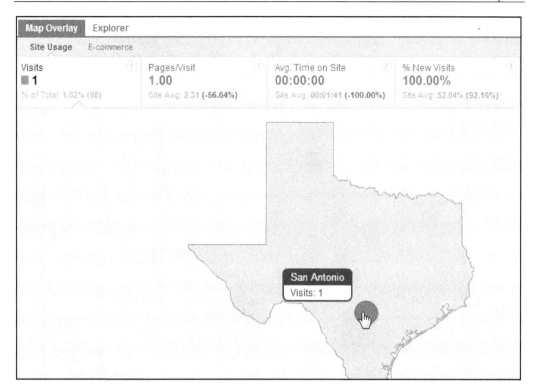

Clicking around on the map is not only useful for your blog stats, but it can also be good fun seeing where in the world your visitors are coming from. You may be surprised by the far-flung destinations!

**Languages** is also an interesting statistic. If you are receiving a high proportion of visitors who are non-English speakers, maybe you should consider providing some of your posts translated into their own languages. However, as we saw with the idea of making content country-specific, monitor things carefully—maybe they are reading your blog to improve their English skills and don't want content in their own language!

Under the **Behavior** menu is the rather self-explanatory **New vs. Returning**. It's good to have a high percentage of returning visitors, particularly for a blog. It shows you are providing interesting content that people want to come back for time and time again.

Also under **Behavior**, you will find **Frequency & Recency** and **Engagement**. This data provides further indications of how *sticky* your blog's content is. The more interesting your posts, the more frequently your visitors will come back and the more engaged they will be.

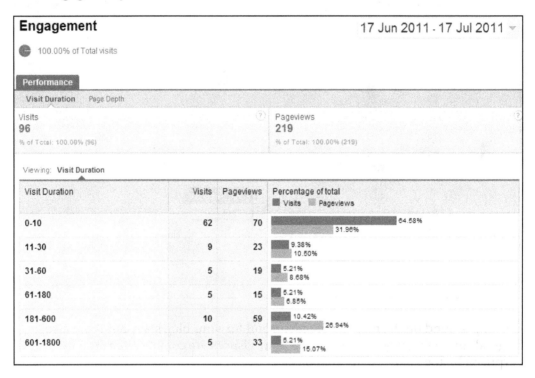

You can also view technical data about your visitors, such as which browsers and operating systems are most used by your readers. Browser type, in particular, is important. It can give an indication of how *tech-aware* your readers are. For example, older versions of Internet Explorer are likely to be used by less technically-aware visitors as opposed to the latest version of Firefox.

It's important to know browser types if you are re-designing your blog or adding new features. You should try to test your blog in the most common browsers used by your visitors as different browsers render some CSS features differently. You need to be sure that your blog looks right in the browsers used by the majority of your readers. Click on **Technology | Browser & OS** to see browser data:

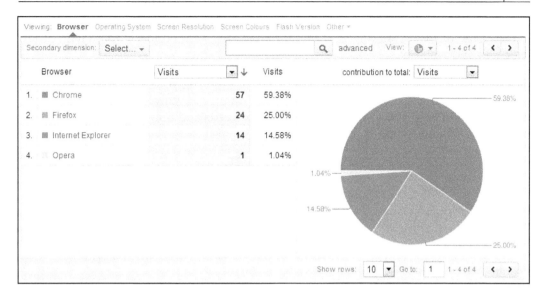

# Traffic sources

Click on **Traffic Sources** in the left-hand menu, then **Overview**. You are now viewing the **Traffic Sources Overview**. It tells you where your visitors came from and is broken down into three main sources: **Search Traffic**, **Referral Traffic**, and **Direct Traffic**.

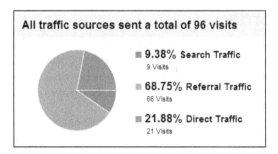

If you select **Incoming Sources | Direct**, you will be shown how many visitors arrived at your blog directly. This means they came to you either by using a bookmark in their browser or by typing your URL into their browser address bar. This can be a useful statistic if you have recently done any offline promotion. For example, people who saw your blog's URL in a newspaper article, on your company letterhead, or in an advert will be direct visitors.

The data under **Referrals** is the same as the information we saw for **Referrers** in WordPress.com Stats. Again, it's useful for analyzing your connectedness with other bloggers and websites.

The data under **Search | Organic** is useful for monitoring your search engine optimization work. Combined with the similar data you receive in WordPress.com Stats, it should help you to hone your list of keywords and fine-tune how you are using them in your posts.

The **AdWords** menu allows you to monitor any **AdWords** campaigns you may have running.

# Google AdWords

**Google AdWords** is the search giant's advertising platform—it's how they generate the vast majority of their revenue. I didn't include AdWords in *Chapter 7, Supercharged Promotion* because, frankly, it's rather beyond the scope of this book. But it does deserve a quick mention here as it is closely integrated with Google Analytics.

As you may be aware, the principle of AdWords is that advertisers bid against each other for certain keywords. The advertisers who place the highest bids get their adverts to appear above all the others. AdWords ads are the sponsored links you see down the right-hand side and at the top of Google search results pages:

It's not a promotion technique that's particularly popular with bloggers, for a couple of reasons. First, it can require a fairly substantial budget in order to see any consistent results. Second, bloggers prefer the more *organic* promotion methods such as the ones we covered in *Chapter 7, Supercharged Promotion*. However, if you have a fairly healthy marketing budget for your blog, it might be something you want to try. It's likely to be particularly useful when you first launch your blog as it may provide an early boost in your efforts to build an audience. You can find out more at http://www.google.com/adwords.

# Content

Much of the data you find here is similar to what's available in WordPress.com Stats. However, there are a couple of interesting extra features. The information under **Site Content | Exit Pages** tells you from which pages your readers are leaving your blog. If a pattern emerges with a few pages having a particularly high exit rate, it may mean that the posts on those pages are not relevant or interesting to your readers. However, it may just be the case that there is a particularly interesting external link within those posts.

**In-Page Analytics** is a very interesting feature that gives you a visual representation of which links on your blog are most popular. For example, you can see at a glance which links people are clicking on your home page. Again, this helps you to build a picture of the kind of content your readers want. The following screenshot shows the site overlay for a post on my own blog — the bars show the percentage of visitors who clicked on each link:

That concludes our very quick introduction to Google Analytics. As you can see, there are a few other features you may wish to explore in more depth. There is detailed documentation about Google Analytics at http://www.google.com/support/googleanalytics/ and http://www.google.com/support/conversionuniversity/.

# Not an exact science

As you use WordPress.com Stats and Google Analytics, you will probably notice some discrepancies between what you think ought to be identical data in both tools. This is largely due to the technical difficulties associated with tracking visitors, some of which were mentioned earlier in the chapter (for example, people deleting cookies or switching off JavaScript in their browsers). It's also down to the fact that they are two different pieces of software developed by different programmers, so each will have its own idiosyncrasies.

The point to bear in mind is that no web analytics software is ever going to be 100% accurate, so it's important not to get too hung up on the exact numbers of visits, page views, unique visitors, or whatever. Instead, use tools such as Google Analytics and WordPress.com Stats to identify trends and monitor your progress over time as your blog grows. Are the graphs heading North or South?

# FeedBurner Stats

As I mentioned earlier in the chapter, counting your subscribers is very important for measuring the success of your blog. FeedBurner provides you with the means to do this. You should be aware that the data it provides is unlikely to be completely accurate because it's very difficult to track RSS subscriptions, but it will give you an idea as to how your feed is performing.

When you log in to FeedBurner you can view your stats under the **Analyze** tab. The **Feed Stats Dashboard** gives you an overview; you can then drill down for more detail using the left-hand menu. There is a drop-down menu on the right that allows you to specify a time period for analysis.

# Subscribers

This section gives you two main statistics: **subscribers** and **reach**. The subscriber count is based on an approximation of how many times your feed has been requested in a 24-hour period. It is the approximate number of people who are currently subscribed to your feed. The reach measurement assumes that a certain percentage of your subscribers will be actively engaging in your feed content. It also assumes that there are people engaging with your feed content beyond your known subscriber base (for example, on a feed search engine or news filter site). The reach measurement aggregates these two groups to provide an indication of your true audience.

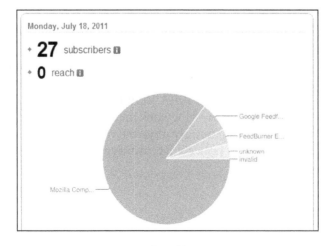

## Item use

This simply tells you how many items in your feed have been viewed and how many clicks back to your blog there have been.

## Uncommon uses

This measurement tells you about any other uses your feed is being put to, in addition to normal views and subscriptions in web browsers, feed readers, and the like. FeedBurner says that uses like these could be *...a neat little news filter somebody wrote, a blog somebody assembled from feeds, or even blog spam.* Obviously, it's useful to know who is using your feed in this way. You should monitor this and if you feel any of these uses are inappropriate, contact the owner of the domain that's listed.

# Alexa rankings

As well as monitoring your blog stats you may also want to keep an eye on your Alexa ranking. Don't get too hung up on the exact ranking, but use it as a way to track your progress. Maybe check your Alexa ranking once a month and make sure it's heading in the right direction. To see your ranking, go to `http://www.alexa.com/topsites` and enter your full URL into the search box. As you can see from the following screenshot, a new blog such as WPBizGuru that has virtually no traffic at present will have a seemingly abysmal ranking—it's way down at 22,794,407. However, you'll soon notice vast improvements even with fairly modest traffic growth.

# Summary

In this chapter, we examined the data needed to analyze your blog and the tools you can use to collect it. We identified five categories or groups of data that comprise your blog statistics: Traffic, Subscribers, Comments, Search Engine Results, and Inbound Links. We looked at WordPress.com Stats, Google Analytics, FeedBurner Stats, and how these tools can be used to measure your statistics.

In the next chapter, we will examine a variety of ways to monetize your blog, including advertising revenue and affiliate programs.

# 10
# Monetizing your Blog

As your blog's traffic levels grow, you may see some potential for revenue generation. Don't expect floods of money—very few bloggers make a fortune from their efforts. But you could reasonably expect to cover your monthly web hosting costs and perhaps a few other expenses, which may at least make your blog self-financing.

Monetization will not be an appropriate option for all business bloggers. This is particularly true for the more corporate blogs. Most cash generating strategies, especially the ones covered in this chapter, involve showing adverts or promoting affiliate programs of some kind. Displaying ads may be completely inappropriate for many corporate blogs; in fact, your company may well have policies that forbid it. However, for smaller, independent operators, selling advertising may be an attractive additional feature for your blog.

You are probably already monetizing your blog, but in indirect ways. Hopefully, you're already seeing the benefits in your business's bottom line. Remember the strategic goals you set for your blog? These may have included things such as, 'building a brand', 'reputation management', and 'improving customer relations'. These are all fairly intangible, but they will certainly add value to your business. If you're achieving those goals, then your blog is already paying you, even if the precise cash amount is hard to quantify.

This chapter is concerned with the direct monetization strategies you can employ. Selling advertising is the most straightforward way of directly monetizing your blog. Advertising, in one form or another, is what this chapter is all about. We'll cover:

- Using Google AdSense to display ads
- Affiliate programs, such as Amazon Associates
- Selling advertising directly
- Using paid reviews for monetization

# Google AdSense

This is one of the largest advertising programs available to web publishers. In Google's own words:

> *Google AdSense matches ads to your site's content and you earn money whenever your visitors click on them.*

It really is as simple as that. AdSense is a straightforward way of introducing advertising to your blog. It may not be the most profitable form of advertising, but it can generate a steady income stream.

As with most Google applications, AdSense has plenty of advanced features. Most of these are beyond the scope of this chapter, but we will run through a quick-start guide for getting AdSense on your blog. Once you have it set up, you can explore the more advanced features with the help of Google's excellent documentation (`http://www.google.com/adsense/support/`).

# Getting started with AdSense

First, you need to sign up for an AdSense account. Go to `http://www.google.com/adsense`, click on the **Sign up now** link, and fill out the registration form. Google will then review your application and contact you within a couple of days to let you know if it has been successful. Your application should be approved. The reasons why Google may reject it could be if your blog content breaches their terms of service (for example spam, pornography, and so on), or if they have reason to believe the account may be used for fraudulent activity.

Once you have your account approved, go to the AdSense home page and log in.

 At the time of writing, there is a new AdSense interface in beta testing. We will be using this new interface for the tutorials in this chapter.

The first page you see is the **Overview** page. It gives a snapshot of your account. Obviously, there's nothing there yet, but when you start using AdSense, you will see information about the number of times your ads are viewed, how many clicks they have attracted, and how much you have earned. The following screenshot shows the new AdSense interface:

# Creating AdSense ad units

To set up an ad, click on the **My ads** tab and then the **New ad unit** button. Begin by giving the new ad unit a name—this can be anything you like, and is just to help you identify all the different ads in your account (call it **Ad1**).

Next you can choose the size of your ads. We'll be placing our AdSense unit in the sidebar, so we need a vertical format. I think it's also a good idea to begin with a relatively small AdSense unit, so as not to clutter your sidebar too much. If you feel that a small size isn't getting good enough results, you can always experiment with larger formats later. Select **120 x 240 Vertical Banner** from the drop-down menu.

Depending on the ad size you have selected, you can choose the ad type. These can be image ads, text ads, or a combination of both, but some ad sizes will only allow text ads. As you can see, the size we have chosen is for text ads only.

You can click the **View examples of ad types and sizes** link to see all the different ads that are available.

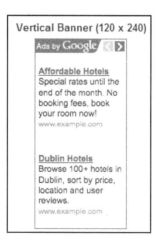

The next section allows you to select channels to track your ads. We'll skip this feature for now; it's something you may want to explore later, when you're more used to the basic functionality of AdSense. For the time being, we'll leave all the **Ad style** options at their default settings.

Click on **Save and get code**. The code for the AdSense unit appears in a pop-up.

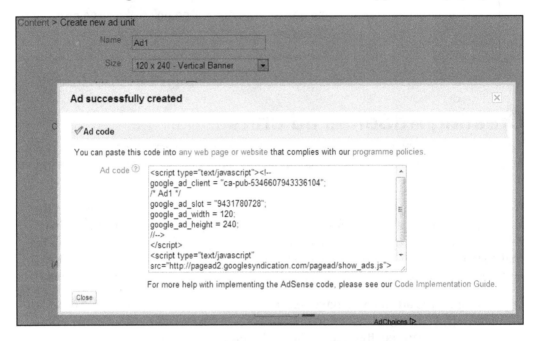

# Using the AdSense code in WordPress

Now, we need to get this code into WordPress. Copy all the code to your computer's clipboard. Log in to your WPBizGuru case study blog and go to **Appearance | Widgets**. We'll begin by placing our AdSense ads in the sidebar, so drag a **Text** widget to the bottom of the **Secondary Aside** widget area. Open up the new text widget for editing. Give it the title **Sponsored links**, paste the AdSense code into the text area and click **Save**.

Now view the blog and you will see the AdSense ads being displayed in the sidebar:

You may want to place some AdSense ads in a more prominent place on the page. Google allows you to display up to three AdSense units on one web page. We will use a plugin called **Awesome Google Adsense** (`http://wordpress.org/extend/plugins/awesome-google-adsense/`), which allows you to place AdSense ads at random positions within a post. Install and activate the plugin in the usual way.

Go to **Settings | Awesome Google Adsense** and begin by entering your AdSense ID.

Your AdSense ID begins with **pub-** and you can find it in the top right-hand corner of the AdSense admin area.

> | Report issue | Return to old AdSense interface | Sign out
> Publisher ID: pub-5346607943336104   Last Login: 21 hours ago
> **You're using the new AdSense interface (beta). What's new?**

In the **Display Configuration** section you can set the colors for your AdSense units, if you wish, but we'll leave the default Google color scheme. For **Ad size** choose **468x60**; for **Number of ads per Page** choose **0**; and for **Number of ads per Post** choose **1**. You can leave the other settings as they are and then click **Save Changes**.

| Ad size | | | |
|---|---|---|---|
| Choose more than one to display random. (Width x Height) | ☐234x60 ☑468x60 | ☐728x90 ☐120x600 | ☐160x600 ☐120x240 |

| | |
|---|---|
| Number of ads per Page | 0 ▼ |
| Number of ads per Post | 1 ▼ |
| Ad type | Text ▼ |
| Ad Placement | Center ▼ |
| Do not show ads on these Pages | ☐ Home Page ☐ Static Pages ☐ Posts Pages ☐ Category Pages ☐ Archive Pages |

Now when you view the blog you will see that ads are being displayed in random positions within the body of posts:

You will have realized by now that there are many more features in Google AdSense. Now you understand the basics, take some time to explore the other features and experiment with AdSense to see what works best on your own blog.

# Affiliate programs

Affiliate programs allow web publishers, such as bloggers, to earn commission when they refer customers to other businesses' websites. Affiliate marketing offers you the opportunity to earn revenue by generating sales for some of the Web's biggest e-commerce sites.

# Amazon Associates

One of the oldest and biggest affiliate programs is **Amazon Associates**, which has been running since 1996. Once you have signed up to be an Amazon Associate (or affiliate), you can place links to Amazon on your blog. These links contain your own unique tracking ID. If one of your referrals makes a purchase, Amazon pays you a percentage of the sale. Your tracking ID tells Amazon that you were the affiliate who generated the sale.

The program offers many features that enable you to target Amazon products that are likely to be of interest to your readers. Think about the massive inventory that Amazon carries across diverse departments such as books, electronics, and kitchenware. There is bound to be at least one product on Amazon that your readers might consider buying and, therefore, potentially generate some commission for you.

At the time of writing Amazon is embroiled in sales tax disputes with several US states, most notably California. Because of this the company has withdrawn its Associates program in California and a handful of other states, so depending on where you are in the US, Amazon Associates may not be a monetization option.

There are several ways you can use your Amazon Affiliate links. For example, you may write a review of a new book or product. You could place an affiliate link within the text that points straight to the product page on Amazon. Some of your readers, who may be interested in the product, may click the link, and hopefully buy it. You can also showcase products on your blog—the sidebar is a good place for this. You can choose a specific product, or use a widget that randomly displays products from a particular department or category. There are many ways to get your Amazon links in front of your readers. You should take time to look around the Amazon Associates members' area to see what's available—the following screenshot shows some of the options:

# Creating an Amazon Associates widget

Let's imagine that WPBizGuru has written a book about WordPress. He could place an Amazon advert for this book in his sidebar. We'll work through how to do this, but first you need to sign up for an Amazon Associates account. Go to `http://affiliate-program.amazon.com/join/`, click on the **Join Now for FREE!** button, and fill out the registration form.

Log in to the Amazon Associates members' area and click on the **Links & Banners** tab. You can search for the product you want to display by keyword, the ISBN, or the **ASIN (Amazon Standard Identification Number)**. Of course, WPBizGuru hasn't really written a book (because he doesn't exist!). So, you can use any book (or product) you like. Enter your search terms and click **Go!**.

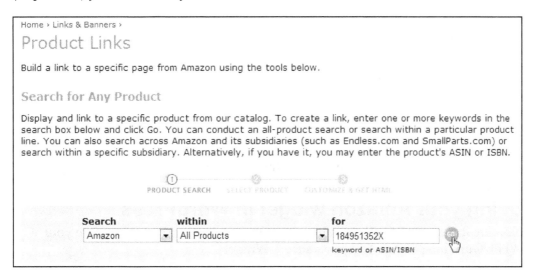

You'll be presented with a list of results for your search. Click the **Get Link** button next to the book you want.

The next page allows you to customize the widget. If you look at the **Live Preview** of the link, you'll see it's a fairly simple design. Try selecting different options and see how they look in the preview (I recommend you stick with the **Text and Image** link type; I've also removed the border). Once you're happy with your option choices, we can change the color scheme to match WPBizGuru a little better. Enter the following values in the color fields: **Background Color: FFFFFF; Text Color: 666666; Link Color: 004B91**:

Copy the HTML code, which appears in the box below the link editor.

## Using your Amazon widget in WordPress

Now we'll paste the HTML code into a text widget in WordPress. Log in to your WPBizGuru blog and go to **Appearance | Widgets**.

Add a **Text** widget at the bottom of the **Secondary Aside** widget area:

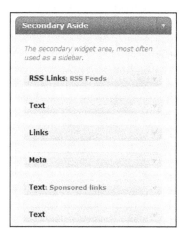

Open up the new **Text** widget for editing and paste the Amazon HTML code into the text area. Give the widget a title: **My Book**. Click the **Save** button.

When you view the blog, you'll see the link in the sidebar. Go ahead and click on the image or one of the other links, and you'll be taken to the product page on Amazon. Your tracking ID is embedded into the link, so if anyone clicks through and buys the book, you earn commission. This is how the widget looks in the sidebar:

# Affiliate networks

Along with Amazon Associates, there are many other affiliate programs and networks that you may wish to join. Some companies (for example, Amazon) manage their own affiliate programs; others use affiliate networks, such as Commission Junction, Share Results, or ClickBank to take care of their affiliates for them. These networks manage affiliate programs on behalf of hundreds of companies from household names to small independents.

If there is a particular company for which your readers may be potential customers, check to see if they have an affiliate program. You should also consider signing up to a couple of affiliate networks and see if they are promoting programs that might earn revenue on your blog. For example, WPBizGuru might find affiliate relationships with WordPress theme and plugin providers beneficial because his readers are likely to buy these products and, in doing so, earn him some commission.

# Direct ad sales

AdSense and affiliate programs provide an easy-to-manage, quick-start advertising option for your blog. However, if you're prepared to do some extra work, you may find it more profitable to sell ads directly. This will involve finding your own advertising clients, in other words, **sales**. If you don't have the time or inclination to take on yet another role for your blog, then stick with AdSense and let Google do the selling for you — they seem to be quite good at it!

Don't even think about direct ad sales until your traffic hits a respectable level. There's no point me recommending any precise traffic volumes — it will vary from blog to blog, depending on your industry, and who your readers and potential advertisers are. However, suffice to say that your daily page views will probably need to be in the thousands, or even tens of thousands, before you'll have anything like an attractive proposition to take to potential advertisers.

# Banner sizes

The web advertising industry uses a range of standard banner sizes. This helps advertisers save money on their design costs. They know that once they've had advertising artwork created to industry-standard sizes, it will be acceptable to a wide range of publishers. So, when you're deciding how much room you need for advertising, you should think in units of space that match the standard sizes. The **Interactive Advertising Bureau (IAB)**, a trade body for the online advertising industry, maintains guidelines for the standard ad sizes (see `http://www.iab.net/ Ad_Unit` for details).

When it comes to choosing which banner sizes you want to display, there are a few standard sizes that seem to be popular with bloggers. One of the most common sizes on blogs at the moment is the **125 x 125** square button. The following screenshot shows this type of ad on ReadWriteWeb (`http://www.readwriteweb.com/`):

As with most things blog-related, it's difficult to generalize. Yes, **125 x 125** is a popular size, but it's by no means the only one in common usage. Many blogs, particularly the big players, use ads of all sizes. Personally, I think that smaller ads look better and are more appropriate on small business blogs. I recommend you start your banner advertising venture with fairly small banners. If your advertisers suddenly start demanding **160 x 600** skyscrapers, and are prepared to pay for them, you can consider up-sizing then.

Interestingly, the IAB now lists 125x125 as a delisted standard ad unit; however, it is still widely used by bloggers and is also still available as an AdSense ad unit size.

# Where to place banner ads

There's always a trade-off when it comes to advertising. You can charge more for the most prominent positions on your blog, but then these will be unavailable for your own content. Placing your ads in less prominent positions means they don't get in the way of your content, but they are worthless to advertisers. In fact, you will find it difficult to sell ads that are tucked away below the fold, right at the bottom of the sidebars.

To stand a chance of making any money from banner advertising, you have to be prepared to let go of some of your best screen real estate. This probably means at the top of your sidebars. You don't need to sacrifice a whole load of space to begin with—I suggest you start with maybe two **125 x 125** banners. If your ad sales really start to take off, you can consider devoting more space. Luckily, the widgetized sidebars in WordPress make it fairly easy to move stuff around.

# How much to charge

The simple answer to this is: Whatever you can get! It's going to be tough to get advertisers on board in the early days of your sales efforts. Making your prices attractive will be a big help in closing those crucial initial deals. You may even consider giving advertisers a free trial as an incentive to sign up.

There are various pricing models used in web advertising. Probably the most attractive to advertisers is **Cost Per Click** (CPC), for example, you charge, say, 20 cents each time someone clicks on your advertiser's banner. Advertisers like this model as they are paying for objectified, clearly visible results. Another pricing model is **Cost Per Thousand**, or **Cost Per Mille** (CPM), where the advertiser pays an agreed amount for every 1,000 times their banner is viewed. Finally there is a simple time-based pricing model, known as **Tenancy**, where advertisers pay an agreed price for their banners to be displayed for a certain period; a month, three months, or whatever.

Your prices will also vary depending on the position of the banner. As I already mentioned, the most valuable (and easiest to sell) position is at the top of your sidebar. However, if you were to offer ad positions below the fold at the bottom of the sidebar, your price would have to be adjusted downwards in order to be attractive.

As to the exact dollar amount you should be charging, it really depends on your sales skills and the abundance (or lack) of advertisers in your niche or industry. In working out your prices, do some research—see if you can find out what other bloggers are charging. If your sales drive is not going too well, it could mean your price point is a little high.

# Your media pack and rate card

A media pack gives prospective advertisers all the data they need before deciding whether to buy advertising in a publication. If you're intent on selling adverts on your blog, you will be taken far more seriously if you have a detailed proposition for your advertising customers. In the world of offline publications, the media pack is usually a glossy brochure. On the web, publishers often present it as a well-designed PDF or fancy online presentation. You don't necessarily need to go to these lengths. Your media pack can be in the form of a static page on your blog. The important thing is to include all the pertinent information. Remember, prospective advertisers want to know the **benefits** they will receive from advertising on your blog — what's in it for them? Your media pack might include:

- Page views and visitors per month (these are essential stats for advertisers)
- Number of subscribers by RSS and e-mail
- Google Page Rank, Technorati Authority Ranking, Alexa Ranking (only include these if they are reasonably good; if your Alexa rank is way down in the millions, omit it)
- The number of links in to your blog
- Average number of comments per month
- A description of your target audience
- Any demographic data you may have about your readers (for example, gender, age, income, and so on)
- Any awards your blog may have picked up
- Any testimonials and reviews you can get
- Details about the type and size of adverts you will accept
- Where the ads will appear (use screenshots, if possible)

A rate card is a price list for all the advertising options you're selling. While a rate card can help enhance your professional image, it might not be such a good idea to publish your rates in the early days of your sales efforts. You might find a rate card useful for your reference, but hang fire on publishing it until you've spoken to a few prospective clients. Gauge their reaction to your prices and see if you're in the ballpark. Another reason for not publishing your rates up front is that you may be able to negotiate higher prices for some clients than others. On your media pack page, provide contact details for requesting more information about rates. You might consider setting up a special e-mail address (for example, `advertising@ yourcompany.com`) or a dedicated contact form for advertising enquiries.

# Rotating banner ads

Once you have more than two or three advertising clients, you may decide to rotate their adverts. This means you can display several ads in a much smaller space. Each time the page is reloaded, one of the adverts will be displayed at random.

We'll set this up for WPBizGuru so that there are two advertising spots in the sidebar. One will rotate three **125 x 125** ads and the other will rotate three **120 x 240** ads. I've supplied six JPG images in the code bundle for this chapter, which you can use as dummy adverts for testing. They're in a folder called `ads`.

Unfortunately, there are no reliable plugins that handle banner ad rotation in WordPress, so we will be using a third-party ad server called **OpenX**. It's free to use if you are serving fewer than 100,000 ad impressions per month, and if you go over that amount you can pay for the extra impressions you need. There is also a self-hosted version of OpenX, which is completely free and has no limits on the number of ad impressions you can serve. However, it requires you to install the software on your own web server, which is beyond the scope of this chapter. We will be using the community version of OpenX hosted on their servers. It's called **OpenX OnRamp**.

 OpenX also offers a marketplace where publishers can sell their advertising inventory to a wider audience of advertisers. It's completely optional, but signing up to the marketplace could give a nice boost to your ad sales.

To get started, go to `http://openx.org/sign-openx-onramp` and sign up for an account. During the sign-up process you will need to supply the address of your live blog, but we can test the ad serving capabilities of OpenX on our local development server. Once you have confirmed your account by clicking the verification link in the sign-up e-mail they send you, log in to your account.

From the home page of the OpenX admin area, click on the **Inventory** tab. First, we need to set up a website where the ads will appear. Click on **Websites** in the left-hand menu and then **Add new website**. You'll need to enter the details of your live blog, but we can still run the rest of this tutorial on your local development server for WPBizGuru. You can leave the **Category** and **Country / Language** blank for now, if you wish. Once you're done, click **Save changes**:

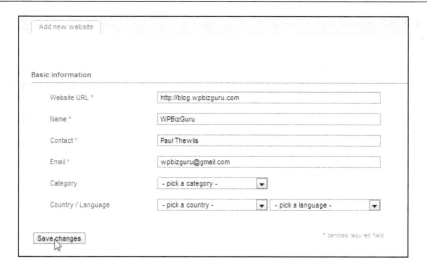

Now, you need to set up the zones for your ads. This is the area of the page where the ads will be displayed. Remember, we want one 125 x 125 button and one 120 x 240 banner in our blog's sidebar, so we'll set up a zone for each of these ad sizes. Select **Zones** from the left-hand menu and then **Add new zone**. Enter a name for the first zone—I've called it **Sidebar 125x125 button**. Choose **IAB Square Button (125 x 125)** from the **Size** drop-down. Uncheck the box for **Serve ads from OpenX Market** and click **Save Changes**:

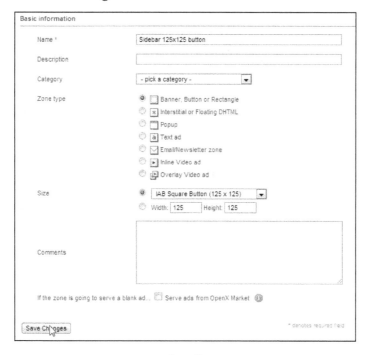

Create another new zone. This time call it **Sidebar 120x240 banner** and select **IAB Vertical Banner (120 x 240)** for the size.

Now you have set up your website and ad zones, you need some advertisers. For the purposes of this demonstration, we'll set up a couple of fictitious advertisers. Select **Advertisers** from the left-hand menu, then click **Add new advertiser**. Enter a name and contact for the advertiser, but make sure to use a real e-mail address in case you want to test the e-mail functions later. Leave all the other fields as they are, and click **Save Changes**:

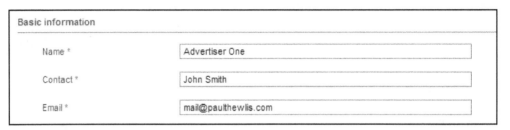

Repeat the process for a second fictitious advertiser:

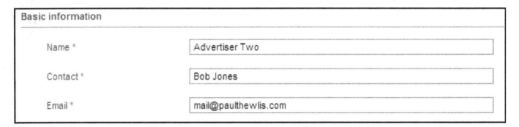

So, let's imagine that **Advertiser One** wants to place three 125 x 125 buttons on your blog. You've closed the sale and agreed the CPC (cost per click) for all three buttons. He has supplied the buttons, so you now need to set up his campaigns and upload the images. We'll run through that now.

Select **Advertisers** from the left-hand menu and click on **Add new campaign** next to **Advertiser One**:

Under **Basic information**, give the campaign a name and choose **Remnant** for **Campaign type**:

Leave the settings under **Date** at the defaults. Under **Pricing model** select **CPC** and enter **600** in the **Clicks** box:

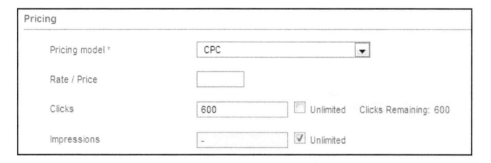

Under **Priority in relation to other campaigns**, enter **1000** in the **per day** box:

You can leave all the other settings at the defaults and click **Save Changes**. On the next page, click on the **Add new banner** link:

Choose to **Upload a local banner to the webserver**. For **Name**, enter **Ad1**. Click on
the button to upload a file and choose **ad1.jpg** from your computer (it's one of the ad
images in the code bundle for this chapter). Enter a destination URL—I've entered
the Google home page for test purposes, but in a real situation this would be the
URL that the advertiser wants visitors to reach when they click on his ad. You can
leave all the other settings at the defaults and click **Save Changes**.

Repeat the upload process to add two more banners for Advertiser One's 1st
Campaign—you can use ad2.jpg and ad3.jpg from the code bundle for this chapter.

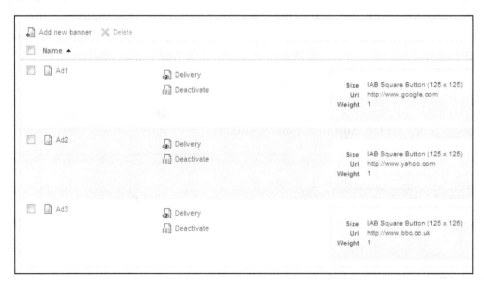

Now select **Advertisers** from the left-hand menu. This time click **Add new campaign** for **Advertiser Two**. Set up a campaign for this advertiser and upload three banners—you can use ad4.jpg, ad5.jpg, and ad6.jpg from the code bundle. Note that these are the 120 x 240 banners.

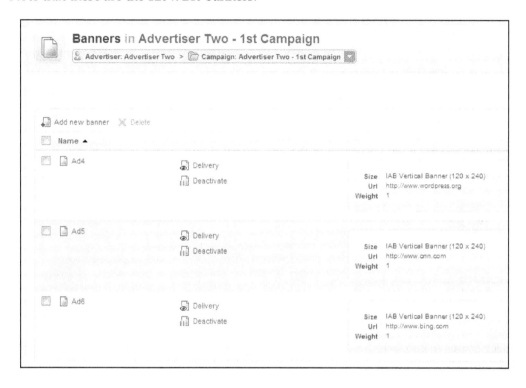

Now we need to link the banners to the appropriate zones. Select **Zones** from the left-hand menu and click **Linked Banners** for the **Sidebar 125 x 125 banner** zone:

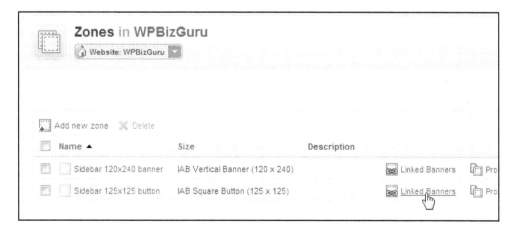

From the drop-downs, select **Advertiser One** and **Advertiser One – 1st Campaign (3 banner(s))** and click the 'arrow' icon:

You'll see the banners are linked to the campaign:

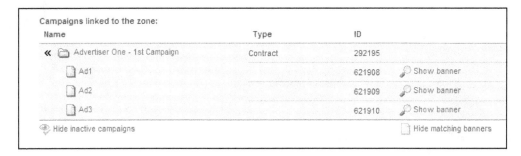

Select **Zones** from the left-hand menu and link the banners for **Advertiser Two** to the **Sidebar 120x240 banner** zone.

We're now ready to display the rotating ads on our blog. There is a plugin that makes this a simple process—it's called **OpenX WordPress Widget** (http://wordpress.org/extend/plugins/openx-wordpress-widget/). Install and activate it in the usual way.

Go to **Settings | OpenX-WP** to view the settings page. Enter the **Url to OpenX-AdServer**—because we are using the hosted version of OpenX, this is **d1.openx.org**. Click **Save**.

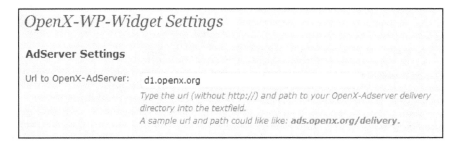

The plugin includes a widget that we can use in our sidebar, but before we can use it, we need to get the **ZoneID** for each of the zones we created in OpenX. To do this, go back to OpenX and select **Websites** from the left-hand menu. Click on the website we created earlier—**WPBizGuru**. Click on the **Invocation Code** tab. Leave all the settings as they are and click the **Generate** button. On the next screen you will see a list of tags for all the zones we set up. These tags include the ZoneID—to find it, scroll down to the **Ad script** section and look for the id in square brackets. Copy the ID for both of the zones we created earlier. I've highlighted it in the following screenshot:

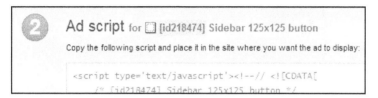

Now go back to WordPress and select **Appearance | Widgets**. We will place the ads at the top of the **Secondary Aside** sidebar. Drag an instance of the **OpenX Widget** to the top of the **Secondary Aside** sidebar. Enter **Our Sponsors** for the title and select **2** from the **Number of banners** drop-down. Enter the ZoneIDs you just copied from OpenX, omitting the letters 'id' (so just the numbers). Click the checkboxes to append a `<br/>` tag, which will insert a line break after the ads. Click **Save**:

Now view the blog. You will see that the **OpenX Widget** has been added to the sidebar. Go ahead and reload the page a few times and you will see the ads rotating at random. Click on the ads and you will be taken to the corresponding destination URL.

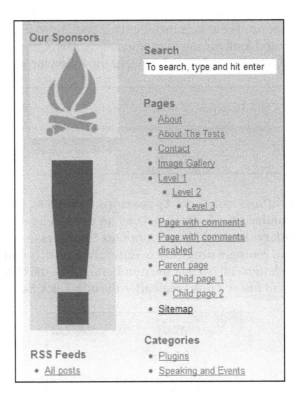

OK, so the dummy images look a bit weird, but you get the idea! Hopefully your advertisers' banners will be a little more attractive. You might also think that the **125 x 125 + 120 x 240** banner configuration takes up too much space. If so, consider just one or two **125 x 125** banners. It's really up to you.

You've probably realized that OpenX has lots of features I haven't even mentioned. It's a powerful ad serving platform that offers you plenty of flexibility. If you'd like to find out more, there's a useful book published by Packt called *OpenX Ad Server: Beginner's Guide (ISBN 1849510202)* by *Murat Yilmaz*.

# Paid reviews

Paid reviews are a contentious issue in the blogosphere. As the name suggests, the practice involves bloggers receiving a payment from a company in exchange for reviewing that company's product or service. Many bloggers have ethical objections because they believe paid reviews can mislead readers, and distort the spirit of blogging, which, in its early days, was not about making money. I mention paid reviews here because they can be a useful source of revenue. But think carefully before using them as you could upset a sizeable proportion of your readers (and other bloggers).

**Disclosure**

If you do use paid reviews, I strongly recommend that you disclose this to your readers. Having a disclosure statement on your *About* page, outlining how you make money from your blog, is a best practice you should implement. If you're in the USA, you should also be aware of the FTC guidelines about commercial endorsements (`http://ftc.gov/os/2009/10/091005endorsementguidesfnnotice.pdf`).

You're the best person to judge the likely reaction of your readers and whether they would appreciate paid reviews. If you're not certain, ask them. Write a post about it to canvass opinion and/or conduct a poll. There are paid review networks that can help match you up with companies who want their products reviewed and are willing to pay—a couple of the biggest are **Pay Per Post** (`http://payperpost.com/`) and **ReviewMe** (`http://www.reviewme.com/`).

**WP-Polls plugin**

On the subject of polls, you may be interested in the **WP-Polls plugin**, by Lester Chan. It's a little off-topic for this chapter, so we won't go through a full installation here. However, it's a very simple plugin to install and use. You can have reader polls up and running in no time. Go to `http://wordpress.org/extend/plugins/wp-polls/` for full details.

# Case study review

We've now completed all the work on the WPBizGuru blog. I've made one final change and that's to hide the extra pages that were included in the dummy content we imported.

I hope the work we've done on the case study has shown you how straightforward it can be to create a feature-rich, professional-looking business blog using WordPress. You should also now realize how easy it is to extend WordPress, thanks to the large and active community of developers who have created so many cool plugins.

Just because the case study is over for the book, that's not to say it's finished. Likewise, you'll discover that your blog is never *finished*. You will be constantly tweaking it and adding functionality. The beauty of web publishing is that things will always evolve.

I will be adding updates and additional tutorials to my own blog at `http://blog.paulthewlis.com`. WordPress is constantly developing with new versions and plugins. I'll try to cover as many of these as possible on my blog, and show you how they can be applied to the WPBizGuru case study.

# Summary

In this chapter, we looked at how you can place advertisements on your blog to generate revenue. We began with an introduction to Google AdSense and the Awesome Google AdSense plugin, which allows you to place AdSense ads in a variety of locations on your blog. Next, you learned about affiliate programs, in particular, Amazon Associates. We set up an Amazon book widget and placed it in the sidebar. Finally, we looked at display advertising and how you can set up ad rotation using OpenX.

In the next chapter, we will look at strategies to help you cope as your blog grows and the number of visitors increases.

# 11
# Managing Growth

If you've applied the tips, techniques, and methods you have learned throughout this book, you should be well on your way to having a successful blog that's attracting lots of visitors. Hopefully, it won't be long until your blog grows into something big. Of course, that's great—it's what every blogger wants. But success can bring with it a whole host of issues you need to deal with. In this chapter, we will explore some of these and discuss how you can address them, including:

- How to manage your workload
- Ensuring your blog is available to mobile browsers
- Managing increased traffic
- Moving your blog to a better web server
- Bringing in other writers
- An introduction to WordPress Multisite

## Keeping up with the workload

As the number of visitors to your blog increases, so will your workload. You'll notice your inbox filling up with e-mails from your readers and you'll spend more and more of your time moderating and replying to comments. If your traffic volume really starts to take off, you could soon find yourself snowed under with correspondence from your blog.

If you find yourself in this situation, it may well be worthwhile bringing in some help. Many of the e-mails and comments you receive will be of relatively low-level importance. You will inevitably receive a high volume of *Great Post!!* comments that require no response from you and just need to be moderated. You may also receive a lot of e-mails all asking the same or similar questions. You could easily make a list of stock replies to these FAQs. You may well find that only a small proportion of your correspondence requires your personal attention, in which case, get someone to filter it so you only see the stuff that matters.

You may already have a PA or admin assistant who is good at vetting your e-mails. You could set them to work moderating simple comments and responding to FAQ e-mails using your list of stock replies, while only passing on the correspondence which needs your attention. It may be difficult to let go this amount of control of your blog, but it will certainly free up a great deal of your time for more important tasks, like writing new posts.

# Going mobile

As your visitor base grows, there's a good chance that more and more of your readers will want to access your blog on mobile devices such as PDAs and cell phones. Mobile computing is a growth sector, and savvy web publishers are doing all they can to ensure their content is compatible with as many devices as possible. You can provide a great service to your expanding readership by giving them a version of your blog that is optimized for mobile viewing. Granted, most modern smart phones have web browsers that are capable of displaying full websites very accurately. However, not everyone has a smart phone and even those who do may wish to access the web when they are away from a Wi-Fi hotspot and have no 3G/4G reception. It's in these circumstances that a mobile-optimized version of your blog will be useful to your readers.

There is a plug-in called **WordPress Mobile Pack** (`http://wordpress.org/extend/plugins/wordpress-mobile-pack/`), which makes mobile optimization a cinch to set up.

Log in to your admin area, and install and activate the plugin in the usual way. Depending on your server setup, you may get an error message telling you that some directories are not writeable. If so, change permissions on the server then deactivate and reactivate the plugin to remove the error.

Go to **Appearance | Mobile Switcher**, and enter the following settings, then click **Save Changes**:

---

*Mobile Switcher*
*Part of the WordPress Mobile Pack*

| | |
|---|---|
| Switcher mode | Browser detection ▾ |
| | The switcher can detect whether the user is using a mobile device or has requested a mobile domain. It will switch theme accordingly. |
| Mobile theme | WordPress Mobile (base) ▾ |
| | The theme that will be sent to a mobile user. Desktop users will receive WPBizGuru |
| Browser detection | User-agent prefixes ▾ |
| Desktop domains | |
| | Use comma-separated domain names. eg: **mysite.com, downloads.mysite.com** |
| | Desktop users who mistakenly access a mobile domain will be given the option to return to the first domain in this list. |
| | This is also the domain used for switching when 'browser detection' is used, and in that case should be your site's primary domain. |
| Mobile domains | |
| | Use comma-separated domain fragments. eg: mysite.mobi, m.mysite.com |
| | Mobile users who mistakenly access a desktop domain will be given the option to return to the first domain in this list. |
| | NB: The plugin does not create theme domains. You must be sure they DNS entries already resolve and are served by this web server. |
| Footer links | ☐ |
| | Places a link in the theme footer to allow users to override the detection. You can also enable the widget that contains this link. Both the footer link and the widget will only appear when a switcher mode is enabled. Regardless of this setting, the switcher link will always appear on the mobile admin pages. |

( Save Changes )

---

These settings tell the **Mobile Switcher** part of the plugin to activate the **WordPress Mobile (base)** theme, if it detects that the visitor is using a mobile phone browser. The theme we have selected came with the plugin, but the **Mobile Switcher** can use any one of your installed themes, so you may want to use a different mobile-optimized theme. A quick Google search will show you plenty of existing mobile themes, or you could create your own using the Thematic framework.

As you can see from the following screenshot, the theme we have selected strips out most of the styling and delivers a very simple page that is quick to load and easy to navigate on a mobile device.

The plugin has some other features that you may want to experiment with. For example, if you go to **Appearance | Mobile Widgets** you can select which widgets are available in your mobile theme.

# Managing increased traffic

As your traffic increases, there is a chance you could run into technical issues related to your web server. You may well notice your blog running slow. This is a particular risk if your blog is getting *spikes* of high traffic that place a sudden strain on the server. These spikes can occur for a number of reasons, for example, one of your posts making it onto the front page of Digg, or a couple of major bloggers linking to you. Of course, this is all good, but only if your server can handle it.

If you work in a corporate environment and your blog is hosted on your company's web server, then these performance issues are a problem for your IT department—submit a support ticket.

However, if you're an independent operator or a small company, you may not have the luxury of a dedicated IT team. If you notice your blog slowing down or even crashing completely, and you suspect it may be caused by high traffic volumes, the first remedy to try is installing a great little plugin called **WP Super Cache** (we'll go over what to do when you've outgrown your web host in the next section of this chapter).

# Installing WP Super Cache

This plugin is designed to reduce the server load for high-traffic blogs. It could be the solution to your slow performance problems. It works by converting your blog's pages into static HTML files and serving them to your visitors instead of the dynamic pages from the database. Static files are quicker and easier for your web server to handle, so it will be able to deal with far greater volumes of traffic before it slows down.

We'll run through the installation process, which is slightly different from most of the other plugins we've used. Go to `http://wordpress.org/extend/plugins/wp-super-cache/` and download the plugin. Unzip the package and use your FTP software to upload the entire `wp-super-cache` folder to your blog's `plugins` folder (`/wp-content/plugins/`). Log in to your admin area and activate the plugin, then go to **Settings | WP Super Cache**.

You may see a warning message advising you that `wp-content` is writeable. If this is the case, use your FTP client to change the permissions for your `wp-content` directory to `755`.

Select the **Caching On** radio button and then click **Update Status**:

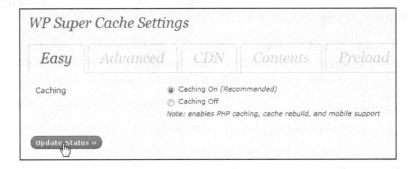

The plugin is now set up. If you click the **Advanced** tab on the **WP Super Cache Settings** page, you will see that by default PHP is being used to cache files. This is a slightly slower method of caching than using mod_rewrite. However, setting up mod_rewrite caching is slightly more complicated. If you'd like to switch to mod_rewrite, the plugin has plenty of documentation and an active support forum to help you out. For new users, PHP caching is recommended and it works just fine.

You can check that the plugin is working by viewing your blog and opening a few random pages. Now go back to **WP Super Cache Settings** and click on the **Contents** tab. Click **Regenerate cache stats**, and you should see that some pages have been cached:

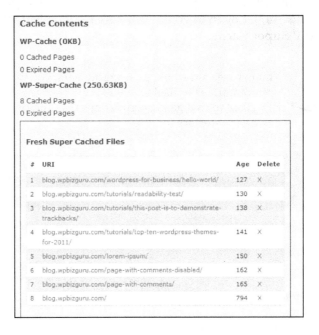

# Outgrowing your web host

This won't be a problem for you if your blog is running on your company web server, managed by the IT department. However, many readers will have installed their self-hosted WordPress blog on a shared hosting account. This means it's on a web server alongside lots of other people's websites, all of which have to share the server's resources, such as memory (RAM) and processing power.

Shared hosting accounts have limits set on disk space and bandwidth. As the traffic volume to your blog increases, you may well start to exceed these limits. You may also experience performance issues (remember you're sharing memory and processor with lots of other websites). There may well come a time when your blog simply outgrows its shared hosting space, and you have to think about upgrading. If this happens, you need to move to a dedicated server.

As its name suggests, a dedicated server is all yours. There will be no more sharing of resources, which should improve performance. Also, the bandwidth limits on dedicated servers are usually much higher. The downside is that you will see a considerable increase in your monthly hosting bills. Unfortunately, that's an unavoidable cost of your new-found success!

As with desktop computers, server specs are constantly improving. Choosing a dedicated server is a bit like choosing a new desktop computer — you should go for the fastest processor and the largest RAM you can afford. For most standard blogs, disk space is less of an issue. These days, even low-end servers come with at least 250 GB hard disks. That should be more than enough, unless you have a lot of media files such as video, audio, and images.

With a dedicated server, you also need to consider server administration. Web servers don't just run themselves; they need to be constantly monitored and maintained. With your shared hosting account, all of the server administration is done by the hosting company. However, for a dedicated server, essential routine tasks such as backups, operating system patches, virus scanning, reboots, and monitoring are not necessarily included in your monthly rental costs. You're probably not a dab hand at server administration via the command line, so you'll need to buy in this expertise. Most hosting companies will offer server admin as an add-on service, or you may be able to find it cheaper if you outsource to a specialist server admin company (you provide them with access to your server and they carry out all the maintenance tasks remotely).

You should also check that your new dedicated server has all the software you need to run WordPress. Many web hosts will provide their dedicated servers pre-configured with a similar setup to their shared hosting plans. But some web hosts might just provide an *empty box* and you may have to ask them to do the initial setup for you. As a minimum, you need to have installed: a Linux operating system, Apache web server, a control panel (for example cPanel or Plesk), PHP (version 5.2.4 or higher), and MySQL (version 5.0 or higher) with phpMyAdmin.

The web hosting industry is a very competitive market, so it's well worth shopping around and doing some research. There are literally thousands of hosting companies out there. I've listed a few of the best known and established hosting companies next, all of which offer dedicated servers. This is in no way an endorsement of these companies, nor is it anywhere near an exhaustive list. I've just provided them as a starting point for your own diligent research:

- Rackspace: http://www.rackspace.com
- Media Temple: http://www.mediatemple.net
- GoDaddy: http://www.godaddy.com
- Host Gator: http://www.hostgator.com
- Lunarpages Dedicated: http://www.lpdedicated.com

 Of course, you may decide to remain loyal to your existing hosting company if they offer dedicated servers! In fact, there could be advantages of staying with your existing web host; they may offer to move your WordPress blog and database for you, if you upgrade to one of their dedicated servers.

# Virtual Private Servers and Cloud Servers

Dedicated servers are no longer the only alternative to traditional shared hosting accounts. You may also wish to consider a **Virtual Private Server (VPS)** or a **Cloud Server**. A VPS is a server that resides on a Virtual Machine, which is a completely isolated guest operating system within a normal host operating system. I know that sounds a bit complicated, but all you really need to know about VPS hosting is that, in terms of cost and performance, it sits between shared hosting and a full dedicated server.

**Cloud hosting** has developed into a mainstream product over the last couple of years and is the latest buzz word in the web hosting marketplace. Cloud hosting gives you all the features of a dedicated server but with the added benefit of almost limitless scalability. So instead of renting a single physical server with its finite resources (disk space, memory, processor speed, and so on), you can take all the resources you'll ever need from the *cloud* and just pay for what you use. Think of it as hosting provided as a utility, in the same way that power is provided by the electricity grid.

# Moving WordPress to a new server

Once you've chosen your new dedicated hosting package, you'll need to move your blog to it. Moving WordPress is not a particularly difficult task, but as with any job involving a remote web server, things can go wrong. Check with your new web host and see if they offer any assistance in moving websites for new customers—some companies do offer this service and it's always good to have some personal assistance from experts who have done it before.

If you're taking on the task yourself, here are a few preliminary guidelines before we look at the detailed procedure:

- Make a full backup of your WordPress files and database before you begin moving your blog, just in case things go wrong (see *Chapter 5, Content is King* for backup instructions).

- Try to figure out the time and day of the week when your blog is quietest, in terms of traffic. Use Google Analytics to work this out. Moving your blog to a new server will inevitably mean it's unavailable for a certain amount of time. Doing the work at a quiet time will minimize disruption for your readers. It's worth choosing the slowest time of the week, even if that's 4 a.m. on a Sunday morning!

- Be sure to warn your readers in advance that your blog is likely to be unavailable at the specified time. Try to give as much notice as possible, in a prominent place. Maybe use a text widget in the sidebar to make the announcement, or mention it in a blog post and on Twitter.

- Any delay is most likely to be caused when you change your domain's nameservers to point at your new server. It will take time for these new DNS settings to propagate across the Web. Ask your domain registrar and new web host for advice on how to keep this delay to a minimum.

We'll now run through the process of moving WordPress. These instructions assume that you will be keeping the same domain (and subdomain, if you're using one). They also assume that you have already downloaded your blog's database as part of the backup process.

First, use your FTP client to download your entire WordPress installation to your computer — *entire* means all the files and folders in the WordPress root directory. This may take quite a long time. The following screenshot shows the entire WordPress installation for WPBizGuru:

Once it's all downloaded, you can upload it to the correct directory on your new server (for example, if your blog was installed in a directory called blog on your old server, place it in a directory called blog on the new server).

Next we need to create a new MySQL database for WordPress. The best way to do this is to use phpMyAdmin. If your new server doesn't have phpMyAdmin installed, ask your web host if they can install it for you. When you create the database, try to use the same database name, username, and password as you had on your old server (this is not always possible, it will depend how your new web host has configured MySQL).

If you can't use the same database settings on your new server, make sure you change them in the `wp-config.php` file in the root directory of WordPress.

Once the database is created, you can upload all the WordPress tables using the backup copy of the database from your old server. Again, use phpMyAdmin for this. Select your new database from the list in phpMyAdmin:

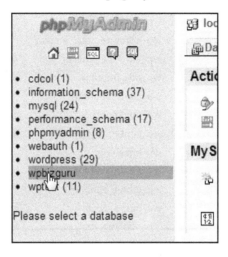

Click on the **Import** tab:

Click on the **Browse** button and locate the backup `.sql` file (remember, this is the file you downloaded when you backed up the database from your old server):

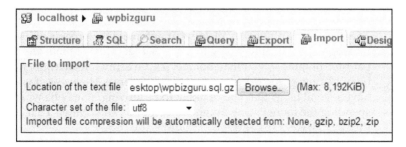

Now click the **Go** button and your database will be populated with all the WordPress tables from your old server:

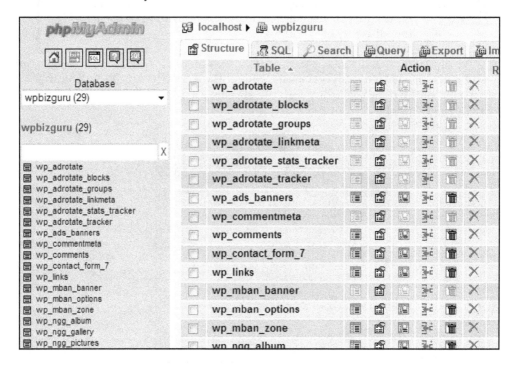

Now all you need to do is change the nameservers for your domain so that it points to your new server. If you're not sure how to do this, seek advice from your domain registrar and web host. This is the point in the process where your blog is likely to be unavailable for a few hours while the new nameservers propagate. If you're using a subdomain, set this up for your new server using the control panel.

Do not delete the WordPress files or database on your old server until you are sure the move to your new server has been successful. Once the changes have propagated across nameservers, view your blog. Make sure the content is all there and that all the permalinks are working. You may need to re-confirm the permalink settings (go to **Settings | Permalinks**).

 There are some plugins available that automate the process of moving your WordPress blog to a new server. Most of them are paid-for plugins so you may not feel it's a worthwhile investment if you're only going to be moving your blog once. However, if you have several blogs that you're likely to be moving, it may be worth spending the money. One plugin to look at is called **Move That Blog** (http://www.23press.com/movethatblog).

# Bringing in other writers

This is a strategy that can bring a number of benefits as your blog grows. As we discussed earlier, as your blog traffic increases, so will your workload with an ever increasing number of comments and e-mails to answer. You may well find that the time you have for writing new posts diminishes. This is where bringing in guest writers can be a big help. You can use them to create content so you don't have to.

There will also be periods when you can't devote time to your blog, for example, during vacations or when other work activities have to take priority. Again, a guest writer can provide a much-needed break from your blog work.

Unless you are very lucky, you will also experience a common problem faced by most bloggers: writer's block. If you can't think of anything to write about, bring someone else in to plug the gap.

Guest writers will also add variety to your blog, which may help to keep your readers interested and provide them with a new perspective. Working with guest writers will also demonstrate your connectedness with the blogosphere, as most of them are likely to be bloggers themselves. They will undoubtedly tell their readers that they are posting on your blog, which can bring new visitors for you.

# How to find guest writers

Often the best people to approach to be guest writers are your most active commenters. These are people who already know your blog and have already taken the time to contribute content. They also enjoy your blog because they keep returning to view your posts and add comments.

You could also approach other bloggers who you follow on a regular basis—maybe ones who you have included in your blogroll. Pay particular attention to bloggers who appear to be keen networkers; these are the ones who are active commenters on several other blogs that you read.

Other possibilities for guest bloggers could be well-known people in your industry. They may not necessarily have their own blogs but could have done some offline writing in industry journals and magazines. Your colleagues, associates, and even clients may also make very good guest writers.

If your blogging budget is big enough, you may even consider hiring a freelance writer. This should guarantee some good copy. However, it's not always necessary to pay your guest writers. Most of them will be happy to gain the exposure and links back to their own blog (if they have one). You could also engage them on a *quid pro quo* basis, where you agree to do some guest writing for them some time.

You stand a better chance of having prospective guest writers accept your invitation if you don't demand too much from them. Don't set them a challenging *assignment* that requires lots of research and writing time. Help them out by keeping your request fairly open ended so they can choose a topic they feel comfortable with.

# Introducing WordPress Multisite

As your blog grows and you see the benefits it brings to your business, you or your colleagues may decide to set up other blogs. You may want each member of your team, or each department in your company, to have their own blog. Or maybe your CEO is so impressed that he or she wants his or her own blog, too. You could run each of these blogs with their own individual installations of WordPress. However, WordPress has built-in functionality that allows you to run multiple blogs from a single installation. It's called **WordPress Multisite.**

WordPress Multisite allows an unlimited number of blogs to run off one installation. All the blogs on such a network operate completely independently of each other. Each can use different themes and settings. The administrator decides which plugins to install, and can give different permissions to different users.

We'll look at the basics of WordPress Multisite so that you can see just how easy it can be to get multiple blogs up and running for your business.

# Getting started with WordPress Multisite

You could set up WordPress Multisite on any existing installation of WordPress (3.0 or higher). However, as this will be a test installation for you to experiment and play around with, I suggest you make a fresh installation of WordPress on your local development server. This way if you play a little too hard and break something, it won't affect anything on your live blog.

Note that on our local development server we won't have full functionality of WordPress Multisite. On a live web server, you would have the option to install each blog in the network on its own subdomain (for example, `firstblog.mydomain.com`, `secondblog.mydomain.com`, and so on.). However, to mimic this functionality on a local test server running on XAMPP, it would require lots of Apache configuration work that is beyond the scope of this chapter. So we will be using a directory structure for our blog network (for example, `http://localhost/wpmulti/firstblog`, `http://localhost/wpmulti/secondblog`, and so on).

As you can see from the previous example URLs, I have installed WordPress in a directory called `wpmulti` — you might want to do the same so that your URLs are identical to the ones in the rest of this tutorial.

# Installing a network

In your new WordPress installation on your local development server, add the following code to the `config.php` file, just above the line that says `/* That's all, stop editing! Happy blogging. */`:

```
define('WP_ALLOW_MULTISITE', true);
```

Log in to the admin area or, if you are already logged in, refresh the dashboard, and you will notice that **Network Setup** has been added to the **Tools** menu. Click on it, enter the **Network Details** and click **Install**:

On the next screen you are given instructions to follow to enable the network.

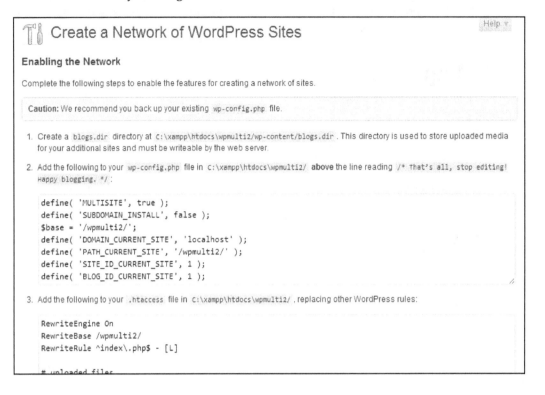

### Creating a .htaccess file

When you get to step 3, you will need to create a .htaccess file. To do this, open Notepad++ and select **File | New**, followed by **File | Save As**. Browse to the root of your new WordPress installation as the location to save the file. Use the file name .htaccess and for **Save as type**, select **All types (\*.\*)**.

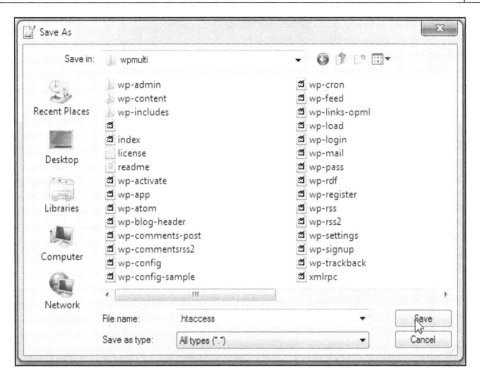

When you have completed all the steps, click on the link at the bottom of the page to log in to the admin area again:

# Managing your network

To manage your network, click on the **Network Admin** link, which is on the drop-down menu in the top right-hand side of the main WordPress dashboard:

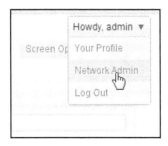

You're now in the **Network Admin** dashboard.

 When you need to switch back to the main **Site Admin** dashboard, you'll find the link in the same place — in the top right-hand corner.

As you can see, the network options and settings are fairly extensive, so we won't be going through all of them in this chapter. There is plenty of documentation at WordPress.org and elsewhere on the web to help you manage your network.

However, we will create a blog on your network so you can start to experiment with the WordPress Multisite features.

Click on **Sites | Add New**, enter a **Site Address**, **Site Title**, and **Admin Email** then click **Add Site**:

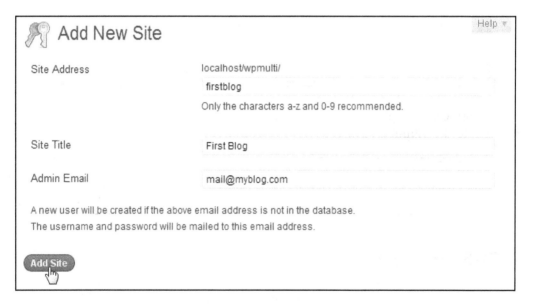

If you go to **Sites | All Sites**, you will see the new blog in the list. Hover over it and click **Dashboard** to access its admin area:

The admin area should be familiar because it's very similar to a standalone WordPress blog. One difference you will notice is that you cannot install plugins and themes. This is a task that can only be performed by the main network admin user. For example, if you go back to the **Network Admin** dashboard and go to **Plugins | Installed Plugins**, you will see the option to activate a plugin for the entire network:

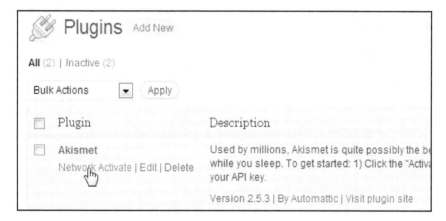

# Developing a blog network

Hopefully you're beginning to see how easy it is to set up a network of blogs using WordPress Multisite. You could set up blogs for anyone in your company in no time at all. You could even configure WordPress Multisite so that your colleagues can register for their own blogs without having to bother you. We'll set this up now.

In the main **Network Admin** dashboard, go to **Settings | Network Settings**. In the **Allow new registrations** area, select the radio button for **Both sites and user accounts can be registered**:

**Registration Settings**

| | |
|---|---|
| Allow new registrations | ○ Registration is disabled. |
| | ○ User accounts may be registered. |
| | ○ Logged in users may register new sites. |
| | ⦿ Both sites and user accounts can be registered. |

This setting will allow anyone to register their own blog on your network. However, you only want people within your company to be able to do this. So scroll down to the **Limited Email Registrations** area and enter your company's domain:

| Limited Email Registrations | mycompany.com |
|---|---|
| | If you want to limit site registrations to certain domains. One domain per line. |

Click the **Save Changes** button. Now registrations are restricted to people who have an e-mail address for your company. No one else will be able to sign up.

We can try this out. Log out from the main **Network Admin** dashboard. Go to `http://localhost/wpmulti/` and click on the **Register** link. You will be taken to the registration page:

Get your own WP Multisite Sites account in seconds

**Username:**

(Must be at least 4 characters, letters and numbers only.)

**Email Address:**

We send your registration email to this address. (Double-check your email address before continuing.)

⦿ **Gimme a site!**

○ **Just a username, please.**

Next

In the **Username** box enter **secondblog**. To test the sign-up restriction, enter an e-mail address that does *not* end in @mycompany.com and click **Next**. You should see a message telling you that the e-mail address is not allowed:

So now enter an e-mail address ending with @mycompany.com and click **Next** again. You'll be taken to the next page, where you should enter **Second Blog** in the **Site Title** box and click **Signup**. You will be taken to the 'success' page:

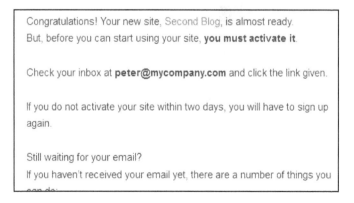

As you can see, WordPress Multisite will now send a confirmation e-mail, which contains an activation link.

Of course, we don't have e-mail functionality on our local test server. However, we can work around this for the purposes of this demonstration. Go to `http://localhost/phpmyadmin`. Select the `wpmulti` database, and click the **Browse** icon for the `wp-signups` table. There should be a record for `/wpmulti/secondblog/`. Look for the **activation key** and copy it to your clipboard:

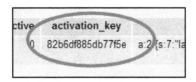

The activation link that the new sign-up receives in their confirmation e-mail looks like this:

`http://localhost/wpmulti/wpmu/wp-activate.php?key=82b6df885db77f5e`

Replace the activation key with the one you copied from the database and then enter the activation link URL into your browser's address bar. You should see a page telling you that the second blog is now active:

Copy the password and use the **Login** link to access your new blog's admin area.

That was a very quick run through some of the basic features of WordPress Multisite, but hopefully it has shown you how easy it is to create a network of blogs for your business. You now have a test installation of WordPress Multisite to experiment with and explore the features in more detail before deciding if you'd like to use it on a live server.

# Summary

In this chapter, we have discussed some of the issues that may arise as your blog grows. You learned how to improve your blog's performance by installing WP Super Cache. You should now know how to choose a dedicated server for when you outgrow your shared hosting account, and how to move your blog to the new server. You also had an introduction to WordPress Multisite and saw how it can be used to easily set up a network of blogs for your business. We also looked at how to make your blog *mobile-friendly*; how to handle the increased levels of correspondence you'll receive; and how to find guest writers.

# Index

Atom 176
attachment 107
attachment page 107
authority 242
Automattic 55
Awesome Google Adsense 270

# B

background-color property 62
backup file
  database, restoring from 145, 146
banner ads
  placing 278
bashing. *See* flaming
BBC 176
blog
  about 9, 11, 16, 43
  About page 138
  availability, ensuring for mobile users 292-294
  backing up 141 case study review 289, 290
  comments, moderating 221, 222
  examples 9-19
  key feature 13
  KPIs (key performance indicators) 238-240
  monetizing 25
  paid reviews 289
  promoting 24
  success, measuring 25
  tactical goals 10
  favicon, adding to 121, 122
  guest writers, searching for 303
  moving, to better web server 297, 298
  promoting 175
  traffic, managing 294, 295
  usability and accessibility 53
  workload, managing 291, 292
  wp-content, backing up 141
  writing tips, backing up 126-129
  writing tips, restoring 126-129
blog, components
  color 49, 50
  layout 44-48
  typography 51, 52
blog design
  implementing 54

principles 43
bloggers 8, 125
blogging 7, 8, 211, 128
blogging strategy 10
blog network
  developing 309-312
blogosphere
  about 8, 9, 211, 128
  engaging with 212, 213
  feeding off 218, 219
blog plan 29, 33, 34
blog promotion
  RSS syndication 175, 176
  search egines, using 190
  social bookmarking 205
  social network used 193, 194
  specialist blog engines, using 190
  Twitter used 198
  WordPress feeds 176, 177
blogroll
  about 214, 217
  links, adding to 214- 217
  managing 214
  SEO issues 217
blog URL
  subdomain, using in 30
blog writing tips
  backing up 126-129
  ending with proactive question 130
  killer headlines 126
  links, to other blogs 128
  post frequency 127, 128
  post length 126, 127
  post structure 129
  quick checklist 130
  restoring 126-129
  tone, establishing 128
  voice, establishing 128
body selector 62
body tag 60
Boeing
  URL 13
brochure style sites 17
business blogger 7, 10
business blogging
  about 9
  strategic goals 10-19

## G

gallery 112
Garmin
  about 11
  URL 11
Gawker 165
Generate Tag feature 233
Genesis
  URL 55
GIF 99
gigabytes (GB) 100
GigaOM
  URL 22
Gizmodo 165
GoDaddy
  URL 298
Google 205
Google +1 205
Google AdSense
  about 40, 266
  ad units, creating 267, 268
  overview 266
  URL, for documentation 266
Google AdWords 258, 259
Google Analytics
  about 25, 247-249
  content 259
  tracking code 248
  Traffic Sources option 257, 258
  URL, for documentation 260
  using 250
  Visitors menu 253-256
  working 250-253
Google Analytics for WordPress
  URL 249
Google Blog Search
  URL 213
Google Fonts API
  URL 52
Google Page Rank 173
Google PageRank. *See* PageRank
Google Reader 176
Google robot 164
Google Sitemap
  about 160
  adding 161

Google Toolbar
  about 26, 242
  URL 26
Google Video
  about 120
  videos, incorporating from 120
Google Voice number
  URL 231
Google webmaster tools 148, 170-172
Google XML Sitemaps 160
growth, WPBizGuru makeover 41
guest writers
  about 303
  searching, for blogs 303
Guy Kawasaki's blog
  URL 23

## H

header 60
header, WPBizGuru design 84, 85
head tag 60
hexadecimal RGB color system 50, 51
hits 238
home page
  excerpts, using on 165-167
Host Gator
  URL 298
HTML 55
HTML document
  stylesheet, applying to 63-68
html tag 60
Hybrid
  URL 55
HyperText Markup Language. *See* HTML

## I

ID selector 61, 65
image gallery
  NextGEN Gallery 111-117
  page, creating 117-119
  setting up 110
image measurements
  dimensions 100
  file size 100
  resolution 100

# X

# Y

# Z

## Thank you for buying
# WordPress 3 for Business Bloggers

## About Packt Publishing

Packt, pronounced 'packed', published its first book "*Mastering phpMyAdmin for Effective MySQL Management*" in April 2004 and subsequently continued to specialize in publishing highly focused books on specific technologies and solutions.

Our books and publications share the experiences of your fellow IT professionals in adapting and customizing today's systems, applications, and frameworks. Our solution based books give you the knowledge and power to customize the software and technologies you're using to get the job done. Packt books are more specific and less general than the IT books you have seen in the past. Our unique business model allows us to bring you more focused information, giving you more of what you need to know, and less of what you don't.

Packt is a modern, yet unique publishing company, which focuses on producing quality, cutting-edge books for communities of developers, administrators, and newbies alike. For more information, please visit our website: www.packtpub.com.

## About Packt Open Source

In 2010, Packt launched two new brands, Packt Open Source and Packt Enterprise, in order to continue its focus on specialization. This book is part of the Packt Open Source brand, home to books published on software built around Open Source licences, and offering information to anybody from advanced developers to budding web designers. The Open Source brand also runs Packt's Open Source Royalty Scheme, by which Packt gives a royalty to each Open Source project about whose software a book is sold.

## Writing for Packt

We welcome all inquiries from people who are interested in authoring. Book proposals should be sent to author@packtpub.com. If your book idea is still at an early stage and you would like to discuss it first before writing a formal book proposal, contact us; one of our commissioning editors will get in touch with you.

We're not just looking for published authors; if you have strong technical skills but no writing experience, our experienced editors can help you develop a writing career, or simply get some additional reward for your expertise.

## WordPress Complete

ISBN: 978-1-904811-89-3     Paperback: 304 pages

A comprehensive, step-by-step guide on how to set up, customize, and market your blog using WordPress

1.  Clear practical coverage of all aspects of WordPress

2.  Concise, clear, and easy to follow, rich with examples

3.  In-depth coverage of installation, themes, syndication, and podcasting

## WordPress Theme Design

ISBN: 978-1-847193-09-4     Paperback: 224 pages

A complete guide to creating professional WordPress themes

1.  Take control of the look and feel of your WordPress site

2.  Simple, clear tutorial to creating Unique and Beautiful themes

3.  Expert guidance with practical step-by-step instructions for theme design

4.  Design tips, tricks, and troubleshooting ideas

## WordPress 3 Site Blueprints

ISBN: 978-1-847199-36-2          Paperback: 230 pages

Ready-made plans for 9 different professional
WordPress sites

1. Everything you need to build a varied
   collection of feature-rich customized WordPress
   websites for yourself

2. Transform a static website into a dynamic
   WordPress blog

3. In-depth coverage of several WordPress themes
   and plugins

4. Packed with screenshots and step-by-step
   instructions to help you complete each site

## WordPress 3 Plugin Development Essentials

ISBN: 978-1-84951-352-4          Paperback: 300 pages

Create your own powerful, interactive plugins to
extend and add features to your WordPress site

1. Everything you need to know to develop your
   own plugins for WordPress

2. Walk through the development of five plugins
   from ground up

3. Prepare and release your plugins to the
   WordPress community

Please check **www.PacktPub.com** for information on our titles